THE KEPT WOMAN
MISTRESSES IN THE '80s

THE KEPT WOMAN
MISTRESSES IN THE '80s

by Edna Salamon

ORBIS·LONDON

CONTENTS

This Book is Dedicated to Paul Rock

PREFACE

In September 1980 I came to London with the intention of doing research on marital deviance for a Ph.D at the London School of Economics and Political Science. I wanted to compare the reasons why women stayed with alcoholic husbands, physically incapacitated husbands, battered husbands and unfaithful husbands. With regard to the first three, I thought collecting a sample would be relatively easy in that organizations such as Al Anon (for the families of alcoholics), societies for the disabled and shelters for battered women all exist in London and are fairly accessible. As for unfaithful husbands, I was clearly at a loss. Rather discouraged, I mentioned my problem to my hairdresser who breezily informed me that while he could not introduce me to unfaithful husbands or their wives, he could arrange introductions to numerous friends and customers who were being kept by married men. So the cart drew the horse and my topic was redefined by the availability of a potential research sample.

In researching 'kept women' it was felt that it would not be appropriate to use statistical sampling techniques. The chances were that knocking on every nth door in a block of flats, for example, could result in more slammed doors than study participants. I therefore followed the more informal method of enlarging my sample by including friends and companions of original members of the group who had been put in contact with me by them. From autumn 1980 through most of 1982, I interviewed hundreds of 'kept women', their lovers and their friends. There is no way of telling how representative my sample is. Although the method I followed may be criticized as being unlikely to produce a representative collection of all kept women/lover relationships and although I am unable to say whether the incidence of women being kept is increasing or has decreased since, say, the eighteenth century, it is a viable method for collecting information on a group which cannot be identified through unions, club membership listings, or participation in a particular activity.

I have investigated as many divergent groups as possible, and in order to gather an international sample I sent 'Letters to the Editor' to newspapers and magazines, inviting people who were involved in such relationships, or who had been involved at some time, to contact me by post. I wrote to every North American newspaper with a circulation of over 100,000 (my newspaper contact was necessarily confined to the United States and Canada because of anticipated language difficulties). Where it appeared that geographic areas with small populations would be entirely excluded, I tried to contact the largest local newspaper despite its smaller circulation. The staff of newspapers and periodicals tended to be rather disbelieving about my intentions and interests. The editor of one paper on the West Coast of the United States, which did eventually publish the letter, wrote:

> Enclosed is a copy of our 'Letters to the Editor' column of 1 October in which your letter was published concerning your thesis on 'kept women'. Although several colleagues charged me with making the whole thing up, I wish you well on it, even if it is indeed, a ruse.

Others rejected the idea entirely and accused me of having a less than professional interest, of seeking vicarious excitement or with the intent to blackmail respondents:

> In response to your letter of October 1, 1981, concerning your research on 'kept' women we do not carry such letters to the editor. We fear that some irresponsible persons could use such letters to take advantage of unsuspecting women.

In Great Britain, I attempted to enlist the cooperation of London daily newspapers, but enjoyed little success in terms of having my 'Letter to the Editor' published. The reticence of publishers in this respect is symptomatic of the 'invisibility' of the extramarital affair and also tells us something about the character of taboo. The ostrich mentality that hides the issue from public consciousness does not prevent its existence; it merely avoids confrontation.

Getting my letters published in magazines proved to be an even less successful sampling method. Even when a letter was accepted there was a delay of approximately two months before it appeared in print. This resulted in the practical difficulty of feverishly juggling an interview schedule for the weeks immediately following a magazine publication so that the women who responded would not lose interest. Magazines were selected from trade listings under 'Women's Interests', 'Men's interests' and 'Fashion' sections. New, unlisted publications were also contacted when their names were brought to my attention.

There was a general unwillingness to admit that 'such women' read the magazine in question. One somewhat grand editor looked utterly aghast and stammered 'Why US?'. In one instance, two responses were received from the same magazine, one giving me an unequivocal 'NO' informing me in bellicose terms that my letter was entirely 'unsuitable' for publication, while the second denied even having a 'Letters to the Editor' section! I received the latter reply several times. One London monthly magazine which regularly extols the 'female orgasm' and recommends 'How-to-find-and-attract-sexy-men' was straightforward in its reply:

> It may sound a bit prissy, but I'm sure you will understand my feeling when I say that I think our readers might well be offended at the inevitable implication that I felt that they had at some time been in this position. This isn't a moral judgement of my own, merely good publishing sense in relationship to the market at which — [name of magazine] aims.

When my letter was accepted and published, this did not ensure serious or genuine responses or a positive reception from the magazine's readers. I collected some cranky letters written in crayon and coloured felt pens, a letter full of hate from a member of the Moral Majority, an American clean-up-society organization which told me in no uncertain terms that my research was 'disgusting' and that I must be a tramp to pursue it. I later learned that people unknown to me were harassing people they suspected of being kept by telephoning them and pretending either to be me or to be affiliated with my work. Even an old friend (who calls me Adie) who spotted one such 'Letter to the Editor' wrote:

> Adie! How could you! (My friend Adie writing about kept women!) – all indignation aside, *what's his name*? Nobody writes about kept women without good reason. How old is he? Is he a good Catholic? And most important, is he keeping you well? Where did you meet him?

Apparently in writing on sexual deviance you are thought at least marginally deviant yourself. Had I done research on admirers of babies and small animals I probably would have gathered a larger sample and far more easily.

It is to be expected that my sampling techniques produced a particular type of respondent – one that is more self-advertising than reticent about his or her relationship, and I was largely dependent upon networks and referrals so I can only guess at how the participants would compare with kept women who prefer to maintain their anonymity. My method of exploration lays no claim to being representative or typical, and is best described by Dr Ken Plummer's term 'Ad Hoc Fumbling Around':

It involves fumbling upon a whole area, e.g. transvestism, sado-masochism, pedophilia, and thinking widely about a range of problems associated with that area.

I freely acknowledge that there are several limitations in this book, and must emphasize that it represents only a part of my original 160,000-word doctoral dissertation which I submitted to the University of London in March 1983.

The first problem in doing research on 'kept women' is simply that of being female. The sex of the investigator affects the informants' reporting so I can only guess if a male interviewer would have received identical responses. Contrasting my own research with Lewis Yablonsky's *The Extra-Sex Factor: Why Over Half of America's Men Play Around*, for example, I note that his respondents repeatedly and routinely used the word *fuck* as an adjective, noun, verb and adverb whereas my own male respondents did not; it could be that the men I interviewed felt it necessary to monitor their conversation when talking to a woman – a constriction not felt when simply 'talking among the boys'. While I don't regret the absence of the word, it is possible that other, more important omissions were made as well.

One of my most notable difficulties while interviewing men was negotiating the line between close rapport and mistaken personal sexual interest. After spending hours at a time talking to men about their views of sexuality non-judgmentally and sympathetically, it was often difficult to assert my lack of interest in becoming socially involved with them. I then took to offering a polite excuse with the phrase 'I'm involved with someone already.' This sounded rather feeble when the man countered with 'I'm married already.' The most stark illustration of this complication was with a ponce who offered to take me with him to Acapulco for Christmas in 1981 and assured me, 'You don't have to fuck me unless you want to.' Yablonsky fails to mention such interview dialogue and others similar to it.

The extent of my direct observation was to a degree curtailed by the exclusiveness of certain social meeting places with private membership, and as this research was undertaken without any type of financial grant, I could not blithely follow respondents on expensive jaunts abroad to continue observing their behaviour. It is possible that the relations between two people are not fully apparent when an interviewer is present at a double interview, and in some cases I was only able to see one of the two people concerned. The duo relationship is innately vulnerable and while one of them might talk freely, he or she was often loath to invoke the lover's wrath by directly bringing her or him into the interview situation. This fear is not without foundation. One of my female respondents is a 24-year-old woman who has been kept for the last five years by a prominent London businessman. The man is in his late forties, originally from the East End of

London and has five children from two marriages. Elaine, the woman he keeps, was originally his secretary but was re-located by him in a Bond Street shop (in which he has financial interests) when his wife learned of the affair some two years ago. The wife left her husband and returned only when he pledged that the affair was totally over and that Elaine was no longer even in his employ. Elaine lives in a £500-a-week Knightsbridge flat which the man owns in addition to rental properties in England and on both coasts of the United States. My interview with Elaine was straightforward; what was unusual was the aftermath.

A few days after seeing Elaine I received a visit at about 8.30 in the morning from her lover, accompanied by a younger man, a visit which was totally unannounced and unexpected. With the nonchalance of the blissfully obtuse, I assumed the men had come to be interviewed and only too happy to enlarge my sample size, I invited them in. It soon became rather obvious that it was they who were doing the interviewing. Although I thought it rather odd that Elaine's lover would bring a friend along, I attached no special significance to the fact. This 'friend' asked me if I was writing for a newspaper and I answered no. He replied that the man's 'brass' had told her lover I was doing research and they wanted to know exactly for what purpose I had spoken to Elaine. I asked the man why he referred to Elaine as a 'brass' and he said that in the East End the slang for money was brass and since keeping a mistress costs money she was a brass. Intrigued by this information, I asked him if there were any other terms differentiating the mistress from the wife. He looked rather perplexed at the direction the conversation was taking and told me that while you would say you slept with your wife, you had 'caseo'* with your mistress. It was an extremely odd situation – while I was compiling my dictionary of East End slang, Elaine's lover quizzed me on my family, my morality and my financial background. He appeared inordinately impressed by a photograph of my parents in which they are posed in the style of Grant Woods's 'American Gothic' (minus the pitchfork) in the front hall of their home. After 45 minutes or so, the man's friend said to me:

> I knew as soon as I saw you you're a good girl and not the sort to make trouble. You're like the old East End factory girls – cor, I remember when I was young having to go with a girl for six months and still not get anywhere. It drove me potty!! But then, you're from a proper family – you can tell that. I've never met a writer before – you never know do ya? [*Know what?*] Well, you know, most writers like to make trouble and I'd say nine out of ten girls in this area would do anything for what it'll get them. [*What*

---

*'caseo': variant of *casa* (a house) and 'case' which since the seventeenth century have been slang for a brothel and the female pudenda respectively; 'to be cased up with' denotes living with a woman/mistress.

do you mean?] This is a fancy area, you need a lot of money, right? Girls here do anything for money. If I ask you out and some other bloke does and me, I got a Ferrari outside, can take you to Annabel's and you'll be sitting next to Prince Charles and the like – who you going to go with? [*Depends who I like more.*] Na, say you don't know me and you don't know the other guy – you'll go for the guy with the money, right? It's the same thing – some girls wouldn't mind causing trouble if it could get them good money. But then, you're an American [*Canadian*] – same thing, you don't need the money.

The friend was, in fact, the man's 'minder' or strong-arm. The task of the minder is to suggest, firmly, that his employer's interests are in everyone's best interests. The man Elaine was involved with had been unnerved by the fact that someone other than the people he himself selected to tell knew of his relationship. Since his wife had already left him once because of the affair, were she to be furnished with evidence that in fact the liaison was still continuing, she was thought able to wipe him out financially in a divorce action for adultery. His friend had been brought along to suggest that I had better not cause trouble but luckily the consensus appeared to be that I was not the trouble-making kind. Whether the man assessed me as non-threatening because I am female, five-foot-three tall, a student, an 'American' (with the assumption that all Americans are so filthy rich they do not have to resort to blackmail), stupid or a combination of any or all of these characteristics, the episode passed uneventfully. It does relate, however, to the enforceable 'invisibility' of the affair.

In all cases where I have included verbatim quotes the names and places although retaining their character have been changed so as to disguise their identity. The body of my research was conducted without tape-recording which might have inhibited the flow of talk and created an unnatural climate for conversation. When I did use a tape recorder I always obtained permission to do so from the respondent. I took notes during the interviews wherever possible and at no time did I attempt to conceal or disguise the nature of my research from respondents. While I have attempted to record answers as precisely as possible, there may be slight differences due to my own nationality, as with the word 'flat' in my notes which became 'apt.' and so in transcribing conversation the word apartment may remain.

Finally, each chapter in this work could be expanded and warrants further research. Limitations of time and space have meant that I had to prune or omit entirely certain areas. For example, I have not included a section here on the homosexual kept relationship or a discussion of the gigolo. I hope that my findings on these subjects will be published at a future date.

EPITAPH
FOR A DARLING LADY

All her hours were yellow sands,
Blown in foolish whorls and tassels;
Slipping warmly through her hands;
Patted into little castles.

Shiny day on shiny day
Tumbled in a rainbow clutter,
As she flipped them all away,
Sent them spinning down the gutter.

Leave for her a red young rose,
Go your way, and save your pity;
She is happy, for she knows
That her dust is very pretty.

DOROTHY PARKER

(Collected edition *Enough Rope*, 1926)

INTRODUCING
THE KEPT WOMAN

The relationship in which a woman is kept by or receives some financial support from an already married man outside marriage is not necessarily a love affair – what is popularly depicted as the poignant relationship of two lovers who meet at the wrong time, or a casual fling which is pleasing but ephemeral, or indeed an orgy of fervid passion. The following view comes from a man who has kept three women:

> The reason men 'keep' women is not sexual, nor is it the reason women allow themselves to be kept. I think it's a need for a form of security; part of it, for the woman, financial, but for both emotional. There is a large measure of ego involved, more on the male than on the female side of the bed. Macho is involved. (*58-year-old man, San Francisco*)

Views from the other side come from two of my kept women contacts:

> I am somewhat asexual. If the moon doesn't happen to be in the right quarter, neither am I!! However, I am extremely sensual – and therein lies my successes to date. He remains my true friend honestly believing that if I do not have sexual intercourse with him it is because that is the way I am. Not with him, then not with anyone. A delusion on his part, yes, however not a selfish hope for he would not begrudge me or my partner (whomever) as long as he gets his!!... No, he is not unintelligent. 'Tis only delusion in some subjective areas and illusion to the greater extent in that I remain for him the ultimate experience. My men are virgins! Something of a vicarious experience for him isn't it? And yet, he knows the reality

of it, he is the first to point out that this is his choice. (*35-year-old woman, Toronto*)

A kept woman is basically someone who provides a service to the man in return for a financial sop to her pride. [*Can you explain that?*] A sop to her pride? Something that soothes the fact that he's not going to marry her. It salves his conscience and it gives me respect from other women. It also gives me security – emotionally because I know he won't find another fool like me – this was true with the other men in my past who were also married – and financially, because I know he can afford to support me. (*32-year-old woman, London*)

These three quotations provide an introduction to three of the themes which will re-emerge in subsequent chapters: the social reinforcement of male and female attitudes towards sexuality and the interpretative work that accompanies them; the connection between fantasy and romance, and the presentation of self to others for confirmation of status.

It would be too simple to say that kept relationships are motivated and sustained by lust alone, whether emanating from one or both parties. In the past the kept woman has largely been regarded as a glorified prostitute and the kept relationship as a form of prostitution. Writers of fiction and non-fiction alike have presented lurid images of boudoirs with mirrored ceilings, reducing the relationship of the kept woman and her lover to heavy breathing and nocturnal pyrotechnics. In the few works which do exist on extramarital affairs, men and women are shown singularly obsessed with sex and the affair is seen as the way in which people attempt to gratify their sexual desires. I found no evidence to suggest that the kept woman was a champion of sexual liberation and few respondents who were as focused on sex as Xaviera Hollander, 'Emmanuelle' or their current rivals. With few exceptions, the kept relationship was a sexual one but it was much else besides. Trumpeting the fact that sex is involved is, to draw an analogy, like photographing a bear's nose, blowing up the photograph to gigantic proportions and saying '*Voilà*! This is what a bear looks like.' The importance of the relationship as a sexual one varied, not only from one couple to the next, but also from one partner to the other in any specific relationship. My research revealed that the role of the kept woman was not strictly sexual and that it would be over-simple to present the kept relationship as if it existed solely for coitus.

A kept woman clearly denotes someone who is not married to her (already married) male partner but is nevertheless dependent on his financial support. The implication is that the relationship is one of some duration. Unlike the 'one-night-stand' or the encounter with a prostitute, keeping a woman implies a sustained relationship albeit for variable amounts of time. The term 'kept woman' has been used synonymously with mistress, courtesan, *hetaira*, adulteress and as a euphemism for a prostitute by writers who argue that any activity underwritten by a financial calculation is prostitution:

> Courtesan, *demi-monde*, and *fille de joie* are euphemisms, for prostitution in its deepest sense can exist within marriage. It is consistent with complete marital fidelity. A woman who marries for money or social position may better deserve to be called a prostitute – hotly as she would resent it – than a mistress. (*Live and Let Live* by Eustace Chesser)

> The first difficulty we have to face is that, strictly speaking, there is no such thing as a prostitute type ... It is really absurd to talk of large remedies for prostitution without first establishing a reasonably exact classification of prostitutes. For that part, we might also have to have an accurate survey of allied groups, including, for example, the 'enthusiastic amateur' and 'gold digger', or the type of individual who marries for money. And if we go so far we might as well consider the significance of the 'dowry' and the 'marriage settlement'. (*The Psychopathology of Prostitution* by Edward Glover)

It is not my intention to build a metaphor out of prostitution such as 'All the world's a whorehouse' but if I offer several definitions of prostitution it will become clear that any attempt to decide its character is fraught with problems. The term 'common prostitute' has been legally expressed as:

> . . . a female who offers her body for acts of sexual intercourse for payment and includes a woman who offers her body for acts of lewdness although no act of ordinary sexual connection takes place.

However, in the work of H. Benjamin and R. Masters, *The Prostitute in Society*, several other definitions by specialists are cited, including the following:

> Prostitution starts when the giver becomes a seller. What is love if it isn't a gift? (*Psychoanalysis of the Prostitute* by Maryse Choisy).

> A prostitute is an individual, male or female, who for some kind of reward, monetary or otherwise, or . . . and as part- or whole-time professions, engages in normal or abnormal sexual intercourse with various persons. (*A History of Prostitution* by George Ryley Scott)

> Any person is a prostitute who habitually or intermittently has sexual relations more or less promiscuously for money, or other mercenary consideration. (*Prostitution in Europe* by Abraham Flexner)

> If the woman offers to satisfy sexually in any manner whatsoever any man who meets her terms and conditions, she's a prostitute.
> (*Sex and the Law* by M. Ploscowe)

Although these definitions may not at first appear to be very different from each other, each has a particular emphasis. Prostitution is defined as (1) a fraudulent display of affection; (2) a professional career in which access to your body is exchanged for monetary reward; (3) spiritual compromise, and (4) indiscriminate promiscuity. The plurality indicates more than a pedantic preoccupation with exact meaning. The definition of prostitution itself can have moral, ideological and cultural overtones. It is important to recognize that labelling a woman a prostitute uses a term in which an artificial line is drawn between the behaviour of some women and others. Although the *hetaira* class of Ancient Greece were kept women, they were not looked upon as invariably immoral or parasitic; theirs was an open concubinage. In *Fallen Women*, M. Seymour-Smith offers a self-regarding male definition of what is admirable in the *hetairae*:

> In as much as any class of women may be said to be admirable as a whole, they were admirable; they were witty, intelligent, and (so far as we know) good lovers. They performed a useful social function, and were well integrated. They, and not the wife – whose task it was to produce children – were the companions of men. Consider then, in the light of our own time in the West, they were not prostitutes at all.

In existing works on prostitution the kept woman is generally mentioned only briefly. Since the population of kept women in a society is assumed to be relatively small because of the inherent cost of keeping a woman compared to buying a common prostitute's time, she is generally dismissed as the individual man's problem rather than as a symptom of society's moral decay or a cause for righteous panic. Nevertheless, there is a strong tradition in academic literature connecting the kept woman to the prostitute as the 'flaunting, extravagant Queen' of prostitution. In *World Famous Mistresses*, C.E. Maine notes:

> Mistresses are usually associated with men of power, of wealth – they have to be 'afforded' and kept in proper style. They are usually more than just playthings . . . Too often a mistress has not only been a 'woman illicitly occupying place of wife' but also 'woman illicitly occupying place of Queen', for mistresses throughout history have been very much the sport of kings – although even the humblest proletarian may have a mistress rather than a prostitute. [Despite] the indefinables of infatuation and emotion there is invariably some kind of reward for service rendered.

Identifying the kept woman as a prostitute simplifies her role – she becomes the bad type of woman who lures men into her parlour and sells sex.

An American, Melissa Sands (who founded Mistresses Anonymous, a self-help group like Alcoholics Anonymous for women who are addicted to married men), strongly denies the idea that the majority of mistresses are kept. In *The Mistress' Survival Manual* she writes:

> Historically speaking, the term mistress referred to a woman who was involved with a married man and was financially supported by him. In my love affair there was no money. Yet I still call myself a mistress. I just updated the label. Why? Because the word mistress gets right to the heart of the issue. Mistress immediately brings to mind a woman catering to a married man. That was me, catering to the needs of my married man, but not for money, but for love.

Similarly, Wendy James and Susan Jane Kedgley, co-authors of *The Mistress* and self-proclaimed participants in their study's sample as former mistresses, deny any affiliation with the kept woman. They view accepting financial support as characteristic of the Predator type of mistress:

> The cold, hard, calculating mistress . . . using men as vehicles to give her all she wants . . . She's made a conscious decision about her role and she's willing to commit herself fully to it for the rewards alone. She is the most exotic of the mistresses and she uses her wiles and her body to insinuate her way into the lives of wealthy men, men with power, men who can raise her status . . . She is a predator in the sense that she cannot exist alone. Her emotions are involved only to the extent that she knows best how to use them for effect.

For James and Kedgley, what distinguishes the predator is the fact that she is kept. In my view, however, to describe the kept woman as a calculating predator is naive and to claim that while an affair is acceptable if the female partner does not receive financial support it is deplorable and parasitic if she does, is unsatisfactory; that is saying that it is fine to accept a married man's love but not his rent cheques. Sands and James and Kedgley seem to agree that the mistress's role must include a degree of martyrdom: through selflessness the mistress atones for her sins. The maligning of the predator type of kept woman as the Scarlet Woman totally distinct from the good, unsupported mistress may reflect society's self-righteous hypocrisy when confronted with behaviour which deviates from the monogamous ideal. The prostitute is the general cat to kick in identifying the bad type of woman and the kept woman becomes the sort who gives mistresses a bad name.

In John F. Cuber and Peggy B. Harroff's *Significant Americans*, a study of upper-middle-class sexual mores, the authors refer to the upholding of traditional, acceptable sexual ethics as a colossal unreality founded upon a collective pretence, a supposition which is somewhat intolerant of human failing. It is debatable whether or not collective sentiment or individual consciousness is acute enough to misrepresent acts and/or beliefs intentionally. Nevertheless, the fact of financial support lends itself to aligning the kept relationship with prostitution. This may go some way towards explaining why the kept woman is disparaged as an utterly different type of mistress or woman in general. Whether the kept women themselves saw the affair as a tragedy or a success story, the question of financial reimbursement was the one area which they regarded with the greatest reluctance during my interviews. Men, too, who would speak freely about their sexual proclivities, shrank from discussing specific amounts of money given. A lifestyle of comfort and affluence would be mentioned rather than that of offering payment for companionship and sexual favours.

All of the women I interviewed were self-labelled kept women. Not all of them regarded being kept as discreditable, however. For some it was a case of 'taking life into my own hands', an assertive effort to promote self-gain. These women defined their experiences as success stories. One 21-year-old woman said: 'You have to take advantage of the world or be taken advantage of by it.' For others it ended in stalemate. The allowance, gifts, rent and trips abroad are all seen as tantamount to proof of the man's true affection and concern for their well-being.

There is a popular fallacy concerning the difference between the kept woman and the wife (or girlfriend) of the married man, neither of whom is deemed to be kept. The wife and unsupported girlfriend are sentimentally depicted as altruistic lovers, while the kept relationship is shown as a self-indulgent act between 'man on the make and girl on the take'. The presumed difference may be more exaggerated than real: marriage may be a social expedient, a relief from loneliness or an economic shelter and it is debatable whether people are as selfless as a kamikaze pilot and plunge into a marriage in the name of love alone.

Challenging the predator stereotype of the kept woman, an article in the American edition of *Cosmopolitan* magazine, 'Playing the Game' by Patricia Morrisroe (August 1982), drawing largely upon interviews with Melissa Sands, created a new caricature:

> . . . Mainly the old-fashioned paid mistress is someone over fifty who's been relatively unaffected by the Woman's Movement . . . Florence . . . assumed the mistress role in the late 1940s, when the only real alternative was being a housewife. Florence wanted a career, but after eight years as a secretary she wasn't exactly moving up the corporate ladder at top speed. So there she was at thirty-four, toiling away at a dead-end job, unmarried and living in a small New England Town where her friends, family and neighbours figured she was a born spinster or – heaven forbid! – a lesbian.

The article proceeded in benevolent tones to exonerate Florence for being kept. Born too early to profit from the enlightened consciousness of the woman's liberation movement and faced with the horrifying prospect of being thought a lesbian, Florence's situation supposedly represents the grim choice of the devil or the deep blue sea. In *The Rich Boy*, F. Scott Fitzgerald wrote: 'Begin with an individual, and before you know it you find that you have created a type; begin with a type, and you find that you have created – nothing.' To present Florence as a typical kept woman is misleading for it suggests that the only kept women in society are ageing spinsters regretting their past. This is nonsense. Nor do the facts bear out the implicit suggestion that modern society has so fully indoctrinated women into new roles through feminist rhetoric that the kept woman is a phenomenon of times past.

One of the lingering images of the kept woman is that of a languid female draped idly on a *chaise longue*. In proclaiming the liberation of women, employment is often pointed to as the great emancipator. Although some women in my research were totally dependent upon the man, the majority did have jobs or a career, whether or not employed by him. Nell Gwynn may have identified herself as the 'King's whore', but she was still active as a popular actress. Whether the women I interviewed earned some income independently or were totally dependent upon their lovers did not generally deter them from identifying as kept women. Subsidized or totally supported, my respondents considered the term applicable to their situation. When conducting my research I did not advance with pointed finger on unsuspecting women as if accusing them of being kept. On the contrary, it was they who identifed themselves to me.

No special philosophical insight is required to see that becoming a kept woman is a result of a decision made and acted upon. Approximately 80 per cent of my respondents said that the decision to formalize the relationship with financial support comes from the male but it is interesting to consider how great a part women play in promting this move. Certainly the statements made suggest that there is a gradual process whereby the support given becomes ever more complete. It is unusual for the two to meet, the man immediately to inquire 'May I keep you?' and the woman to assent (though it does happen). One of my respondents, a professional call girl, received a car in addition to her fee after her first meeting with an Arab client and was shortly after installed as his mistress. More commonly, however, the early period is one of wining and dining and gifts given as tokens of affection. To start with, financial support generally comes about in the form of helping out with day-to-day expenses such as rent, groceries, clothing and so on.

Approximately three-fifths of my contacts live in rented accommodation and have their rent paid for by the man, or live in a company- or embassy-owned flat. Generally the purchase of a flat specifically for the woman, and/or the transfer of a lease to her name, is dependent upon a relationship having existed for at least a year or two. The typical process is that the woman would have her rent paid for or be moved to a flat that is grander than her own and, financed by the man, live there for a few months or years. The remaining two-fifths of my contacts are made up of a mixture of women who are given their own flats or houses and those who have the free run of a place but whose claims on it are more dubious.

It could be argued that women who pursue a job or career are not really kept women, but the fact that total support is not always given and that some of my contacts pursued careers or were employed may simply reveal one way in which the role of the kept woman reflects more general changes in women's position in society, as well as changes in employment opportunities for them. I doubt that employment and the role of the kept woman are mutually exclusive or fundamentally antagonistic. I would be surprised if the role of the kept woman became obsolete whether being kept means being given total support, financial subsidies or career perks by a married man. To satisfy everyone's assumptions of what constitutes a kept woman I would have had a fruitless search for a type who, I suspect, only exists in salacious novels. All my respondents were involved in relationships with married men and identified themselves as kept women.

A degree of self-support should not be considered incompatible with the idea of the kept woman. Some of these women had jobs that were indirectly linked to their relationship. For example, a woman who had been given her job on her lover's recommendation or was employed by him often received perks of employment which were not strictly related to the job itself. In the kept relationship there are variations in the amounts of money, gifts and so on given. There may also be huge differences in the amounts regarded as acceptable by the woman. To conform fully to the stereotype each respondent would have to have been an idle, avaricious, 18-year-old nymphomaniac. This was not the case.

It seemed helpful to trace four sub-groups of kept relationships in order to provide a more detailed investigation of the social worlds involved. The boundaries of these groups are arbitrary. I do not pretend to have made a definitive classification of all types of kept relationships or that these role types are based on complete scientific objectivity. Rather, my identification of sub-groups constitutes a surrender to subjectivity and the Humpty Dumpty notion that a category means 'just what I choose it to mean – neither more nor less'.

'Kept woman' is an opaque umbrella term for a multitude of types and my classifications mark rough divisions between the various forms of behaviour they display and the conceptions of their roles expressed by the women themselves. To present the kept woman as if she were a member of a homogeneous group in terms of social network, motivation and self-definition is to obscure the different forms the role takes. The writers of pulp fiction suggest that she is to be known by a flashy car, racy lingerie and a 'Deep Throat' attitude towards sexuality. This is patently untrue. Although some relationships seemed to approximate the stereotype – the woman living on a lavish scale with a spectacular display of material possessions – there was no evidence of a consistent 'kept woman mentality' or standard of living throughout the sample. It was possible, however, to observe certain similarities in terms of attitudes towards their position within each of the four sub-groups. Anecdotes about the various women who constituted the sample will elaborate this observation in each of the chapters. The categories are:

1. The Mistress: the adulterous affair in which the woman professes love for the male partner and which, divested of the impropriety of the union, resembles monogamy.

2. The Career Woman: this has been crudely referred to as 'sleeping your way to the top'.

3. The Professional Opportunist: the relationship is basically a marriage of convenience. Unlike the Career Woman/lover relationship, the manifestly ambitious strategy is missing or tangential. It lacks the extended participation in a network group that characterizes the Smart Set and also lacks the emotional fervour of the Mistress's commitment to her male partner. While the Smart Set Woman is a team player the Opportunist is a solo performer whose relationship may or may not be part of a professional career of being supported by interchangeable men.

4. The Smart Set Woman: an approximation of the form of prostitution encapsulated in the 'party girl'. The lifestyle is a calculated career of being kept by a series of different men. The term Smart Set is drawn from two sources: *Smart Set* magazine, a New York publication of the 1920s and a predecessor to the *New Yorker*, *Tatler* and other journals which pander to the rich and fashionable, and second, John D. Spooner's *Smart People: A User's Guide to Experts*, a book which stresses the desirability of cultivating profitable friendships. Together, these sources provide my definition of the Smart Set Woman as one who deliberately attempts to gain entrance and secure membership among society's elite. In this sub-group the kept woman is not isolated but exists among an extended network of others who support her role and make it viable.

Placing the respondents in the correct group poses real problems, and there is some overlap between categories, reflecting a horizontal mobility between types of kept women. A notable irony exists in that should any of my respondents marry their lovers, their actions and their role definitions would neatly be subsumed by the title of wife. At this point it would be superfluous to speculate on the sincerity of their affections although it does not necessarily follow that the women's conception of their role would have fundamentally changed. The woman who is kept by a man may later marry him for love, or money or convenience, and marriage may be just a slip of paper. One of the women I interviewed – a former, high-priced call girl – was kept by her married lover and later married him after he divorced his wife. Although she receives frequent attention from the press, her life before her marriage is never mentioned. Marriage seems to have acted as the metaphorical birth to her new persona and to have conferred retroactive virginity and respectability. It is assumed that a wife loves her husband and that marriage makes an honest woman of her. The role of the wife may, however, like that of the kept woman, be based on a number of different ideas.

It seemed important to base my categories on the reasons the women themselves gave for being involved in their present relationships. Given that a substantial number of my respondents had had previous kept relationships, it could be argued that the dividing line should simply be between 'prostitute' and 'mistress'. I chose not to do this for various reasons. First, if the number of previous relationships was the only factor taken into account in determining which women were prostitutes, this would presume a commitment to a career of prostitution which in fact might not exist. Certain women did make a career of being kept while others had simply had previous kept relationships. The difference may seem slight, but it is very real. To draw an analogy, it is the difference between a soldier and a mercenary or hit-man. The soldier may decide to fight for a number of reasons; with the mercenary or hired killer, killing is a professional career role. Second, identifying certain women as prostitutes might encourage the assumption that these women entered each and every relationship for the identical reason and that the reason remained constant within the course of the relationship. Unlike the mercenary, the prostitute does not always regard her target with stoic indifference. To insist that 'a leopard cannot change its spots' ignores the fact that people's patterns of behaviour and attitudes are not fixed but subject to change. Finally, although certain forms of behaviour may constitute prostitution the tendency in previous works discussing the kept woman, however briefly, is to judge her as a 'prostitute type' on the basis of her receiving financial support.

The prostitute type is ostensibly avaricious, sexually loose or promiscuous, immoral and so on. The act that contravenes the normal female role (having sex with a man in return for money) is thought to provide conclusive information about her character. It is more than a moral flaw or character fault that motivates a woman to make a career out of being supported by interchangeable men. The social context and practical feasibility of the relationship are important, for it is neither consummated nor conducted on a desert island far from civilization: the rules of society impinge on the most personal or intimate relationships.

In reading biographies of the famous courtesans of history, you inevitably learn something about the mores and manners of the time. While this study is like the photograph of the bear's nose, focusing on a particular aspect of modern society, nevertheless it attempts to conduct an autopsy of a sub-group in the society that sustains it and to analyse the role of the contemporary kept woman in the society in which she lives. Any type of descriptive research is grounded in a specific social setting. While *Dialogues Among the Courtesans* by Lucian, the second-century Greek satirist, glorifies the courtesan and William Acton's *Prostitution*, written in 1857, vilifies her, both inadvertently reveal more and less than objective reality. The former displays a certain social tolerance, the latter an antipathy towards the role of the kept woman. If Acton takes the tone of someone writing from Mount Parnassus it reflects upon the time in which he wrote, the time of the Contagious Diseases Acts. By describing the minutiae of how the kept woman occupies her time and with whom, her social environment is unveiled. The aristocracy are no longer the only men wealthy enough to keep a mistress, nor is the life of the kept woman strictly linked to the royal court, although the kept relationship financed by an Arab man may be reminiscent of a royal court and its courtesans, underlings and lackeys. The role of the Career Woman, however, reflects a different lifestyle and type of kept relationship.

The social worlds of the kept woman in this book could be portrayed as a series of concentric circles, some of which overlap while others only touch at specific points. It is a grand hotel whose register includes Arabs, Europeans, Africans and North Americans and where people may linger or depart quickly, know others well, have a nodding acquaintance with still others or stay largely to themselves. I should emphasize that my research represents work undertaken in London during 1980–1982 and cannot claim to be representative of all kept woman/lover relationships. The social setting is important and determines the scope and character of information collected. This book is not a 'how to' manual, a salacious treatise or a moralistic one. It should be read simply as a piece of social history.

Despite the licentious image of the kept woman, the following inform-ation (expressed to the nearest percentage) garnered from my cor-respondents and interviewees does not bring to mind a confirmed nymphomaniac, or as some writers on prostitution suggest, a lesbian:

1	Participated in an orgy or had sex with more than one person at a time	9%
2	Still had occasional lesbian relationships	3%

3	Experienced a lesbian relationship in their past	11%
4	First sexual intercourse between ages of 15 to 20	72%
5	Generally slept with a man on the first date	20%
6	Sex was generally enjoyable	40%
7	Sex was almost always enjoyable	15%
8	Were 'thinking of England' during sex	9%
9	Enjoyment of sex variable, depending on the partner, feeling towards him, his attractiveness and so on (i.e. occasionally enjoyable/neither expressly enjoyable nor disagreeable)	36%

I have found that much of the ambiguity about the role of the kept woman is not due only to the dearth of material on mistresses or on affairs but to the presentation of the extramarital affair in the works which do exist. The 'If it feels good do it' philosophy which characterizes much popular fiction disregards anything other than hedonism as the basis for the relationship. Conventional society is totally ignored or ridiculed while protagonists congratulate each other on being 'liberated'. Medico-theological writers on prostitution, adultery and wantonness, on the other hand, preach the inviolable ethics of righteous living and punishment for transgressors, drawing on the Bible (Proverbs 6:24–28) for their beliefs:

> To keep thee from the evil woman, from the flattery of the tongue of a strange woman. Lust not after her beauty in thine heart; neither let her take thee with her eyelids. For by means of a whorish woman a man is brought to a piece of bread: and the adultress will hunt for the precious life. Can a man take fire in his bosom, and his clothes not be burned? Can one go upon hot coals, and his feet not be burned?

There seems to be a tendency for writers dealing with morally sensitive areas such as prostitution and adultery to present their arguments with what amounts to religious fervour. In dealing with either topic many authors have given their interest as rising out of a desire for moral reform. They have distanced themselves from the topic by penning maudlin dedications to their wonderful and devoted spouses and 2.2 cherubic-faced children and gone on fistwaving, spurred on by avowed moral indignation. Adultery (or prostitution) they argue, is a moral sin. Every man should have one God and one wife. With logic firmly based in ethnocentrism and neo-Darwinism they suggest that the monogamous marriage which is observed in Western society has evolved and represents a higher stage of civilized social life – that is, that polygamy and polyandry are characteristic of a primitive or uncivilized society. The monogamous ideal is not a universal norm, however. In Clellan S. Ford and Frank A. Beach's work, *Patterns of Sexual Behaviour*, the authors reported that of the 185 societies they studied, only 16 per cent formally restricted infidelity and, within that percentage, less than a third totally disapproved of both premarital and extramarital liaisons. Additionally, in *Of Time, Work and Leisure*, Simon de Grazia wryly notes that: 'among the remote Baluchi of western Pakistan, the penalty for adultery is death. If it were enforced, there would be few Baluchi left alive. The rule is served only to supply a dash of danger.' Although monogamy in a global context may not be the norm statistically, the social organization of the monogamous marriage is sanctioned and sanctified by church and state in Western society. Regarding the extramarital affair as behaviour that breaks the rules is an aspect of social and cultural setting. Pronouncements about the rights and wrongs of adultery and prostitution are inessential to my study; they only become relevant when and if the woman herself was conscious of the possibility of being labelled an 'immoral woman' and sought to negotiate a label for her behaviour which was sympathetic rather than derogatory. Branding the kept woman as moral or immoral is not my concern.

Recent surveys on sexual behaviour suggest that having a mistress has reached epidemic proportions, but if this is true a vast amount of 'passing' must go on. Combined with giving an appearance of unquestioned respectability is a pervasive reticence about revealing an indulgence which may offend some people. The maxim 'Do not fornicate in Old Etonian braces' has been updated to read 'By all means fornicate in Old Etonian braces but do so with style and a sense of propriety!'

> Americans are not particularly tolerant of this sort of behaviour – if it is brought to light. It's a different thing if done discreetly and not the subject of common gossip in the wrong circles. (*56-year-old man, Sacramento*)

> [*Does your wife know?*] My wife has the most immaculate sensitivities – she has her boyfriend as well – the idea of my keeping a mistress does not bring a tear to her eye. As long as I don't embarrass her – and I wouldn't – we have a perfect marriage. (*51-year-old man, London*)

> As for mistresses, I know lots and lots!! It's more a matter of knowing the right people than there not being any. Unlike the traditional English tea, the practice of keeping a mistress is not dead. (*62-year-old man, Edinburgh*)

The kept relationship is not covert but is generally restricted to certain people and places. There is no general encouragement of individuals who are having extramarital affairs to 'kiss and tell'. This feature, combined with the sanctity of private places and the reticence of the press to expose powerful people aids the participants to escape being pilloried for their behaviour. The popular press is no moral vigilante squad. It is more likely that an affair would be reported on the lines 'So-and-so seen dining with his new blonde gal-pal' than as an outrage to decent citizens. None the less, wealthy and powerful people exercise a certain veto. I became aware of affairs which were common knowledge in the social world of a man's network group – homosexual liaisons, the eminently respectable government minister and his seventeen-year-old girlfriend – which have totally escaped becoming known at all outside it. Newsworthy stories are passed over by reporters in exchange for remaining in the good graces of people who would steadily throw out a minnow of gossip in order to keep the whale of scandal in their unpublicized sanctuary. More than one 'exclusive' London nightclub admits photographers and journalists on the understanding that they direct their attention in specified directions only. It seems rather hard to believe that I could so easily find many skeletons in the cupboards of the highly placed and that no ambitious reporter could have stumbled on to the same information. For whatever reason, much goes on that never makes the news headlines.

The anthropologist, T. Gregor, has suggested that what differentiates the extramarital affair from marriage is the disparate amount of publicity given to the relationship. That is, marriage is a public event, in fact, it is often a three-ringed circus, especially for those who are wealthy. On the other hand the code of etiquette for 'affairs' in a Western context demands discretion in the relationship. The men and women I interviewed acknowledged their concern that the affair should not embarrass the man or jeopardize his career or his family. It is therefore not surprising that the lifestyle of the kept woman has escaped the exhaustive examination to which others like the street-walker have been exposed. The behaviour of the street-walker is of course by definition more conspicuous and, paradoxically, the wealth of the kept woman's lovers has led to a poverty of research, a result of limited access and curtailed visibility.

One of the problems encountered in researching kept women has been the unwillingness of people to associate themselves with the subject, like the magazine editors mentioned in the Preface, since identification with kept women might lead, they imagine, to the discrediting of their moral standing. To be furnished with a label of immorality can be distressing for a woman – or man – who does not believe in sexual liberation or libertinism *per se* but drifts into an affair or falls in love with her or his partner. Over three-quarters of my female respondents admitted to disclosing their involvement with a married man to other people who recognized that there was an ongoing relationship while concealing the fact of financial support in order to reduce the chance of being badly thought of. It was this fact which they felt laid them open to accusations of immorality more than simply having an affair with a married man. Women who made a career of being kept used this strategy in dealing with people who might have been critical or intolerant of the way in which they chose to earn their living. While recognition of being kept may be actively sought in order to establish status among a network of women who are similarly involved, the kept relationship can pass for a straightforward love affair to those who might be severe in their judgment.

Generally women seemed to think that being kept would be looked on as more discreditable than being the girlfriend of a married man. A woman may tell her friends that she is involved with a married man in the hope that they will be sympathetic and guard her secret. It was expected that a comrade would understand and be supportive of her actions. In this way, the onus is on the friend to fulfil the duties of being a true friend. Another strategy used to head off attacks was to discredit the critics. Women would say that their actions were less disreputable than those of women who slept around, or who were married and cheated on their husbands; men would say that their actions were more honourable than those of husbands who deserted their wives and families. By claiming that 'nobody really minds any more' or that society is hypocritical and only paid lip service to the idea that adultery is wrong, the respondent could deny the supposed impropriety of his or her behaviour.

A fourth way in which my respondents sought to explain their behaviour was to claim to be in love with their partner, as if this was sufficient justification for any anti-social behaviour – rather like pleading incompetence in a legal trial. Falling in love may be thought governed by rather less reason than choosing a dry-cleaner, so that if a person's behaviour deviates from the norm or breaks society's unwritten rules, being in love – that renowned condition of diminished responsibility – may be presented as an excuse. Furthermore, the presence of love in a relationship may be believed by the person to confer on it a degree of respectability. A woman may claim that she loves her male partner so that she will not be thought of as a prostitute or an immoral woman. Thus, love may be used to whitewash the relationship, denying that it is merely one of social or financial expedience. In saying that she simply fell in love, a woman may seek to deny that she can be held accountable for her actions or be chastised for them.

My female respondents generally presented their particular relationship as the exceptional case. They implied that their unique circumstances, whatever they may have been, warranted their behaviour. They were not particularly tolerant of others in the same position. The women themselves judged each other's relationships in terms of a respectability depending upon variables such as the length of time spent in the relationship, the social status of the woman's lover and the style in which she was kept. Style, in its turn, was a matter of being subsidized or totally supported, living in luxury or restricted to a budget, and enjoying sexual exclusivity or promiscuity. Among the various categories of kept women the importance attached to any one variable differed. For example, the Mistress type stressed the longevity of the union, her fidelity and her love for her male partner as testament to her respectability. In contrast, the Smart Set woman and the Professional Opportunist would stress the man's wealth or fame and the elegance of her lifestyle. In both cases, however, they would attempt to present being kept as other than disreputable and there was a consciousness of relative respectability in status. One woman, who was kept by a Middle Eastern man, was triumphant when he declared that he would never buy her rubies, since within the network circle they were a trademark of the common prostitute or female lackey who was passed from man to man. She felt his statement testified to her superior status within the network of girls that accompanied the man and his friends. Another woman was told not to mingle with a group of agency girls sent to provide window-dressing and light relief at a social function. This distancing was important in establishing that her role was unlike that of a prostitute; mingling with the girls would have threatened her status and might have brought guilt by association upon her.

Different people look to different sources when seeking to have the label of respectability conferred upon them. The respectability attached to being a kept woman may be based on a logic which is little influenced by traditional ways of thinking. For example, the social world of the woman who makes a career out of being kept is a caricature of the taken-for-granted world. It exaggerates the ethos of conspicuous consumption, the life of glamour and the desirability of spectator participation in the lives of the wealthy and/or powerful. Traditionally, women have been encouraged to better themselves through marriage. With few exceptions, the women in my study regarded being kept as a means to moving up the social ladder. They saw themselves as meeting and being accepted by a better class of people, attending social activities and enjoying spontaneous holidays – activities in which they would otherwise have been unable to participate. They thought that moving in circles of high social status conferred on them respectability and gave them lustre. The kept woman basked in the reflected glory of her male companion.

In *Deviance and Respectability*, Jack Douglas notes:

> . . . The various categories of social status . . . have become themselves morally meaningful categories . . . it is apparent that the categorical status of poor (and, even more, that of lower class) has as one of its abstract meanings that of being immoral, at least to the large middle-class groups. On the other hand, being well off, successful and so on, means (in the abstract) being virtuous to these same groups.

If the woman attaches little importance to the opinions of people who 'don't count anyway', placing a high value on herself may follow from identifying herself with the 'beautiful people'. The woman who makes a career of being kept bases the legitimacy of her role on her belief that living well materially is synonymous with high social status and respectability.

Although being the supported girlfriend of a married man may be thought of as a 'deviant' role, the way she lives may be a caricature of rather than a challenge to the traditional roles women are encouraged to adopt in their relationships with men. This should not be surprising, for the totally liberated kept woman is a contradiction in terms. What she does and what she says may tell us more about things than an improper romantic involvement. As one woman remarked:

> Are you including wives in your study? [*No, why?*]They certainly form the largest amount of women who are kept don't they? When I was younger we used to have debutantes' balls – have you heard about them? Girls brought up with one aim in life and that was to attract a rich man, marry well, and sit at home while someone else took care of her meals, her cleaning and her children. Most married women are better called kept women. (*56-year-old woman, London*)

Whether or not you agree with this woman's comment, titillating portrayals of kept women in fiction and films obscure traits which may be common both to the role of mistress and to women in more conventional types of relationships. If the relationship can be viewed as verging on prostitution it is also reminiscent of ways in which men and women react to each other when playing their conventional roles. Unlike the prostitute's encounter with a patron, the kept relationship is more than a market-place transaction exchanging sex for support. The prostitute and her client strike a straightforward bargain – if he wants a specific sexual position or variation he pays the agreed price and if he is especially pleased he may leave a tip. The limited time spent with a prostitute in a hotel room may allow the relationship to remain strictly sexual. The exchange in other social relationships is less precise, however, and the role of the mistress may be more like that of the wife than of the prostitute. Few would deny that the relationship between a wife and her husband involves more than sex and the establishment of financial support. Even if a man marries specifically to ensure himself a regular sex life, and the woman marries in order to be supported, the man and his wife will presumably interact in situations other than the bedroom. The roles of being a wife and a mistress are not dissimilar, and the fact of having once been a wife or a mistress does not preclude the subsequent adoption of the alternative role.

Where the kept woman deviates from the norm is, it is thought, in allowing herself to be supported by a married man. It is this acceptance of support which seems to offend certain moral sensitivities, especially if the woman makes a career of such relationships. There is no suggestion, however, that the numerous women who have made a career of marriages to rich men have committed a moral offence even if they are gold diggers. It may be that to become a kept woman does not require her to undergo a fundamental conversion or refute what society suggests is the proper way for women to conduct their lives. In *Symbolic Leaders*, Orrin Klapp writes:

> Glory is concentrated in hero types, the bulk of which in American culture – possibly eight-ninths – cannot properly be called feminine (for instance: 'pin up girl' has a specifically feminine gender, 'reformer' is shared by men and women, and 'strong man' is specifically masculine) . . . Of course . . . there are important, specifically feminine heroic roles, such as beauty contest winner, prima donna, glamour girl, best dressed woman, Lady Bountiful, and self-sacrificing nurses. Tradition also provides attractive models of heroic women: Ruth, Cordelia, The Patient Griselda, Cinderella, Penelope, Antigone, Helen of Troy, Madame du Barry, Cleopatra, and Queen Elizabeth. But it is interesting to note how much choice has actually been confined to two types of glory: the faithful submissive Penelope–mother–sufferer–helper; or the erotic queen who may use her attraction as a means of power over men but does not strike out for herself.

The kept woman preoccupation with romance or glamour and with cosmetic frills is evident of her need for adult female pacifiers. By and large, the women in my study were not explorers. They did not attempt to set off on their own or become self-sufficient. Rather, they relied on their lover or on a series of lovers to provide for them. Their daydreams of romance or glamour or wealth preoccupied them with the building of sandcastles as Dorothy Parker's poem quoted at the front of this book suggests. Playing happily in a child's sandpit and building majestic sandcastles, the kept woman neglects the intrinsic frailty of the structure she creates. She is not the man's legitimate wife, she has no legal rights in the relationship, nor does she necessarily receive the legitimization or public support of her right to be 'kept' by the man, let alone any redress if the relationship ends. Perhaps the greatest difference between the role of the kept woman and one who makes a career out of marrying rich men is in security of tenure. The kept woman is only the temporary occupant of a sandcastle . . .

Chapter One

THE MISTRESS

I realize that my relationship is the exception and not the rule – but it was filled with much loving, and giving and pleasure. He was, and is my friend, confidant, and although no longer my lover in the physical sense of the word, he is still my lover. Oh, in case it is important, he was the first man I ever had sexual relations with and I was totally faithful to him. (*35-year-old woman, Texas*)

The Mistress type thinks of her relationship as the exception, not as the average affair, which she may denigrate as immoral or unseemly. She does not generally profess any emotional empathy with other women who are being kept; it is more likely that she will look upon them as mercenary, that is, 'in it only for the money'. The Mistress is not sexually promiscuous, she does not pursue the ideal of liberated sexuality for its own sake, nor does she impute that ideal to the man. Sexual intercourse is seen as making a physical bond between the participants in the affair rather than as something that is uniquely satisfying in and of itself. The Mistress implies that her special circumstances warrant her behaviour, justifying her conduct in terms of the ideal of romantic love in which sexual intercourse is a symbolic, rather than a purely physical act, between two people who are 'in love' and intend to be married. She generally maintains that her love for her male partner is unaffected by his ability to provide her with financial support, and strongly denies that the man's wealth makes him a desirable lover. Consistent with modelling themselves on traditional roles such as girlfriend, fiancée or wife, financial assistance is portrayed as equivalent to the husband's role of provider. As such, the pejorative connotation of support being payment for services rendered can be avoided:

He helps me out because he wants to, he doesn't have to after all, it's not like he's paying me; even without the money he knows that it wouldn't change anything. (*42-year-old woman, London*)

It's only natural that when you love someone you want to take care of them and ensure that they're not wanting for anything. Dave helps me out because he wants me to have part of him in my life, a reminder of the times we've had together. (*34-year-old woman, Denver*)

The kept woman and her lover are not sexual renegades or necessarily rebels against the conventional social order. For the majority, the world does not move from left to right or become suspended when they embark upon this type of relationship. Popular fiction suggests that the sexual liberation of women has finally arrived and that the kept woman is particularly liberated in her attitudes and behaviour. I would argue that the sexual liberation of women is as authentic as the Loch Ness monster. Some people believe it exists, others claim to have seen it, and some simply regard it as the invention of the mass media. For women, respectability is still linked to being sexually chaste, and juxtaposed with the maxim 'If it feels good do it' are the admonishments that 'Good girls don't', and 'No woman is worth money who takes it'. There is no reason to assume that the kept relationship is a pornographer's dream rather than a love affair. The difference between the seduction scene in 'Rose of Romance' type novels and soft-porn books is the amount of space given to graphic details. In the former the lights are demurely turned off after the first kiss, leaving something to the imagination, while in the latter every grope is painstakingly recorded. The reality, however, is no more and no less than the act itself and the meaning behind it is subject to interpretation. Even when and if one party thinks of coitus as straightforward fornication, the other may still call it an act of love. The cynic could argue that the kept woman likes or tolerates the man and loves his money. Everyone knows that sexual attraction or lust exists outside marriage, but love is thought to be a misnomer in the context of the kept relationship. What the kept woman professes to feel is thought of as cupboard love, not real love. The argument is familiar to pet-owners – would your pet continue to love you if you did not feed it? It seems unnecessary to question the foundation on which love exists if the woman herself professes its presence. A prostitute's relationship with a man can be viewed as a blatant exchange of sex for money, but the function of financial support in the kept relationship is more opaque.

The adage that 'men give love to get sex and women give sex to get love' is over-simplifying the situation but the phrase captures the uneasy alliance of male and female attitudes to sex as an act of love. For the Mistress, the supposed deviancy or wrongfulness of the relationship is mitigated by the fact that it is a love affair.

The hopelessness of love with a married man may suggest itself as being the proverbial love story. That the mistress or the married man is forbidden fruit can contribute to the tendency to fantasize the relationship. Bound up in the pursuit of a forbidden object is the need for secrecy, intrigue and socially imposed deprivation, making the situation poignant, heroic or even tragic. The great love stories are invariably tragedies; only in fairy tales do the prince and princess live happily ever after. In the love affair that facilitates the fulfilment of intense sensations, love is neither rational nor necessarily bound by social convention.

The power of love may be thought greater than traditional morality. Thinking of the relationship as a love story can transfigure it from something mundane, a false step in the social sense, into a romance. It might be said that there is nothing romantic about an adulterous love affair, which necessarily involves deception, and dishonesty, but thinking of it as a love story suggests that those involved ignore patent reality.

One woman I interviewed has been a kept woman for over 40 years and views herself as the man's polygamous wife. As if to assure me of the durability of their love, she told me that she is provided for in her lover's will. A second respondent, a 25-year-old girl, is not discomfited by the fact that during her lover's professed separation from his wife the latter has given birth to two children. She has broken off with him repeatedly and tends to recite lugubrious elegies every time she does so, telling of the good times they had together – but she inevitably takes up with him again. Both of these women look on their relationships as love affairs and find solace in the fact. Others seem captivated with the artefacts of romance – love-letters and hearts-and-flowers sentimentalism.

In novels, the mistress is typically young, beautiful, and decked with jewels; my first detailed case history is none of these things. If it is difficult for young people to imagine their parents or other older people in the act of making love it may also be difficult to imagine them embracing the ideal of romantic love. Nevertheless, 'falling in love' and seeing the kept relationship as a love affair is not an experience exclusive to the young, the naive and the aesthetically beautiful.

Mary (aged 53) has three children ranging in age from 24 to 29 and lives in England. Divorced seven years ago, she said that one of her only regrets in life was that she did not divorce ten years earlier. She was battered as a wife and only stayed with her husband because she felt her children would not only suffer emotionally by not having a father around but also economically in being unable to afford such things as going to university:

> My parents had a horrible marriage. When I was eight my father disappeared with another woman and didn't come back for nine years. My mother never divorced him, she thought the scandal of being divorced was worse than being married to him and took him

back when he returned. When I told my parents that Alex [her husband] was beating me they told me that they had said from the start he was no good but I had made my own bed and had to lie in it. I used to think if I could make it past 60 I wouldn't care any more what Alex did. One day I realized that waiting meant I'd have to spend the same amount of time in the marriage that I already had spent and I just couldn't stand that. Alex never understood why I divorced him. He told people that it was because I was ambitious and he wasn't. I thought the kids needed a stable family. Then I realized that what they were getting was a mother who was going crazy and unable to cope with life.

By profession Mary is a teacher. She met Bill, her present lover, at an educational seminar at which he was a speaker. Bill is 64 and has been married for over 40 years. He has a married daughter and three grandchildren. Mary described their first meeting to me:

We were both staying in a hotel and a few of us went for dinner and stayed on until the bar closed. Bill said he had a bottle in his room so we went up there for a final drink. Gradually, everyone else left and I don't remember exactly what happened. In the morning I think we both felt 'My God, what have I done?' and were pretty embarrassed by the whole thing. I imagine part of the reason I kept in touch with him was because I wanted to reassure myself that he didn't think me the type that can just go to bed with someone and not think anything of it.

With this last point Mary admits to constructing a context of friendship after the event to make having had sex with Bill acceptable to herself. She wanted to establish herself in his eyes as someone other than the type who is lightheartedly promiscuous. To the Mistress, the bad girl/good girl division exists and Mary's behaviour acknowledges it. It is typical of the Mistress to point to her fidelity within the relationship as proof that she is a decent woman whose conduct is honourable. It is interesting that Mary attempts to reconcile her initial involvement, which was impulsive and physical, with her conception of what is acceptable – to make something more out of a sexual encounter which labelled her as a one-night stand. Mary gets as excited as a young girl over her meetings with Bill, who is a romantic soul himself, frequently sending letters and flowers. A typical letter from Bill would include the question:

Have I told you lately you're wonderful? You are. I am so lucky. Thank you for loving me.

Since Mary's lover is married it is necessary for the relationship to be discreet. Although they live in different cities and cannot see each other every day they still want to remain in frequent contact. Keeping in touch presents problems of its own. Mary can easily receive letters or telephone calls since she lives alone and nobody but the postman knows when she gets a letter. Writing a letter in return to Bill poses real difficulties, however. If she addresses it to his home, his wife might intercept it, read it or merely become curious as to who was regularly writing to her husband. It was decided that Mary would write to Bill via his business address and mark her letters 'personal'. Mary acknowledges that this in effect makes Bill's secretary an accomplice to the affair. If the secretary has acted the unsuspecting innocent she is 'wise' to the relationship: relaying telephone messages, placing dinner and hotel reservations, and so on.

Once the letters are safely forwarded to Bill there is the additional danger that they will be discovered by someone else and read. Mary maintains that Bill has remedied this problem by reserving a locked drawer in his office desk to conceal the letters. When he retires, however, as he will in a few years, a new strategic position will have to be found. This is not a simple matter. If he sticks the letters inside an obscure dictionary or some academic volume there is still an off-chance that someone will want to look at the chosen book and read more than originally intended. If he hides them away in a sock drawer, under the piano lid, in the toe of his ski boots or under his mattress the possibility always exists that someone will inadvertently come across their hiding place. If the man defines the relationship as a love affair it would be callous to destroy these often poetic epistles, whether they represent a loving keepsake or merely a flattering ego-booster.

The vigilance needed to keep an affair entirely discreet is rather like living each day with the expectation of being hit by a bus; that is, a concern that an emergency examination in casualty will reveal nothing but clean under-wear. In dealing with the practical difficulties of having an affair, the when and where to meet, the individuals I interviewed were mostly forced to develop a system through trial and error. Occasionally a close friend was enlisted to give advice or the 'club Casanova' sought out for his supposed knowledgeability but, as Dostoevsky wrote in his *Notes from Underground*:

> In every man's remembrances there are things he will not reveal to everybody, but only to his friends. There are other things he will not reveal even to his friends, but only to himself and then only under a pledge of secrecy. Finally, there are some things that a man is afraid to reveal even to himself, and any honest man accumulates a pretty fair number of such things. That is to say, the more respectable a man is, the moe of them he has.

The affair requires meticulous attention to detail if it is to remain undetected. For example, the man has to be consistent in the stories he tells to explain absences from home. If he says that he spent the evening having drinks with an old schoolfriend he cannot change his mind later and say that he went to the theatre. To protest that the play was so rotten that he and his old friend left and went to a bar would be too lame an attempt to cover up the meeting that actually took place. In the same way, there is a limit to the number of Old School or Sports Club reunions that can be wheeled out as a convincing alibi for more lively têtes-à-têtes.

Finding a time and a place to meet are additional complications. One club restaurant manager seemed especially sensitive to the schedule of the lover/mistress relationship. He told me that week-ends are notoriously quiet in his club, for men could not excuse their absences from home as easily as they could on weekdays. Going for drinks after work, taking a client out for dinner or simply working late at the office are excuses which can be used with certain credibility during the working week. Bill and Mary, however, cannot use these excuses to facilitate their meetings and largely depend on weekend business trips and meetings, or holidays. Conducting a long-distance love affair adds to the romance of the situation, it seems. Mary finds it exciting when Bill telephones and says: 'Meet you in city X on Saturday. I've made reservations at Hotel Y'. The lovers do not have to meet in some squalid hotel or dine in places where they are unlikely to be spotted simply because they are so dreadful nobody they are likely to know would eat there. For the wealthy, comfort does not have to be sacrificed in order to keep the relationship from becoming public knowledge.

Mary admits that she and Bill are both novices in having an affair and as such often jeopardize its secrecy. Although she is not quite sure how much Bill's wife knows about the situation she feels the need to protect him by remaining discreet. Although her children and her intimate circle of friends know about their relationship and accept it, she expressed regret at having told certain individuals. She feels that she may have allowed herself a vanity in giving voice to her pride in Bill and her relationship with him that could harm his career or family life:

> I think I'm more afraid for him than he is for himself. Maybe he'll blame me for it later or say that I broke up his home.

Like many others, Mary adopts an ostrich-like philosophy in regard to Bill's wife. She acknowledges her existence but tries to shut herself off from thinking of her or of the particulars of a divorce. The Mistress generally will deny that she has feelings of ill-will towards her lover's wife. She is more likely to take the attitude that since her lover loves her more than he does his wife, their place is rightfully together:

> Sometimes I wonder how he can reconcile it in his own mind because he's basically a very honest, old-fashioned man. I guess he doesn't bother trying or feels it is right since he loves me.

Mary's relationship seems both to delight and dismay her. She finds it incredible or out of character to be involved with a married man and to accept his financial support. Mary equates Bill's financial support with the husband's role of provider, testimony to his true care and concern for her welfare. The Mistress type looks upon the behaviour of the woman who is officially 'kept' as discreditable and abnormal. While the Opportunist type stresses that the man's support is the most salient reason for the maintenance of the relationship, the Mistress stresses the emotional bond and likens the union to that of marriage.

The 'best friend' relationship will often develop within the love affair. Bill is not only Mary's lover but also her confidant. Since she is aware of his unequivocal acceptance of her, she is completely at ease with him and feels encouraged to discuss her dreams and fears without worrying that she will be thought stupid, over-emotional or ridiculous. This awareness may similarly apply to physical acceptance, giving an assurance that the man – or woman – will not think his or her partner kinky, perverted or a turn-off because of physical attributes or sexual preferences. Beth, a 49-year-old divorced woman, told me that she was able to have oral sex with her lover for the first time because his admiration for her was so continuously reassuring that she never felt embarrassed or self-conscious. It seems reasonable for us to like those whom we perceive to like us. The person to whom we confess all and expose our self-perceived flaws may become someone we love because they consider us as lovable and worthy of love. Each man seemed to hold the promise of a panacea for the woman's self-doubt or problems. He values the woman, or affirms some quality that she feels has not before or never will be noticed or desired, but for him: 'He makes me feel like a desirable woman' and 'he makes me feel like a girl again'. There is a sense of exhilaration that the man finds her so beautiful and/or desirable.

Most women in a long-term love affair stressed how important the man's openness in discussing his feelings was to them. Not only 'feelings' but also talking openly about his past triumphs and failures are seen as professions of his love. The ability to express your feelings without restraint is a quality often emphasized in defining the relationship as a love affair. Sexual intercourse is not necessarily the starting point of a broader relationship as happened with Mary. Nevertheless, one form of intimacy may lead to another.

Although Mary maintains that she is in love with Bill, her feelings about marriage are ambivalent. She vacillates between hoping for marriage and feeling that marriage may change the nature of the relationship for the worse. Her past experience as a wife has not jaundiced her towards marriage *per se*, but she feels that going through a divorce is 'hell' and she said she did not want to impose this on her lover. Not only that, but she is afraid that his behaviour would change with marriage, that he would blame her for his divorce, the estrangement of his daughter and grandchildren, and that the romance of the relationship would become dissipated. This fear was not atypical. Although marriage was the mystical goal, some Mistresses were timid and reticent about the subject. Some seemed to be in love with romance and with being in love more than with the idea of settling down to life in the suburbs:

> I was terrified when he started saying that he'd applied for a job transfer and we could start a new life together. I found myself telling him to take things slowly and to be sure that's what he really wanted. (*21-year-old woman, London*)

This Mistress thus seeks a reprieve from a situation which she is convinced would only serve to diminish the romance of the union. Just as an adolescent who may enjoy dating and being in love but not feel ready for a serious commitment, so the Mistress may be afraid of marriage because of past failure or anticipated problems, such as his children not liking her, or his children being favoured over the ones they might have together and the usual domestic rows. She may feel unprepared, unsuitable for or unwilling to assume the role of wife. As one respondent said:

> The way it is now everything I do charms and delights him. I'm sloppy and he'll follow me around a room picking up things. His wife is supposed to be extremely tidy and organized. He is as well and I just think back to my own marriage where my husband couldn't stand to see things untidy and would yell and fuss all the time. I know that if we were married he wouldn't find it all so charming any more. (*47-year-old woman, London*)

Although the love story is more likely to be applied to the relationship by the female than the male, just under a fifth of my male respondents spoke of a desire for romance or to missing romance in their marriages. These men saw love and romance as two separate ideas. Romance was conceived as synonymous with passion, sexual attraction and excitement while love was more prosaic, perhaps incompatible with marriage but nevertheless a term reserved for the affection you had for your wife and children. Occasionally a man would look rather disdainful when I asked him if he loved his mistress, telling me: 'You shouldn't be so influenced by the movies'.

This separation of love and romance is interesting. Passion is reserved for the chase, for the pursuit of the unattainable. Whether or not the Mistress and her lover identify the relationship as a love affair for the same reasons, the 'love story' may provide the script for it. When I interviewed the male partners of women I had already spoken to I noted with disconcerting frequency how rarely there was any similarity in their understanding of the relationship. Indeed, for a woman to see the affair as a love story does not necessarily require the man to be Tristan to her Iseult, only that she should perceive him as such. For both actors, the romance of the situation may be promoted by the circumscribed nature of the relationship itself. Neither reality nor banality need impinge upon the Utopian ideal. He need never see her in curlers and face cream and she need not see him day in, day out, unshaven and as likely as not in a foul mood. The romantic fantasy is based on being able to place the partner on a pedestal. A fantasy, by definition, is not a head-on confrontation with reality.

The Mistress as a type of kept woman tends to rhapsodize over the relationship and the wonderful qualities her lover possesses, and is likely to point to romantic gestures on the man's part. A Mistress would show me her love-letters, telling me that the man had sent flowers or given her a gift, as if this were unequivocal evidence that the relationship was a love affair. Every time I saw Mary she would show me her latest love-letter laced with effusive professions of love, grin at me and ask 'I think he loves me, don't you?' Nor was it infrequent for the excitement over a relationship to be described as 'really living instead of existing' or being in love for the first time.

> I was married and divorced before I was 30 and thought that maybe something was wrong with me, that maybe I was just the type of person who never would be happy. When Mark came along I knew that it's just that I didn't meet him soon enough. For the first time in years I feel life is exciting and that I'm not just a spectator looking in at life. (*26-year-old woman, Texas*)

> My daughter says that my life is more exciting than hers is . . . I never thought I'd have this excitement in my life and whenever I question if it's right or wrong I just think, well, you only go around once. (*51-year-old woman, Calgary*)

The romance of the affair often seems as important as the relationship itself, but both tend to be depicted in idealistic terms. Just as the 'Lady' of the allegorical sonnet was an ideal image rather than an actual woman with human faults, so the love story is told without regard for its selfish quality or imperfections.

According to Melissa Sands, the founder of Mistresses Anonymous:

> The married man is a man with responsibilities . . . has defined himself . . . has committed himself to a woman for the future. He has pledged his life to family goals and dedicated his energy to achieving them.

The above is but a short quotation, the original (in her book *The Mistress' Survival Manual* in a chapter called 'Ecstasy . . . The Appeal of the Married Man') expands on the pathos of the situation. Melissa Sands, as a former Mistress, can serve as a sterling example of the woman who is in love with love. By saying that part of the appeal of the married man is knowing that he has 'pledged his life to family goals and dedicated his energy to achieving them' she overlooks the fact that having an affair represents a misdirection of energy. Making such a statement without comment, she illustrates the tendency to idealization. Sands's admiration for the married man's pledge might seem somewhat misplaced. It is difficult to see how seriously he is taking his responsibilities so far as the oaths of marriage are concerned. In all her books Sands seeks to present herself as a romantic, lacing the text with her rather maudlin poetry and song lyrics by her lover/husband. The dedication to her first book reveals how fully she has embraced 'romance' and the love story as the model for behaviour. Melissa Sands is the success story of the mistress who marries her lover and the book is dedicated to her husband 'Whose talents have scored all my dreams, whose alchemy has guided my life'.

In my research I found that the fact that the man was married was thought of variously as an escape mechanism, as an obstacle to the couple's happiness, and/or as a source of tension and self-doubt, exemplified by the woman asking herself whether she was the type who would ruin another woman's happiness. Regarding his marital status as a plus seems to be a contentious point. The Mistress was more likely to claim that the man was estranged from his family and that his role in it was more the provider than the husband and father. Both views, however, appear to exonerate the man from being thought liable to cheat in normal circumstances. The Mistress does not believe that because the man commits adultery with her there is a possibility he would cheat on her – although the love you would suppose he once had for his wife did not prohibit him from cheating on her with his Mistress. Similarly, the Mistress disputes the suggestion that her lover's only interest in her is sexual. His present infidelity is not interpreted to mean that he would cheat on *her* should they be married. Mary recounted to me:

> He [Bill] always says to me, 'One day you'll meet the type of great guy you deserve and I'll lose you . . . but I'll kill the bastard'. But I'm not really looking for anyone else. I don't go on dates with other men and I still wear my rings [her wedding band and engagement rings from her marriage to Alex] because I feel married. Once at a party Tom [a male friend who knows of her relationship] said: 'Wouldn't you be afraid if you married Bill that he'd play around?' I told him, 'I'd wear Bill so completely out that he wouldn't have energy left to play around.' It's Tom who's a real tomcat, not Bill. I never think of Bill as even looking at women really. He's not the type to play around in a relationship and neither am I.

Identifying your partner as a beloved often seemed equivalent to presenting him as an ideal, a person incapable of doing wrong. When love was thought to be reciprocated the Mistress did not question that her relationship could be other than a love affair. Peppering the conversation with 'I love you' may signify nothing but glibness on her lover's part, yet the Mistress often revels in the man's professions of love for her. A cynic could say that the married man has little to fear from such disclosures. If a single man says 'I love you', it can be interpreted as 'I'm serious in my intentions towards you'. If a married man says it, it can only be an indication of warm feelings with limited promise; whether or not the single man is speaking sincerely or rhetorically, 'O.K., I love you, I respect you, now let's go to bed', his expression of tenderness is not necessarily qualified by the fact that he has already pledged his love to his wife. The married man can be confiding, eloquent in his profession of love and yet not commit himself to anything permanent or anything other than openness in an affair. Since both individuals are aware of his marital status, the offer is circumscribed from the start. Nevertheless, the Mistress may look upon the love professed as more real than that of single men who are only after one thing.

In the article entitled 'Towards a Sociology of Sex' in *The Sociology of Sex*, J.M. Henslin suggests:

> Linking the concept of love with human sexuality can be viewed as one of the major forms of social control . . . While sex is not an emotion but an innate drive, love is an emotion; that is, sexual love is a learned way of thinking about our drives, a quality that we ascribe to particular experiences. By tying the concept into sexuality and then by tying love and sexuality into expectations of marriage, and then love, sexuality and marriage into expectations of procreation and family, the individual's sex drive becomes channelled along broadly predictable lines highly supportive of the social order. This conceptual ordering of reality dictates the emotions we feel and helps to pattern, shape and determine outcomes of human experiences.

The term making love may be a delicate way of referring to fornication, but it links sex to love and to romance. Coitus becomes an act of love. The absence of a more accurate and generally accepted name for a long-term sexual relationship encourages the use of the term 'love affair' to describe it. The following case history shows how the relationship may be threatened when it becomes obvious that the individuals' conceptions of the relationship are very different.

Sandra, a 27-year-old woman, was kept by her boss Stephen for 18 months. Stephen, a 43-year-old executive, encouraged her to date other men during that period but Sandra felt this indicated his unselfish nature rather than lack of interest in or detachment from their relationship. She told me that he repeatedly commented that he 'did not deserve her', that she was 'too good for him' and so on. She sought to stress her commitment to him and the relationship by remaining faithful , refusing to date other men:

> When I packed it up with all my male friends I think he got a bit
> scared. He took to giving my address to various friends of his which
> made me feel cheap. My feelings changed too. I'd been really keen
> on him but this made me see him for what he was, a middle-aged
> man making a fool of himself – you could say I dropped him.

Sandra had previously interpreted his suggestion that she go out with other
men as the peak of unselfishness when in fact it simply meant that he wanted
to withdraw from the relationship. Being in love may mean that individuals
hang on to their illusions tenaciously even when they receive little
confirmation from their partners that a relationship exists – or still exists.
Ultimately, Sandra was unable to reconcile her lover's behaviour with her
expectations of how a beloved ought to behave.

There is a structure to romance which allows for a certain predictability
in the conduct of the Mistress and her lover. The Mistress bases her
involvement in the kept relationship on role models such as the wife,
girlfriend and/or fiancée and identifies her role by the use of these terms. As
such, being an honourable woman is defined through her willingness to
enact the role of the perfect wife, sacrificing herself, if necessary, for the
benefit of the relationship. The first way in which the wife/husband
relationship is emulated is in the importance attached to being faithful.
Several respondents claimed to be virgins upon entering the relationship
and previously married women would state resolutely that during their
married life they had 'never so much as looked at another man'. When the
Mistress claimed to be a virgin or sexually inexperienced on entering the
relationship, she would emphasize that had she not loved her partner and
thought the relationship would lead to marriage she would not have
become involved in 'just an affair'. Despite commonsense assumptions
about female sexual liberation, women may still discriminate between the
justifiability of sex in the context of a relationship rather than spontaneously between two consenting adults. It seems important to the
Mistress to establish herself as a 'one-man woman'. Sexual exclusivity is
thought important in setting themselves apart from the bad type of woman.
The men, too, emphasize that their mistresses are virtuous and not the sort
of women who would deceive a man in an ongoing relationship.

It might seem ironic that a relationship founded on one member's sexual
infidelity would attach any importance to sexual fidelity. This is the case,
however, in relationships of periods longer than six months and in some of
even shorter duration. Although the man may be returning to his marital
bed, this fact was often described by the mistress as the man's 'marital duty'
rather than as an act of infidelity. Moreover, approximately three-fifths of
all Mistresses that I contacted adamantly denied that the man continued to
have sexual intercourse with his wife even though they still lived in the same
house and/or shared a bedroom:

I asked him pretty early in our relationship if he was sleeping with his wife and I was really shocked when he said 'yes'. I couldn't figure out where he'd find the time. I know he's married to her but he said that even when they first got married there was no great passion. She's from the 'right people' and socially it was supposed to be the perfect match. I was taken aback and asked 'Well, how would you feel if I went out with other men?' He hemmed and hawed, said it would be fine and then said, 'Well, you know, male jealousy'. (*22-year-old woman, London*)

It [the relationship] ended when I learned that she had slept with her former boss . . . The reason for ending the relationship was her predilection for dropping her knickers. Apparently, her former boss was not the only one. There is something comedic about expecting 'fidelity' in a situation as basically unstable as this; particularly if the man is married. (*53-year-old man, Sacramento*)

Although I was certainly no virgin when I met him he was so chauvinistic that I played along and let him 'teach me' – what a laugh! He must have believed that I had an elastic hymen because he really thought that before him I knew nothing. Here I was divorced with a child and he's saying 'Now my dear . . .'. (*27-year-old woman, London*)

The concepts of fidelity and chastity within a kept relationship are less inappropriate when you realize that the pattern of the long-term liaison approximates to marriage. The accounts given seem to emphasize this:

I think the fact that I take money from him sometimes makes him feel that he has the right to treat me like his wife . . . that he has a claim on me and that I'm expected to hold up my end of the relationship. (*22-year-old woman, London*)

I feel that I'm more involved in his life than his wife is. I'm the hostess at his parties. I'm the one he talks to about his business. I'm the one his friends know. He says that he and his wife lead completely separate lives. She doesn't like to go out or meet people and it's part of his life which he really enjoys. (*51-year-old woman, London*)

Feminists tend to portray the idea of sexual exclusivity as another form of repression, the ideological equivalent of the bound foot and chastity belt. To the Mistress, on the other hand, sexual exclusivity is a way of expressing her devotion to the man and to the relationship.

Gillian, an attractive girl aged 24, is the subject of my next detailed case history. She met her present lover when she was 18 years old. Her flatmate had been invited out by her boss and when he arrived to pick her up he brought along a friend on the flatmate's suggestion that she would feel more confortable within a group. The friend was in his late thirties and throughout the evening was attentive and non-aggressive sexually; Gillian noted this and felt it indicated his respect for her. Although her friend ceased to see her boss socially after a fortnight or so, Gillian continues to see the original 'blind date' man. She maintained that she was unaware that he was married until it was too late for her to disengage from the relationship because she was in love with him. Presenting the involvement as accidental – it was not meant to happen, it just did – seemed to be an attempt to neutralize any suggestion of misconduct on her part. She pointedly remarked: 'If I'd known he was married, I would never have gone out with him.' Many other women have similar accounts of how they became involved. They claimed that they were unaware that the man was married or said that they had met him while he was separated or temporarily estranged from his wife. In extenuation, many women would also claim that the man's marriage was already in a bad way before the onset of the relationship, failing to acknowledge that it is they who might have caused the discontent within the marital union. Nearly a quarter of the women I contacted told me that their previous knowledge of the man had made them sensitive to the state of his marriage. One respondent said that as her lover's wife's best friend she knew of the troubles in the marriage, another, who worked alongside her lover's wife, said that she – his wife – would literally weep over the unhappiness of her marriage and say that the woman was the only one who seemed to understand her problems and cared enough to listen. In other cases, their friendship with the man just grew until their feelings were too large to combat. Denying intent seemed important in establishing a respectable identity. In the situation of my first case history, Mary, the influence of a few drinks, like the love potion in the Sonnets, became the scapegoat for adulterous love.

For the Mistress, being kept represents only one part of her life. She will have to adopt a strategy by which to explain to her parents why their perfect daughter is not getting married; have to explain to her friends why her boyfriend does not make an appearance at Christmas or weekends but only on work nights and how she can suddenly afford an expensive flat and glamorous holidays one after another.

Gillian uses her career as a cover story. She works for a publishing house and her lover owns a travel agency. His wife is younger than Gillian and they have a two-year-old son. Her lover is the archetypal entrepreneur, continually investing in various businesses and branching out into sidelines. As with the majority of women I interviewed, the process whereby Gillian became kept was gradual. At first the man's financial help was restricted to his taking the traditional male courtship role by paying her way on dates, and giving her flowers and small 'tokens of affection'. Gradually it extended into more substantial sums to 'help her out', take her on holidays and so on.

Although Gillian has continued with her job, her own salary represents pocket money and does not dictate her budget. For the past three years her lover has paid for her rent on a new, more lavish flat, her household bills, holidays with and without him, and given her gifts of jewellery and clothes. The luxury of her lifestyle creates problems of its own when she attempts to pass as just an 'ordinary working girl'. She has said that she has been promoted in the firm she works for to try to explain her standard of living to outside friends and keeps her social life with working colleagues very separate from that outside the office. She tends to exaggerate to family and casual friends the amount of enthusiasm and commitment she feels for her career in order to account for what seems to them a barren social life.

Materially, she lives very comfortably. Her apartment is in an expensive area of London and is tastefully decorated. Although there is a small collage of photographs of her lover in her bedroom, there are none on show in the living room despite the fact that she has numerous photos of her friends and family displayed there. It seems characteristic of the way in which she seeks to separate her domestic and public lives; her bedroom is a private sanctuary while her living room is a place for entertaining others of variable degrees of intimacy. Similarly, one person can keep others at bay by constructing symbolic rooms of self-disclosure; dialogue can be intimate or trite. This idea can be illustrated by the way in which she presented the relationship to me.

Gillian first contacted me after seeing a brief article on my research in a weekly magazine. Saying that she was not sure how fully she qualified as a kept woman, she arranged for an interview with me. At that time she said that her lover was divorced but did not want to rush into another marriage and was supporting her in the interim before they married. We became quite friendly and about a month later she told me that in fact her lover was separated and they were waiting for his divorce. Two months or so later I was with her while she attempted to get in touch with him. She was concerned because she had not seen him for over a week. She rang his friend but, unable to get a response, gave up. I asked her why she had not telephoned the man directly and she gave a garbled reply that he was never in, that he might be taking a midday nap and she did not want to wake him, and so on. I encouraged her to give it a try nevertheless. She seemed flustered and I asked if he was still married. Had I not broached the subject directly it is doubtful that she would have told me herself. Although my friendship with Gillian originated specifically through my research on kept women, she had continually misrepresented the nature of her relationship. In approaching me for an interview it was obvious that Gillian wanted to discuss her relationship with someone, but until we became good friends, she attempted to pass as other than a mistress kept in an extramarital affair.

Precisely because the stereotype of the 'kept woman' remains stuck in the 'platinum blonde, satin dress and feather boa' image, a real kept woman can generally evade detection. Although Gillian's wardrobe is extensive, aside from her jewellery there is nothing that announces itself as expensive. She wears only the most expensive shoes, has her hair cut at the most fashionable salon and patronizes designer shops and sections of shops for her clothes, but the cost of her quiet elegance is not generally apparent. To the unaware, a dress costing several hundred pounds may seem merely a nice, casual day-dress; and ironically, even if a particular garment or item looks expensive, its cost may still be vastly underestimated. A cashmere jumper may 'look' expensive, but there are £50 versions and others which cost several times that sum. On occasion, I would be startled to see in a store the cost of an item identical to one worn by Gillian. 'Passing' is made easier because people do not expect a secretary to spend, say, several hundred pounds on one outfit, and an expensive wardrobe need not brazenly announce itself.

For the Mistress, self-presentation goes beyond concern with appearance. Gillian frequently dines with her lover and his business associates and is delighted when he introduces her to visiting businessmen as his wife. She spoke of running errands for her lover, arranging hotel accommodation or cars for his friends, and rather resents that he often has an employee attend to such tasks as she wants to play a more active role in their relationship. To counteract the idea in her own mind that her affair is somehow breaking society's rules, the Mistress embraces the mundane non-sexual aspects of a relationship. She looks upon the duties of a pseudo-wife – hostessing, being supportive – as important in defining her conduct as honourable. Again, sexual fidelity is thought significant. Gillian would appear to be prevented by her lover from mingling socially in mixed sex groups or from developing casual friendships with other men. She told me that once her lover's friend had seen her sharing a table at a crowded wine-bar with two men who, she said, had sat down with her because there was no other space. The man informed her lover who was indignant and disbelieving when she maintained that she did not know them. Since the relationship is important to her she has chosen to restrict her social life so that her lover will not have any need for misplaced jealousy. For various reasons, Gillian's life has become increasingly bound up with her lover's. When apart from him, she tends to be rather solitary, occupying her leisure time by going to the cinema by herself, or shopping alone, and she admits that she has lost friends because of the relationship. Those who have voiced criticisms of her lover and of her relationship threaten her self-image as one who is loved and is regarded as a wife. Anne (who was her best friend) has apparently decided that: 'I'm no longer worth having as a friend. She has a nice, neat little relationship with her boyfriend so next to her I must appear a real mess. She told me that she didn't want to hear one more word about my lover and if I wanted to get hurt I wouldn't get any sympathy from her.'

Gillian is a self-professed, hopeless romantic but her friends who are less enthralled with 'romance' voiced their impatience with her or refused to see her lover as worth waiting for. They have voluntarily or involuntarily ceased to be her friends. Gillian defines her relationship as a love affair, and is intolerant of those who are less impressed by her lover or the state of her romance. She spends an inordinate amount of time either waiting for her lover to telephone, to drop by, or simply to contact her. Since they have no scheduled day for seeing each other I found it difficult to make plans to meet her. On occasion a meeting would be set up but later cancelled abruptly because her lover had telephoned to say he would be coming round to see her. That same evening she would telephone me for a chat as all of ten hours later he had still not appeared. She would sound distressed and resolve that she would tell him the relationship was over the next time she saw him. However, when he did turn up he was always welcomed back with all the enthusiasm of a father for his prodigal son. It is readily apparent that Gillian believes her lover can do no wrong. She does not seem to realize that the man's excuses are at times incredibly lame and that her vacillations of emotion become somewhat irritating.

When a Mistress breaks off her relationship more is involved than discarding a lover or leaving a financier. To an extent, ending the affair means negating the justifiability of her role. Since she has often made a strong effort to rationalize her behaviour, terminating the relationship may be viewed as challenging its very foundation, tantamount to admitting that the man did not love her, that he will never divorce, and so on. As one 25-year-old Mistress said: 'I don't want to think that it was all a shameful fraud, a disgraceful thing.'

Often I noted that the Mistress would view her role with alternating feelings of satisfaction and discontent. Mary, for example, occasionally talked about her loneliness – 'everyone has someone but me' – and thought that she may have ruined her chances of establishing a normal relationship in which she could depend on a man for companionship and emotional support. At other times she would lightheartedly say that she would rather have her Bill or 'half a man' than the male partners her friends had or the dubiously eligible men she had met. It may be over-dramatic, but the Mistress would as a matter of course say: 'If not this man then no one':

> If something happened and my relationship ended tomorrow I don't know that I'd try to find someone else. It gets too hard to go through all the work that establishing a relationship requires. Getting comfortable with a man – not only in bed – but just establishing yourself – takes a great deal of work. (*29-year-old woman, London*)

> I don't like dating and there's something comfortable about knowing what to expect in a relationship. You know he's not going to drive out somewhere and rape you or mug you. Here [British

Columbia] they've just convicted a man who murdered dozens of children. He was a married man with a wife and a baby son. You get the idea that no matter what anything looks like on the surface you can't take chances. (*24-year-old woman, Vancouver*)

I believed that when his children were older he'd marry me. I started waiting and other men began to realize that I was involved with someone else and invitations stopped coming. I don't know if I'll ever have a family or be married . . . well, that's the tragedy isn't it? (*35-year-old woman, London*)

Titillating novels might put it otherwise, but a relationship which progresses to – rather than starts with – intimacy is not always easy to accomplish. Unless love at first sight is the way most relationships begin, the process is presumably a slowly developing one. Falling in love need not be an instantaneous process and is perhaps best conceived of as a long drop. It may be that a relationship nurtures emotional attachment that was or was not there at its onset. When interviewing kept women I noted that the longer the relationship lasted the greater the likelihood of a professed emotional attachment to the partner. The sceptic could say that the relationship has been lucrative and that the declaration of love does not cost the individual anything. But that dependency itself can foster an attachment which may be called love. If the love professed by the woman is seen as cupboard love it may be that the woman becomes dependent on the man and loves him as a protector. This does not mean that love is less real or less binding than a romantic love based on other factors. Moreover, staying in a relationship may be self-perpetuating. It offers the line of least resistance, while disengaging from it may also mean the withdrawal from a social identity and a social network. Rather than uproot yourself and change your lifestyle, a comfortable lethargy is allowed to set in. Not only may there be loyalty to the man but to the relationship itself. Idealism and passion may wane, but a consciousness of the previous efforts she has put into the relationship – and the time invested in it – may encourage a woman to keep it going. The situation has been stabilized as a love affair and the relationship, as well as being morally supportive, offers a reliable source of financial support.

My next case study is presented as it was offered to me in a letter written from Texas in late 1981:

I just last week turned 35 and lived ten happy years as a 'kept' woman. The man in my life for ten years turned 65 the same day I turned 35. Our relationship is and was very special for both of us.

I had gone to school with his son and of course had known of the father all my life. He was a very prominent attorney in my home town of 70,000 people. When I was 20, I went to work in his law office on a temporary basis – and our relationship blossomed. From that day (December 1, 1966) forward we grew closer in spite of many, many obstacles. Ours was not an easy relationship to continue. I at first lived at home with my mother, a very strict and moral woman who was no one's dummy. Although she suspected our relationship, accused me of it (which I denied) and fought to destroy it, we managed to continue it. After a period of time, I moved into an apartment which was paid for monthly by my friend (let's call him John). The only problem we had in getting along with each other was that I wanted to have a career and he wanted me to be free to travel with him, to play tennis and do the things I wanted to do. He didn't want me to have any less luxury than his wife. I always had a new car to drive – lovely clothes to wear – memberships at the best private clubs, etc. As time grew on, our relationship became more and more accepted by his peers.

In 1970, much to my dismay, I became pregnant with his child. He was very pleased – but the problem of my mother and society was overwhelming for me. I had a very close friend (being an only child, I had become very close to a classmate – Denis) who knew of my plight – and as a convenience, he and I were married. As soon as my wonderful son Lewis was born, Denis and I divorced. We of course are still very close to this day.

In 1972, my mother was killed in an automobile accident. John was the first person I called – and he assisted me in all the arrangements – and represented me with the probate, etc. When Mom was killed, I went into a state of shock which lasted several months – and John remained at my side. I guess it was during that time that we ceased using any discretion at all – although it was known, we had maintained denial for my mother's benefit.

Our son was put in the finest private school and is doing beautifully. He and John are close and our son is accepted readily by John's 35-year-old son and 30-year-old daughter.

In 1974, against John's wishes, I went to work for an oil company. In 1977, they offered me a promotion and transfer to —. I decided to take the transfer and moved – John was extremely upset about the situation. However, when I moved he continued with his support and flew to — weekly. Later that year, I met a man (Peter) and after several months he asked me to marry him. I cared deeply for him and my son worshipped him so I decided to talk it over with John. I flew home to discuss it with him – needless to say, he came unhinged. However, he is very logical and reasonable and if I want to do something and if I feel it is best, he many times does not agree, but he doesn't try to force me. I married Peter and am quite content with my life.

I don't have all the luxuries, etc. that I once had and I now have to work rather than just want to – but I don't object to that either.

My relationship with John still exists. He gave up his law practice two years ago and was appointed to a position by the Governor which required that he move to —, some 70 miles away (rather than the 350 miles before). We see each other almost weekly and talk on the phone daily. He and Peter have come to like each other and have a mutual respect. My relationship with John is no longer physical – but the love and affection has never diminished. I have never before or after loved or been loved as completely as with him. I frequently think of his age and while he is still in perfect mental and physical condition, I dread the day I no longer have him.

I have no regrets about my relationship with him and I feel that I learned much from it. I certainly benefited from it – and I don't mean materially – but from the mere presence of him and his brilliant mind – and the fact that we have a brilliant son who has developed the best of both of us.

I might add that although he is certainly not legally liable – and that I certainly have never asked for anything – a cheque comes in once a month in the amount of $1500 payable to me – with the excuse being our son's well-being. The money is never spent – but placed in investments for our son – because Peter has adopted our son and refuses to let John support him in any way. Peter, after a battle, rationalizes the $1500 as being a gift for our son's future.

I hope this letter helps you. These relationships are not always as bleak as they are pictured to be.

This letter is interesting for a number of reasons. First, unlike the previous two case histories of Mary and Gillian, there is a significant age difference between the Mistress and the lover. Although it would have been more likely for her to fall in love with the son rather than the father, she did not think that the age difference was a bar to viewing the man as a desirable lover. Second, the distinction she makes between wanting to work and needing to work throws some light on the role of employment for the woman in the kept relationship. The amount of commitment felt towards work varied – some women viewed it as very important while others viewed it simply as a way of meeting people and passing the time – but approximately 65 per cent of the Mistress category were employed in full-time work and an additional six per cent of the Mistress category did part-time or voluntary work. In eight cases the lover had subsidized the setting up of a business; in five cases the women depended on their lovers' support to return to higher education or take some form of training. The image of the kept woman recumbent on a *chaise longue* was not adopted by the majority of Mistresses.

The typical kept woman more often than not met her lover at her place of employment, as was the case with this last respondent from Texas. However, the woman's letter suggests that within the kept relationship, as within marriage, the woman's desire to pursue a career may cause conflicts. While employment in the man's office brought about the affair originally, the pursuit of a career brought about its demise. Her acceptance of promotion meant relocation to a new area and a new network of people. Her disengagement from the relationship was eased by her move to an area 350 miles away. In that new location, where her identity was not, perhaps, specifically linked to her lover, she was allowed or allowed herself to date others. And after her marriage to another man, she likens her lover's financial support in her previous relationship to that given by her present husband. Rather than view economic support in the kept relationship as payment for services rendered, she says that her lover did not wish her to have any less luxury than his wife. This phrase suggests that she saw her role as similar to that of his wife and believed the man thought of her as a polygamous wife. Having a luxurious lifestyle was portrayed as simply a benefit of having a wealthy partner – not the sole reason for the relationship. What is more, her letter does suggest that it is possible to bring the kept relationship to an amicable end and that the nature of the love felt may change over time.

This woman identified the exact day on which her affair began. I was continually surprised that the Mistress would remember and note the days of her first meeting, first date, the first time she made love with the man and so on. Celebrating the anniversaries of such events is common. Females are more likely than males to herald such dates as important hallmarks of a romance, and the Mistress, in particular, is likely to do so. By describing her involvement in terms of legitimate role models, the kept Mistress justifies her position. Celebrating anniversaries may be part of the ritual of romance which normalizes (and neutralizes) any imputed misconduct on her part. Presenting her situation as exceptional is a way of avoiding identification with a reference group of prostitutes or other kept women who deliberately weave a life and a social world out of being kept.

My last detailed case history in this Mistress category describes the relationship of Wanda and Philip. Wanda, a Polish Jewess, was a former professional prostitute and emigrated to England after the Second World War. She was a prostitute in Germany during the war, operating a brothel with her sister for German soldiers. My knowledge of Wanda's history was enlarged by meetings with her friends, several of whom have known her since her childhood, and in particular, an elderly woman whom Wanda calls her 'mother' and whom she introduced as such although there is no family relationship between them.

Wanda married an Englishman in 1949 and was widowed during the early 1970s. She has been receiving financial support from Philip since 1971.

Philip was married until late 1980 and has four children ranging in age from 22 to 29. Wanda tended to be rather coy about giving her age but her 'mother' thought her to be 58. Philip is in his early sixties. Wanda is a physically attractive woman even if she does tend to project an image of an old Mae West. Since the first time I met Wanda she referred to Philip as either her boyfriend or fiancé. When Wanda finally married him (in the summer of 1981) she gleefully told me that now no one could laugh behind her back. She was not being unduly paranoid. Of her friends that I met, none had believed that Philip would marry her although he had been separated from his wife and living with Wanda (despite maintaining a separate residence) on an on-off basis since 1972. A male friend of Philip's had consistently referred to Wanda as the 'old tart' when talking to me about her, and the husband of one of her friends called her a *kurwa* (Polish for whore).

Philip was started in business by his first wife's father and is extremely wealthy. Twice a year he and Wanda go off to Switzerland and on more than one occasion Wanda has been less than discreet in disclosing to me Philip's strategies for avoiding heavy taxation. She is not stupid; she just thinks it is important that I recognize Philip as an astute businessman who is adept in his business practices. She met him through her brother-in-law who had known Philip since childhood:

> My husband had cancer and before my eyes changed until there was nothing left of him . . . in the end I was changing him like a baby. I felt if I didn't go out I'd die too. I used to go places – pubs, clubs and come home feeling like throwing up but force myself to go back. You wouldn't believe what women will do not to be alone. Then I met Philip and he was very good to me. If something had to be done, I'd ring up Philip and he'd send someone or do it himself. After my husband died Philip told me 'You've worked long enough' and gave me everything. We go on vacations all over the world. One thing he did for years though I never understood – every time we'd make love he'd leave me £25.

Philip laughed at this and offered by way of explanation:

> Do you know the joke about the man who gave his wife 10p every time they'd make love? The man tells her, 'This is for you, put it in your jewellery box'. One day he opens the box and there's hundreds of pounds. He asks her where did she get so much money. She replies, 'Do you think everyone is as cheap as you are?'

Wanda was hurt by Philip's joke; to her it implied that he regarded her as a prostitute at the start of the relationship. Although she had been a prostitute, she dismissed the fact as a wartime necessity, her only available means of survival. She maintained that you should be faithful and in love with your partner to warrant a relationship. Incidentally, Wanda's daughter, aged 27 and divorced, has been kept on numerous occasions for short periods of time and her mother refers to her as a prostitute because she is opportunist about it. She sees her daughter's actions as contemptible because her daughter would allow herself to be materially supported by a man she does not otherwise care for. I was present at verbal slanging matches between Wanda and her daughter when they accused each other of being prostitutes and indulged in colourful expletives which gave the term 'nuclear family' an entirely new meaning. Wanda maintains that until the end of her husband's illness she was faithful to him and there was no evidence to suggest otherwise; even her detractors did not suggest this was not so.

I noticed that Wanda took pains to make Philip's children like her: inviting them out for lunch, bringing them gifts when she and Philip went on vacation and giving family dinners. His children said that she was all right in that she made their father happy although they tended to adopt a superior attitude towards her. In one instance I was recruited, along with Philip's eldest daughter, to see the home Wanda and Philip had purchased shortly after their marriage. As we walked through the house and the surrounding gardens, Philip's daughter made occasional comments about what was needed or what was unsatisfactory to her and Wanda inevitably would agree and fawn over her. The daughter seemed rather amused and would purposely contradict herself while Wanda continued to agree and court her favour. In attempting to ingratiate herself with those she felt 'a better class of people' Wanda solicited their views on clothes, general appearance and opinions. She tended to shop at fashion houses in France rather than in department stores and be advised on what to buy by experts there or by Philip's children. She explained this by saying that they knew better in general and that in particular Philip's children knew what he liked. It reflected her unease at 'not fitting in' or potentially being identified as 'not the right sort'. On occasions I would make a comment to her or voice an opinion on a subject, only to hear her deliver it as her own during cocktail chatter later on. She seemed to try very hard to establish her identity as the gracious hostess and wife and sought confirmation that she was succeeding in her conventional status in order to nullify her previous position in the relationship.

Wanda was delighted when she got married. Making the relationship legitimate seemed important because it gave her respectability and demonstrated the fact that Philip loved her enough to marry her. She does not work and spends most of her time either at her 'mother's' or in tasks related to maintaining her appearance. She swims and goes for a massage every morning, works out twice-weekly with an exercise class and seems to race from her facial to sun-bed treatments to the manicurist in a never-ending regimen of self-improvement. Her day-to-day life has not changed very substantially with marriage; the important difference is the bond that she sees as proof of Philip's love for her and that she was therefore more than just a sexual playmate to him.

From these highly personal revelations from both the 'keeper' and the 'kept' it can be seen that Mistresses today range from adolescents to post-menopausal women, but while they cannot be distinguished from other kept women by their age, height or physical appearance, the Mistress type does share certain attributes in common:

1 A predilection for equating their relationship with a thwarted love story.
2 a determination to pattern their behaviour on the role of the wife.
3 A willingness to structure their social life in accordance with the dictates of the lover, even when in so doing they become isolated from others who either disapprove of him or of the relationship.
4 the conviction that sexual fidelity is important – as is loyalty – not only to the man but to the relationship.

This form of kept relationship does not pattern itself on the modern open marriage between sexually liberated individuals, but on traditional marriage, and the Mistress equates the man's financial help with the husband's role of provider, as testimony to his true care and concern for her welfare.

These attributes differ considerably from those of the Career Woman type, as will be seen from the following chapter.

Chapter Two

THE CAREER WOMAN

Disappointment always comes from attempting to turn a sow's ear into a silk slipper . . . I have found in my many years that dreams do not guide the future but rather tell us what not to do in the present. This may sound like an odd comment. It is not in my opinion, since dreams tell you what is possible and therefore help you eliminate the deterrents that exist at the time. Help you weed out the people that these dreams cannot, at any time, be accomplished with. (*29-year-old woman*)

The Career Woman dreams of success in her profession and to her a kept relationship is a means to this end.

An analysis of her behaviour and attitudes suggests that the treatment of the office affair in the popular press, often featured under a 'Sex in the market-place' banner, is over-simple. Three of the most common types of the career-related (or office) affair illustrated are: the Casting Couch victim story (the rise and fall of the bright young thing), the Sexual Harassment situation and the 'Love Among the Filing Cabinets' scenario. All of these accounts have some basis in fact but they are often over-dramatic in their presentation and take for granted assumptions about the importance women ought to attach to work and/or the pursuit of a career.

The casting couch story-line springs from bad Hollywood melodramas where an ambitious (but virtuous) starlet is harassed and ultimately seduced. She becomes a Star but only at Tremendous Expense. As the sound of a hundred violins rises to a crescendo in the background the tormented heroine – amidst much hand-wringing and lower-lip quivering – (a) plunges headlong into a life of unmitigated debauchery and ultimately commits suicide or (b) retreats into a nunnery to repent her ambition achieved in a Faust-like pact. The audience is left with the suspicion that had the woman simply relinquished the goal of success and married that nice-boy-next-door she could have averted her downfall and spared herself much misery. If she elects for option (a) and momentarily enjoys the depravity of it all, there is a suggestion that her conscience will nevertheless chasten her for placing success before virtue. The casting couch is depicted as a sacrificial altar upon which virtue and peace of mind are relinquished. Women who achieve success by sleeping their way to the top are forewarned that their prize will be a moral purgatory filled with guilt and self-recrimination.

A sub-plot in the casting couch victim story suggests that women are not really suited to pursue a career or cope with the pressures attendant on success. In pursuing a career a woman apparently becomes the Frankenstein of her own creation. To paraphrase the anthropologist Margaret Mead, whereas men are unsexed by failure, women seem to be unsexed by success. The woman to whom establishing her career is of paramount importance, ostensibly deviates from her 'natural' role (wife, mother) in her masculine orientation to work and sex. She takes her career too seriously and allows her strident emphasis on success to override what should be fundamental concerns with retaining her femininity. The movie version of the casting couch story generally ends on a tragic note, suggesting that no amount of fame can repair the ravages inflicted by success on these women. At heart a morality tale, it is a parable of what *not* to do. Ambition, for women, is portrayed as a force for evil.

If this picture of the career-related affair is dramatic, it receives indirect support from modern feminist writers. In the sexual harassment polemic, the woman who pursues a career is still presented as a victim but the villain is society, symbolized by the office Lothario. The woman is shown as being forced into surrendering to the man's sexual overtures which may be crude or subtle. In *Sexual Shakedown*, Lin Farley pointedly remarks that:

> Female oppression at work is the result of nearly universal male power to hire and fire. Men control the means of economic survival. This control is also used to coerce working women sexually. Institutionalized male power has thus created its own means of maintaining its superior position – by socially enlisting women's cooperation in their own sexual subservience and accomplishing this by rewarding them when they do and punishing them when they do not. Work, the ostensible equalizer, the location of women's hopes for equality, and the means to her economic independence is subsequently transformed into new enslavement. In the meantime, we condemn women as whores for being coerced, fail to acknowledge the daily economic hardship of thousands who fail to yield, and deny help to those who seek it.

Farley sees the office Lothario as symbolic of the subjugation of women. I do not dispute the injustice of making employment or promotion conditional on sexual favours, but Farley presents all women as victims as she makes no distinction between incidents where a woman elects to promote her position by having sex with a man and where she was physically assaulted.

Sleeping your way to the top may not be a widespread strategy or even particularly effective, but the response given to sexual harassment or perceived sexual interest at work is not always one of submission, acquiescence or indignation. The interpretation women give to a 'pass' or proposition determines whether the response is seen as submission to sexual harassment or as an instrumental career move.

In 1980 a Gallup Poll recorded a sample of European womens' experiences of discrimination in the workplace. The women's places of work included shops, factories, offices, schools, health and beauty establishments and the home. They ranged in age from 15 years upwards, with or without professional qualifications and were of differing marital status – single, married, widowed or divorced. Their experiences of discrimination were keyed to six alternatives, with the following results:

1	Interesting job intended for a man only	8%
2	Obliged to accept a lower salary	12%
3	Pregnant women refused a job or transferred	12%
4	Rebuked for absence due to children	15%
5	Employer asked if woman was pregnant at job interview	16%
6	Sexual blackmail	6%

In contrast, a survey conducted by Liverpool's NALGO membership (National Association of Local Government Officers, Britain's largest white-collar union) found that 52 per cent of women surveyed reported sexual harassment; Canadian research produced a figure of 82 per cent. Unless Canadian employers are markedly more licentious than European ones, it must be that sexual harassment is not defined in the same way in the studies or that the samples tapped very dissimilar groups of women. It may be that a group of feminists who define sexual harassment as 'our greatest occupational hazard' would answer differently from a sample of Career Women who did not view a man's sexual overtures as totally unwelcome.

Sexual harassment obviously requires definition. Jane Root, a feminist author writing in *Spare Rib* magazine in 1982 suggests that:

> Sexual harassment takes many forms – from a hand on your leg every time you use the lift to brutal rape or attempted rape. Sexual harassment isn't a 'jokey' part of a friendship between two people

who work together; it isn't mutual in any way. Sexual harassment is a threat to working women. It may force you into changing your job when you don't want to. It may make you unemployed when you would rather be working. It can ensure that you earn less than you deserve. It may turn your working life into such a nightmare that you suffer from serious depression, or it may even make you physically ill – complaints such as cystitis, vomiting, headaches and indigestion can all be caused by stress from sexual harassment at work.

It would thus appear that sexual harassment is the non-reciprocal, undesired attempt of one person to impose power on another. However, it would be a misnomer to call the male's perceived interest in the Career Woman 'harassment' because this presumes that the woman defines herself as the 'victim' of the situation when she complies with the male's demands or conspires to achieve success by 'sleeping her way to the top'.

It is important to note that male power or perceived power to administer rewards is accepted by the Career Woman as the way life is. She willingly relinquishes the autonomy of her body in exchange for the man's ability to furnish rewards. The man's power is undisputed; she just plays the game and claims a victory by abiding by his rules.

J. Lipman-Blumen in his 'A Homosocial Theory of Sex-Roles' (in *Women and the Workplace*) suggests that women are forced to trade their physical resources to gain access to male-controlled resources:

> Men can and commonly do seek satisfaction for the most of their needs from other men. They can derive satisfaction for their intellectual, physical, political, economic, occupational, social, power and status needs – and in some cases their sexual needs – from other men. The dominant order among men is based upon control of resources, including land, money, education, occupations, political connections, and family ties. Women, forced to seek resources from men, in turn become resources which men can use to further their own eminence in the homosocial world of men. . . . In relationships between the sexes, males have a disproportionate amount of resources under their control. They could bargain their power, status, money, land, political influences, legal power and educational and occupational resources (all usually greater than women's) against women's more limited range of resources, consisting of sexuality, youth, beauty and the promise of paternity.

If a Career Woman seeks promotion by making use of her femininity or if she succumbs to the man's desire for her, her advancement depends on her sexual performance or marginally, upon sexual enticement. While the notion of 'sexual harassment' assumes that it is a reluctant female who allows herself to be demeaned and degraded, the female who deliberately plans to sleep her way to the top also exists. Whether or not this strategy is likely to succeed, certain women may still be motivated to attempt it.

In a short story entitled 'The Secret of Success' published in *Smart Set* magazine in 1922, Donald Ogden Stewart addressed himself to examining the various strategies adopted to achieve career success. In this, his young hero read all the how-to-achieve-success manuals, worked hard, was the first to arrive at the office in the morning and the last to leave at night, reviewed his work in his free time and still failed to better his position. However, he did eventually become the president of the firm – by marrying the former president's ugly daughter. This unusual story of the path to success suggests that access to power may be achieved through sexual sponsorship.

A study which suggests the importance of male sponsorship in female careers is the Dutch sociologist Leena Kartovaara's work on women artists cited in an article in Cynthia F. Epstein and Rose L. Coser's *Access to Power*. Unlike other elite professions, the creative arts include a large proportion of women. Statistics show that more women than men artists are married. She explains this by referring to the traditional male role of provider which the male artist cannot take on because he does not have a substantial or reliable income. She suggests that sexual sponsorship allows women to pursue artistic careers:

> . . . a woman can be active in the arts while supported by her husband, but a male artist is prevented from marrying because he cannot support a family. Thus, the high proportion of women in the arts elite may be partially explained by the low economic rewards of artistic activity. Economically, the artist belongs to a 'leisure class' and is supported by someone else. Wives of wealthy men sometimes belong to that class.

The chorus girl and the Sugar Daddy/director scenario is a caricature of this situation. Affiliation with a powerful man may offer tactical advantages, especially in a world like show business where the process of achieving success is vague or ill-defined. The girl may believe her bargaining strength will be increased by the man's patronage. The attitude of the Career Woman is that it cannot hurt to sleep with the right people and that through sexual sponsorship she can better her position and achieve career advancement. My respondents in this category looked upon the relationship as a stepping stone, an eminently practical career move.

Admittedly, sexual sponsorship can take many forms; it can range from a type of nepotism to sexual harassment. If power includes the ability to furnish rewards, there is no denying that men hold the positions of power in most occupations by virtue of their sex, and furthermore, often have the ability to procure advancement through the 'old school tie' network. If women are blocked in their passage through this traditional system or perceive that the formal structure of a profession is inhospitable to women they may resort to more informal methods and take alternative routes to success.

Women who use a mentor to achieve a rapid career promotion or attempt to sleep their way to the top would appear to be inverted – or skewed – feminists. If the Career Woman sees her power as lying in the ability to manipulate the work situation to aid her goals, the power to bestow rewards still remains with the man. Curiously, the latter idea was usually ignored by my contacts. The women often emphasized that by taking control they were no longer victims. Men, they suggested, were more gullible than threatening:

> You don't get anywhere in this world unless you learn how the world works. You can work it to your advantage or you can scream 'Rape!' whenever a man pats you on the fanny. (*35-year-old woman, London*)

> In California, one of our most militant feminists you might have heard of is Jane Fonda. She is pretty amusing to me because she knows nothing at all about the real world and sees herself as one of the working women because she burned her bra and eats health food. Working women don't have movie star fathers to get them a job, send them to Vassar and producer husbands like Roger Vadim to star them in sexy movies. She doesn't know what she's talking about . . . nobody helps nobody for nothing. (*33-year-old woman, San Diego*)

Sexual isolation in an area of employment relatively unpopulated by females and the professional isolation of the freelance worker may encourage a woman to construct her own career strategy and find personal solutions to situations in which sexual interest is expressed. While the designer who finds that getting commissions depends on having sexual intercourse may not be able to draw upon the experience of others to provide alternative strategies, the secretary may have the support of the secretarial pool, and within the business world generally there may be trade unions or staff associations to whom to appeal.

The majority of the women interviewed in the Career Woman category were involved in professions which have relatively unstructured routes to the attainment of success. Most could be called professional entrepreneurs. Neither the actress, the model, the professional entertainer nor the aspiring fashion designer thought that training or formal qualification in a profession guaranteed success. In a world where success was attributed to luck, who you know and being in the right place at the right time, women justified the relationship as being intrinsic to successfully playing the game. In contrast to some militant feminist strategy (which it is thought antagonizes men, making them act defensively), the Career Woman feels that men rather than other women are her most effective allies. Forming a sexual relationship with a powerful man is a tactic which many women think they can use to their benefit.

The Career Woman's involvement with her lover may be seen as a mixture of what she perceives her environment to offer and what the man is thought to offer in fulfilling her needs for self-enhancement. Like the amount of support desired, the amount of job mobility sought by the Career Woman is variable. At times job security is sought rather than advancement itself, but in all events, the relationship is seen as instrumental in advancing the women's career.

One of my London respondents, Susie, who had no educational qualifications of any kind – no 'O' or 'A' levels – went to work for a man in the City as a secretary. She then decided that her great desire in life was to go to university. With this in mind, she played up to her boss although she did not find him at all attractive. He had an intelligent daughter the same age as Susie who was a great source of envy to her. Before too long Susie managed to get her boss sexually involved, so much so that he set her up in a flat and paid for her to return to college full-time. Her plan worked to perfection, she attained the right examinations at the required level and achieved her goal – a place at university.

A fact common to my experience of Career Women and to more general studies on women in top jobs is that they view their achievement as the result of an intensely personal, individually designed strategy. The Career Woman maintains that her success is a result of her individual effort to succeed and a reflection of her ability. Although they have achieved high positions or career success through dubious means, the members of the Career Woman category uniformly appear supremely confident and aggressively sure of their abilities. When they receive a promotion or job perk they are likely to minimize the extent to which this is due to their affiliation with the man. Career advancement is viewed as demonstrating that she is in fact right to put her career above all. The proof is the progression of the career itself. The woman usually acknowledges that the kept relationship helps in this respect but that any accolades are justified by her ability and do not rest on her affiliation alone. Being kept by a man is seen as incidental rather than central to her self-image of being a success.

In a perfect society, recruitment and job stability would depend on merit alone and the person's gender would be immaterial. However, the traditional assumption is that most women view the workplace as a social arena for meeting potential marriage partners and/or that work is a transient means of self-support which is gladly discarded when someone else agrees to pay the bills. Given this attitude, the effect of the Sex

Discrimination Act in Britain, for instance, may turn out to be about as effective as waving a fly-swatter at a submarine. It may be fashionable to espouse sexual equality as part of a political platform, to include a token woman in the organization and be photographed in the company of fashionable female activists, but legal reforms alone will not change dismissive attitudes towards women as employees. It makes little sense to train someone thoroughly and introduce her into the intimate working of the elite power group of the organization if the expectations are that she will unceremoniously quit her job as soon as a wedding ring or baby clothes are in the offing. Where these attitudes prevail, penetrating the 'in-group' or trespassing on all-male turf may become dependent on the woman's forming an alliance with one particular man. By convention, women can gain access to circles of male elites by being the man's wife, girlfriend or companion.

The strategy of the Career Woman is not, however, without risk. There is always the danger that her professional affiliates will dismiss the validity of her position and treat her as simply the boss's girlfriend. Many of my contacts are conscious of the pejorative stereotype of the woman who is both attractive and successful:

> Get an attractive woman in a high post and someone is sure to say 'She didn't get that far just on her brains'. Women are just as bad as men if not worse. In an office the amount of gossip inspired out of sheer jealousy is enormous. If you try to do your job well and be nice to everyone they'll still talk about how much your clothes cost as soon as you close the door. If you didn't do anything they'd never believe it anyway so if you did you just say to yourself 'I'm in charge so who really cares what they think?' (*27-year-old woman, London*)

> If a man goes into a job interview nicely dressed nobody accuses him of trying to get the job on account of his looks. If a woman dresses for an interview she has to worry if her blouse is too low, too see-through, if her skirt is too short, if the slit in it is too high, even if she can cross her legs without it being seen as a come-on. You name it. You have to be a real dog before people will shut up and take you seriously. (*28-year-old woman, Toronto*)

There is always the possibility that the Career Woman's lover himself may trivialize the woman's work and deny or dismiss her desire for a career:

> He couldn't see that my career mattered to me. He thought I had everything I could want. So he bought me a new car to keep me happy. (*24-year-old woman, London*)

The dedicated Career Woman must deviate to a degree from the traditional social role of a woman by subordinating marriage and motherhood to her career. Her strategy is based on the male attitude that career success confers more prestige than marital status. Similarly, she adopts a 'masculine' attitude towards sex. A man's status is defined by his position, not by whether or not he slept with, or married, the boss's daughter. Just as no one would question a man about how many women he slept with during his career – it would seem both rude and irrelevant, so the Career Woman sees the mechanism which brings about her success as her own business. Not content to wait for the social or sexual revolution that might bring about a Utopian working environment, she makes the best use of herself within the limitations of society as it is.

For my first case history in the Career Woman category I have chosen Felice, a 28-year-old lawyer. She is petite, attractive and very fashionable. Despite her china-doll appearance her 'friends' privately characterize her as tough-minded and manipulative. From an upper-middle-class background, she had originally wanted to become a doctor but settled for a career in law when her school marks did not allow for her to pursue a career in medicine. She studied in the United States for a year and then returned to England to complete her degree at a university in London. When I asked her why she had wanted to become a doctor her answer suggested that her reasons were other than humanitarian. She had coveted the high status and the prestige it would confer. Through her father's influence she was articled to a well-regarded firm. Her lover is her employer and one of her father's great friends – a fact which seems to amuse her. He had promised her father that he would personally make sure that she encountered no difficulties in her new post and thus was recruited to act as her mentor. Although Felice is extremely self-assured about her capabilities, her friends are less confident about them. There seems to have been some precedent for her present tactical strategy of being professionally sponsored. She acknowledges having had an affair with a college tutor while at school and her friends imply that she achieved her degree largely through his work and by his being able to warn her in advance of questions his colleagues had set in examinations.

If Felice does not enjoy the demands of her profession she certainly revels in the glory of it. She recalled counselling a man who had been involved in a minor automobile accident and used particular emphasis when repeating his many thanks and his comment that after hearing her words of wisdom he 'would be able to sleep for the first time in weeks'. According to her, the man regarded his conversation with her as a devout Roman Catholic would an audience with the Pope. Her arrogance, however, entirely dissipated when her mentor–lover was around. On one occasion I met her at her place of work and while I waited for her to tie up some loose ends the man returned a brief he had been vetting for her. Her voice dropped several decibels and she thanked the man profusely for his help, saying how grateful she was, and so on.

Being a professional 'teacher's pet' – or an 'apple-polisher' – involves ingratiation through flattery, seeking advice (the helpless female syndrome), contrived or real adulation, and deliberately establishing herself as the boss's spoilt protégée. This attitude may also be characteristic of relations between superiors and subordinates in general, as V.A. Thompson has pointed out in his *Modern Organization*:

> Subordinates must create the impression that they *need* to be told what to do; that they *need* to be told how to do it; and, in general, that they could not get along without the boss.

Since the soft-soap performance may appear not to differ greatly from ritual female–male verbal exchanges or the stereotypical versions which are thought characteristic of the dialogue between the sexes, the female 'teacher's pet' type may be less obvious than her male counterpart, the obsequious employee. The fawning female may be complimented for her femininity rather than disparaged as one who is obviously seeking to ingratiate herself. Moreover, such subservient congeniality may even suggest that she is a good sort who will fit well into the organization and not one of those pugnacious 'woman's lib lesbians'. By manipulating the feminine role, the dumb blonde type may use tactics of ingratiation, bluffs and/or deceit to increase her bargaining strength *vis-à-vis* her male lover. Similarly, the attributes of femininity can be exaggerated in order to gain a tactical advantage in relations with men.

The use of charm as a tactical strategy was emphasized by one woman, a British Broadcasting Corporation executive in her thirties who termed this approach 'twinkling'. Although it is difficult to describe the precise mechanics of this approach she claimed it made those she talked with feel that they were the most scintillating conversationalists, that they held her undivided attention and received her unequivocal admiration. In part this was accomplished by maintaining direct eye contact with the speaker, 'spontaneously' exclaiming 'how fabulous' and 'how fascinating' at periodic intervals, being generally sycophantic and playing the wide-eyed admirer. This performance is a caricature of stereotypical male–female relations – the man being applauded for being a strong, stalwart figure worthy of awe by the admiring female.

Felice, the young lawyer, feels that by virtue of being 'teacher's pet' she is allotted cases in the particular area of law in which she is interested, that she benefits from her boss–lover's tutelage and his guiding of her pen in the presentation of briefs, and that she generally receives preferential treatment. She said that her salary greatly exceeds those of her peers and feels that her position is assured by her relationship with the man. She has accompanied him on several trips abroad to visit international clients and firms, a benefit which might usually be denied to a novice. She sees such trips and her inclusion at social functions as self-enhancing, and believes they will further her career. She wants to leave London in the next five years and feels that through her boss's clients and connections she can meet potential employers and clients. She does not view the relationship as long-term and although her 'affection' for the man takes an exaggerated form, she does not feel that their levels of interest in the relationship are greatly unequal.

In some cases, corporate bigamy, that is, being married to your job, seems to precede a man's having an affair with a fellow employee. Similarly, defining career success as the primary goal may encourage a woman to channel her energies into work and discourage her from allowing time for the development and maintenance of a relationship. One respondent justified her series of relationships with married men by claiming that at the present stage in her career she was unable to maintain or cope with relationships other than those which she conceived of as being intrinsically transient. She felt that an affair with a married man satisfied her need for companionship while demanding less of her time and attention than a relationship with a single man. She referred to herself as a 'hiccup' in the man's marriage and did not feel that their relationship was other than a practical solution for both the man and herself.

Even a long-term relationship may still be thought of as a 'fling' if the person does not invest a great amount of time or energy into it or feels that it is relatively unimportant. Felice does not wish to marry her lover and believes that he is unlikely to disrupt a comfortable social and married life by marrying his friend's daughter. Her relationship with her lover seems to be deliberately misrepresented rather than hidden from others. Since he is a family friend and his wife is a friend of her mother's, Felice thinks the relationship is construed as demonstrating his paternal interest in her. Not from the start, however, did she interpret his attentiveness to her as fatherly. Indeed she had courted it by contrasting him with her father to the man's advantage, telling him how much younger than her father he looked and acted, how she could talk to him far more easily, and so on. Since she had already known the man before starting the job their relationship was never precisely formal nor were his communications with her strictly limited to aloof, professional dialogues. Felice's relationship with the man and her job placement combine two alternative opportunity structures for gaining access to power; nepotism and an intimate personal tie to a man in a position of power.

The ambitious Career Woman lays particular emphasis on the establishment of potentially profitable friendships. The woman who aspires to become an opera singer may never perform at La Scala or the Met, despite the power of her protector or her eager attendance at gatherings of influential people if she has a tin ear and a voice as musical as chalk on blackboard. Marion Davies, for example, never became a successful actress, although her powerful patron–lover, William Randolph Hearst, strove to promote her career. Nevertheless, Career Women with a working knowledge of the 'way the world works' point to the importance of an informal system of relationships with men within the environment of the job. One respondent commented:

> More deals are completed in a restaurant or in a lounge rather than in an office. A business relationship invariably involves more than just business. It means becoming friends and giving and expecting favours, being loyal to your friends and expecting loyalty in return. Men realize this more than most women do and when you work with men you come to realize just how important it is. Sometimes I'll help a client out and say forget it, no charge. It's a sound move because that client will feel favoured and will also feel that next time it will be his turn to do me a favour. I don't think you can leave it all up to just doing your eight hours on the job and expecting the boss to notice that you're always on time and have a neat desk. You have to recognize the social side of the work and be willing to make work almost the centre of your life. You don't wait for a promotion, first you show that you deserve it and you do this by not just sitting and thinking that people always get what is coming to them . . . He [her lover] wants people around him he likes, and that means going for drinks and getting friendly. (*34-year-old woman, London*)

'Who you know' is often considered as important, if not more so, than 'what you know' and the women believe that knowledge itself is gained by participation among certain network groups. The Career Woman is prone to 'expose' or accuse other highly placed women of having acquired their positions through mechanisms similar to her own. This supposition may be false or made out of sheer malice, but it suggests that the woman prefers not to see her act as anomalous or singularly deviant. It becomes a career strategy used by other women and defined as commonplace.

The etiquette of the Career Woman–lover relationship reiterates the importance of maintaining the positive evaluation of her role and retaining social and professional links with her lover even when the affair has ended. This is no more than prudent, for, as one woman remarked, 'You never know when you'll need a friend.' The higher you climb the career ladder, the loftier the heights from which you can fall. The course of one respondent's career seemed to be governed by the 'Peter Principle' and she rose to her own level of incompetence. However, her on-the-job performance was not good enough to justify her place on the pay-roll when she joined a new company, despite her glowing references and mighty friends. She went back to her former company, where she handled the account of its biggest client – her lover. She had sensibly discouraged him from transferring his account when she left the firm and said she did so because she was uncertain about her job future with her new firm and, moreover, did not wish antagonism and resentment to develop with her former employers.

It is interesting to note that despite the relatively young age of the women in this Career Woman category (81 per cent under 35 years old), 46 per cent had already been involved in a kept relationship and approximately 19 per cent had been involved in two previous kept relationships. This would suggest that whether or not 'sleeping your way to the top' actually improved their chances of career success, they thought it did. It also suggests that sexual advances in the workplace are not always thought of as harassment. It should not be assumed, however, that the Career Woman bases her strategy on prancing into a potential employer's office and seducing him. The relationship itself is not so simple, nor is it necessarily the result of premeditation. Admittedly, it could be argued that the Career Woman is a 'victim' who is simply not astute enough to realize what is really going on. Unless the relationship of the Career Woman and her lover is a sentimental story in the 'love among the filing cabinets' mould, it is impossible to avoid considering her as a victim. Look on the office affair as a love affair and you have neatly side-stepped the issue of sexual politics. In my opinion, however, to presume that every Career Woman is a wistful lover is as absurd as suggesting that every Career Woman is a victim.

One of my respondents, Kate, an American in her mid-twenties, came to London with the aim of auditioning for a drama school. She arrived too late to enrol and as a result decided to spend her time in London seeking what she termed 'useful connections'. Her grandparents were British so she had a relatively easy time being allowed to stay in England. She went along to several 'cattle-calls' for touring puppet and pantomime companies and at one met Bill, a 30-year-old stage manager who subsequently became her boyfriend. Through Bill, she was invited to a house-party where she met Tony, a theatrical agent in his fifties:

> The three of us talked together for quite a while and he seemed quite nice in a fatherly type of way. Then Bill left to drive some people home and as soon as he left Tony moved closer to me on the sofa and started rubbing his leg against mine and saying how he thought we could be great friends. He had one of his arms just laying across my thigh so I just lifted it up, took his hand and said, 'I think we're already great friends' as if I didn't know what he was talking about. When I got back to London I told Bill and he said he should have seen it coming because Tony was a real mover . . . Tony phoned a few days later and I played it really straight with him. I basically told him, first you show me how you can help me and then we'll see. I'm not so naive that I believed that he'd come through after I put out . . . I'm meeting a lot of important people . . . I think knowing the right people in this business helps a lot –

they know your name and face and it helps get you in the door. Right now I need all the help I can get. [Kate told me that she did become involved with Tony.] . . . [*In five years from now, do you think you'll be needing Tony's help?*] Hopefully no. I think we'll still be friends but neither of us really looks upon this as a life-time deal. [*Could you see yourself becoming seriously or emotionally involved with him?*] I doubt it.

Precisely because this woman referred to the formation of a relationship as a career-advancement strategy, a conscious and deliberate act, the man's advances were not defined as 'harassment'. Additionally, although the woman denied that she viewed Tony as other than a 'Sugar Daddy', she did refer to the friendship which existed between them.

The original incident that brought about a relationship may be redefined in retrospect so that the question of who seduced whom and for what reason is forgotten or reinterpreted. The element of threat or coercion intrinsic to defining an act as sexual harassment may be retrospectively erased or negated as the relationship progresses. Moreover, behaviour that occurs in a relationship which is fostered, rather than jeopardized by, expressions of intimacy, may not be defined as 'harassment'.

The role of the Career Woman is also a bridging one between 'types' of mistresses. Although the Career Woman may enter into a relationship with a 'work mentality' and judge the affair as if by a balance sheet of costs and benefits (Will this hurt or help my career? Is it financially worthwhile? Will it be too time-consuming?), what was originally conceived of as a form of survival in the jungle of the working world can develop into a relationship valued for qualitatively different reasons. Three sub-divisions: the token lover or flirting relationship, the office marriage and the mentor–protégée relationship can suggest further reasons why the label of sexual harassment is not invoked.

Of my sample of Career Women, those who are professional models are the sub-group least likely to comment that their affair is an attempt to circumvent sexual harassment or that they have been sexually harassed in their jobs. Several reasons may account for this. First, modelling necessarily involves exhibiting yourself and a greater tolerance of attention being concentrated on your body. The occupational ideology of modelling is largely geared towards being every man's fantasy of the perfect woman. This may encourage the woman to interpret compliments or propositions as signs that she is performing her role well. I am not suggesting that the model is the sort of woman who is invariably sexually immodest. Rather, I would suggest that the ambience of the workplace may be as important as the occupational ideology of the profession in determining whether the term harassment will be invoked. Models said that men are frequently present backstage when they dress for a fashion show, working as dressers, make-up artists and hair stylists, and that direct comments about their physical attributes are part of the standard dialogue between the photographer, hairdresser and others who interact professionally with the model. Thus it may be that compliments, caresses and suggestive remarks are simply considered par for the course and of little significance. What could be inappropriate behaviour between a business executive and his female accountant may be acceptable for a photographer or designer and his model.

A second reason why models are unlikely to define suggestive remarks and caresses as harassment is that they identify their male professional colleagues as predominantly homosexual. Models were likely to remark that the men they worked with were simply not interested in women and that they did not feel sexually threatened by them. The hairdresser who introduced me to my original group does a fair amount of work preparing models for fashion shows and photo sessions and his conversation with them is often lewd and punctuated with pawing. He is a homosexual, professes no sexual interest in women, yet engages in a ritual show of flattery and flirtation. Since his actions are thought harmless by the models they are not perceived as sexual harassment.

Whether or not a man is homosexual, vocal or physical overtures of this sort may simply be thought of as a type of play used to minimize the boredom or tedium of a situation. Spending hours in a hairdresser's chair while he straightens curls, braids or dyes a woman's hair often gives rise to a flirting relationship in which certain verbal and physical expressions of intimacy are allowed for. Most Career Women acknowledge that working with men involves developing a certain tolerance for suggestive comments, being stared at and so on, and that this is inevitable when working as part of a mixed-sex group. Although it can be defined as harassment it may also be defined as a form of play or kidding around. P. Loizos has suggested in his article 'Images of Man' in *Not Work Alone* that play, including humour and even obscenity is part of work:

> We know from the sociology of work, and our own experiences, that 'at work' a great deal of what goes on is not work. That is, it is joking, horseplay, courtship, making friends, relieving boredom and so on. Even in some jobs where the worker must keep up a formal and disciplined public style (as with waiters, who are expected to control their bodies, not sing, pick their noses, whistle or audibly break wind, etc. while serving customers) there is usually an 'off-situation' (out in the kitchen) away from customers, where a very different set of behaviour takes place. We are not always at work, at work.

It may be that forms of play between men and women are never precisely devoid of sexual overtones but become sexualized because of the difficulty in negotiating male–female roles.

The ambiguity of male–female friendships is shown in the awkward distinction made in saying that someone is a 'girl friend' and not a 'girlfriend', a 'boy friend' and not a 'boyfriend'. In forming a friendship with someone of the opposite sex, recognition of their gender may not totally be dismissed. When the man is heterosexual, the girl friend may feel a certain amount of jealousy if he speaks of his 'girlfriend' even when she is perfectly content with the platonic nature of their relationship. Similarly, when a man is homosexual, the woman may still regard him as a pseudo-lover. Men whose roles are interdependent with those of the woman may occupy the role of a token lover. Even though a flirting relationship is a parody of a true relationship, genuine intimacy may be promoted in this situation.

The office marriage suggests how the structure of the professions may encourage the development of intimacy. The role that women traditionally hold at work is largely modelled on that of the conventional wife figure. Boss and secretary, doctor and nurse, headmaster and teacher relationships all involve characteristic displays of deference and loyalty on the part of the subordinate. Not only may women be encouraged from childhood to become wives and mothers, but this may be reinforced by the occupational ideology of traditionally female professions which expect them to assume or recreate these roles in their professional life. While women play the role of the supportive wife, it should not be surprising that romantic relationships in the business organization are commonplace. Where gender role distinctions exist (the all-female secretarial staff, the all-male board of directors, the 'female' nurse, the 'male' consultant), it is predictable that there will be sexual byplay. Add to this the length of time spent with the man in a sustained working relationship, and an intimacy may develop which is expressed in the woman's assumption of the role of 'office wife'. The occupational infrastructure of certain professions can be regarded as pseudo arranged marriages which bring men and women together in the roles of 'husband' and 'wife'.

In February 1982, the *Telegraph Sunday Magazine* published 'Next to the Room at the Top' by Jane Ellison, an article on some of Britain's top secretaries. I must point out that these women are not respondents in my study and I am not suggesting that they had sexual relationships with their bosses. Their comments suggest that a certain intimacy may develop due to the time spent in a 'relationship' even when it is conducted according to a formal code of behaviour. The relationship of the boss and his secretary may become intimate over time, an intimacy which may or may not be expressed in the formation of a sexual relationship. The 'office marriage' need not be a sexual relationship.

Of the five women interviewed in the *Telegraph Sunday Magazine*, three were unmarried. They said their jobs made it impossible for them to marry. The two married women were childless, and maintained that children would make it impossible for them to continue in their jobs. The comments of these perfect secretary types who spoke of being 'tied to the office' seemed markedly similar to those you would expect from a dutiful wife. This 'office wife' role is reflected in various studies which show the high proportion of secretaries who are agreeable to running errands, shopping for their boss or for his family, making dental appointments for him and so on. As such, the role of the office wife may be seen as a type of informal back-up system to the function performed by the man's wife.

The office wife–employer husband relationship seems to mime the traditional male–female roles. It suggests that women, by convention, are expected to be content with a career that offers vicarious glamour and to find satisfaction in being a spectator to or participant in the man's career success:

'I never dreamt when I became a Senior Personal Secretary just how closely I'd be involved with affairs of national importance. You take notes for your boss at high level meetings, arrange appointments for him (and remind him to keep them!) and organize his diary generally. Depending on whom you're working for, you could be dealing with telephone calls and correspondence from Cabinet Ministers, MPs, important businessmen and specialists of every kind . . .'

Although this magazine advertisement for a secretary offering the testimony of a well-satisfied one might be thought obnoxious, it shows that the advertiser – in this case a government department – must have believed it would be effective in recruiting potential secretaries and that it offered an attractive picture of a career as a secretary. The woman's comment that she never realized how closely she would be dealing with 'affairs of national importance' is none the less ironic. To draw an analogy, it is like the stage doorman of a theatre saying that he is closely involved with the production of a 'hit' show and believing himself to be part of the cast. The woman's description of her role identifies it as that of an adjunct, a player in the shadows.

Ellison goes on to suggest that the role of the top secretary is based on her devotion and loyalty to her boss and her ability to be inconspicuously efficient:

. . . while her boss may enjoy the glamour of public attention, her role is still self-effacing and anonymous. If a top secretary does her job properly, few should be aware of what she does. She protects her boss . . . from unwanted visitors and telephone calls; she supports him in every area of his life, from organizing his diary to paying his personal bills . . . Like their bosses, top secretaries are often expected to work overtime, at weekends or at home. But while there are few recognized perks, they will usually benefit from flexible arrangements which allow them to go home early when things are quiet, make a hairdresser's appointment in working time when the boss is away, and most important, feel they are doing something useful and worthwhile.

The final comment here is worth noting for it suggests that the secretary basks in the man's professional success and is gratified to play the shadow role of an adjunct because she believes that her help is instrumental to the man's success. If it is true, it mirrors the comments made by the wives of professional men in various studies. For example, wives of doctors often identify so closely with their husband's professional role that they take pride in being a doctor's wife. They feel their shadow role is worthwhile and admirable in that it contributes to their husband's success. Whether or not the relationship between the office wife and her employer becomes a sexual one, the setting for the office affair, the assumption of traditional male and female work-roles and the patterns of interaction between male superiors and female subordinates may encourage intimacy.

The environment of the workplace seems important to the development of the kept relationship. As Melissa Sands says in her *The Making of the American Mistress*:

> In the mistress community, working is common: 85 per cent of all mistresses turned out to be working women . . . Nearly 50 per cent of all the mistresses told me that their affair started on the job. The high correlation between the trend of women going out to work outside the home and the trend of having an affair is not coincidence. Working has a tremendous impact. Working seems to be a definite catalyst for affairs. Working leads to the making of thousands of mistresses at least. As working women aspire to new heights of success, they still carry the old weights of chemistry and biology. There is new respect for women and their capabilities in the working world, and yet an attraction for their womanhood.

While I am wary of Sands's comment that there exists a 'new respect for women and their capabilities' and would suggest that her metaphor of the 'weights of chemistry and biology' juxtaposes the lingo of the sociobiologist and the 'love among the filing cabinets' story writer, I would agree that working, especially in traditionally feminine jobs, may promote the mistress–lover relationship. If the married woman makes a career out of marriage, the working woman may make a marriage out of work. In this connection it should be noted that when the kept relationship began at the place of work the conception the woman had of her role was not always that of the Career Woman. With the exception of my Smart Set category of kept woman, the original introduction to the man (and therefore the relationship) commonly occurred at the woman's place of work. Flirting behaviour was not always premeditated or designed as a method of ingratiation, and career advancement was not always at the core of establishing the office affair. Admittedly, the Career Woman's perception of the man as 'useful' may suggest that her actions are guided with a practical end in view. His being powerful may, to a degree, be the attraction of the relationship. However, achieving a mentor–protégée relationship may not be the result of concerted effort or the deliberate attempt by the woman to find a mentor; it may simply be a fortuitous event.

My second case history centres on Jenny, a senior executive in an international cosmetics company, who was promoted to her present position by her lover, the joint managing director. She says that her sincere admiration for his professional ability, together with his willingness to talk to her as a serious employee, formed the basis of the relationship:

> At first I didn't think of him as a man really – just as a marvellous colleague and boss. When you work closely with someone, putting all you can into the job, you develop an almost telepathic rapport, a sort of mental intimacy that's incredibly satisfying. If he hadn't been so good at his job I wouldn't have looked at him twice. But as it was, he was such a professional that I was fascinated by him – I'm very ambitious myself and I need that mental stimulation in a relationship. Men usually are threatened by women who are ambitious and intelligent. I've dated men who just will refuse to believe that a woman really enjoys talking about work . . . I did not have to play-act at all. I've always found power incredibly attractive. Knowing that I held the cleverest man in the company sexually attracted was a tremendous turn-on. So was the fact that we talked about work much of the time.

Although Jenny was already in a position of some importance when she met the man, there was an established precedent for her aiding her career in collaboration with a benefactor. Her first job, after leaving college with a degree in business administration, was with an advertising firm. After being asked to act as hostess to an elderly client visiting from New York, she established an affair with him. She felt encouraged by her firm to do so and said that her former boss had told her to show their client every consideration and treat him well. She said that she was not ashamed of the relationship in that it proved to be professionally advantageous and the man's sporadic visits represented a lavish interlude in her ordinary, budget-conscious life. She was married for a brief period during her early twenties, but felt constricted in her relationship with her husband and stressed that she resented being known as 'Ken's wife' rather than as a person with an identity of her own. The only drawback in her relationship with the client from New York was that she became known in the office as 'Mr Smith's girlfriend' and thought that, joking aside, her professional peers and superiors did not always view her as a 'serious' career woman:

One thing I learned was to keep my mouth shut. If people don't actually know what you're doing, or plan to do, you operate from a position of much greater strength. One of my bosses started getting rather too friendly – he thought if I was having an affair with one man, why not two? That got pretty rough. If I said no he'd say, 'You shouldn't play hard to get, it doesn't suit you' or ask me if I thought American men were better in bed. Then he would sulk and say that I was pretty full of myself and maybe I thought I was too good for him and that sort of talk.

Jenny left her firm and found her new boss's lack of sexual interest in her refreshing. She stated that for the first two years their relationship was strictly formal and only when a campaign necessitated them working closely together did their relationship progress to a more intimate one:

I had been determined to succeed in my own right and while I valued his advice, I didn't want to be one of those girls who cried behind the potted palms when their boss decided there's not enough challenge in it any more and wants a new secretary. First I made pretty sure that I had a secure job and then I thought about my social life – which at that time was horrible. There was just not enough time for both. Really there still isn't. One night after work we went to dinner and then I asked him back to my flat. I think if a woman finds a man sexually attractive there's nothing wrong with taking the initiative. You have to be aggressive to get what you want – it doesn't matter if it's in business or day-life. Being quick to see an advantage or make one for yourself – that's the way to be successful. The next day at work I just acted as if nothing had happened.

Jenny believes her ability to divide their business and personal relationship impressed her lover. Her dress and entertainment allowances have been enlarged substantially as perks of her new job position, and she now undertakes frequent travelling which she particularly enjoys. She emphasized, however, that her lover satisfied her emotional need in respecting her professional opinion and acting on her advice. She stressed that he was not attracted to the dollybird models who were commissioned by the company to illustrate advertisements and was attracted to her for her professional abilities rather than for her appearance. She does not look like a centre-fold *Playboy* bunny or a magazine cover girl and she does not, she implies, want to be seen as such. Since her position is in a fashion-related industry she feels it important to be well-groomed and well-dressed, but outside work feels it unnecessary to look as if she 'had just stepped out of *Vogue*'.

Her lover has recently bought a four-bedroomed house for her just outside the London district where the company's office is located. She calls it a disaster – the roof is collapsing and the upper floor would be 'impossibly hard' to heat. Nevertheless she seems to be delighted by the gesture. Jenny adamantly rejects the idea of marriage to her already-married lover because working together and living together would cause an intolerable strain on their relationship. The way things are at present, she thought, would allow them to remain best friends much more easily than if they were to marry.

Since the precise nature of her relationship is unknown to others at her workplace she feels herself able to forewarn him of internal scheming – who is critical of him or speaks disparagingly of him, and so on. I noted that she guards the exclusivity of her position. At one interview she mentioned that she would 'have to do something' about a co-worker who was attempting to trespass on her professional terrain. Besides being an internal spy she judges the relationship's communication structure as useful to her interests as well as her lover's. Her grievances are directly expressed to someone in a position to resolve them. Acting as a troubleshooter for him puts on him the obligation to protect her interests in return.

The Career Woman encountered in my research values the mentor–protégée relationship as a successful pseudo marriage. Its value is thought to lie in the emotional support given, not simply in the support given in terms of maintenance. While the pursuit of a career by other kept women seems to be curtailed because it is considered less important than the relationship, the mentor–protégée situation encourages the woman to pursue a career. One such woman found the man to be supportive regarding her career ambitions:

> My work is very important to me and he's very good to talk to, sincere and dislikes constraint and seeks openness and straightforwardness. He wants his friends to be themselves and after some bad experiences I've had where being open and frank has led to being dumped and avoided I can appreciate that. We have interests (if not opinions) that are similar in many ways. And he's a person who like me has had an unsatisfying married life and has gone through pain
> . . .
>
> At a superficial glance one might say that I want something different – which is exactly what I said to myself upon selecting my eminently normal, healthy, well-adjusted husband. Yet, to expand upon the obvious sarcasm, a normal background I don't think guarantees a well-adjusted or mature individual. Nor does it necessarily reveal the true strengths or weaknesses of a person. Whereas being forged in fire can literally do so, forge a person I mean. He has worked himself up from nothing and I admire him for this. Is it to be desired to get a man who has sailed complacently along and has no empathy or patience for what you're going through? Isn't it true that only experience can make someone

aware, attuned to another individual's load of pain and problems? I've had it with working so hard to maintain a phony status quo. I don't want to be the loving stay-at-home wife to someone who had everything handed to him on a silver platter . . . My lover is my true friend because he wants me to make the most of myself. (*27-year-old woman, Toronto*)

In contrast, a second such respondent wrote:

I remember handling a particularly complicated case and trying to talk to him about it. He just ignored me and complained that the house looked like a pigsty and I just waste my time and never do anything around the house . . . Another time our son was picked up by the police for under-age driving and we both left our jobs to come and get him. Our son was really upset over the whole thing and that afternoon was supposed to write his entrance exams for college. All John was concerned about was that our son should get to the exam center on time. Finally he just told me 'You take care of it, I've got to get back to work'. He didn't care at all that our son was badly shaken up or that maybe I had to get back to work . . . We both had similar types of jobs so I had always assumed we were a good match but it just didn't work out that way. (*49-year-old woman, Colorado*)

A third woman contrasted her lover's behaviour with that of her former husband in terms of the support given for her career ambitions. Her former husband had been a writer and she stated that her willingness to assist him included proofreading and revising his work, typing his manuscripts, financially supporting him while he wrote and offering encouragement and moral support. However, she stated that he had been haughty and dismissive of her own ambitions to write. She stated that her relationship with her lover was founded on friendship and mutual emotional support if not precisely romance and sexual attraction.

Just under half of my Career Woman contacts had been married and divorced by their late twenties. Nearly all of these women made reference to the husband's lack of support for their pursuing a career and often expressed dissatisfaction with their former husband for being unambitious himself. One woman said that when her salary had exceeded her husband's this inspired resentment and led to a breakdown in the marriage. Some respondents maintained that while their husbands had not minded their salary *per se* they had been apathetic or undermining when the woman wanted to share news of successful job performances or career-related topics.

In several cases, the Career Woman's affair occurred while she was still legally married. However, the affair itself was not seen as the cause – but the effect – of marital dissatisfaction. Women would say that they had married too young to realize what qualities they needed in a partner or had married simply to leave home. They claimed that they had outgrown their husbands and found little in common with these men after the first glow of marital bliss had faded. One of my oldest respondents in this category maintained that the only area of conversation that she and her husband could pursue with a similar level of interest was discussions about their children. As such, the support given by her mentor–lover, coupled with the excitement generated by pursuing a clandestine relationship, made obvious the dissatisfaction she felt with her marriage.

For the mentor, there may be a feeling of satisfaction that the woman appreciates his help and recognizes his role as an expert. If 'no man is a hero to his dentist', nor is he to his wife, often enough. It may be gratifying and more than a little flattering to play the role of the hero to someone else. It may simply be, however, that working in close contact with his protégée allows an intimacy to develop which is based on common work goals and shared experiences. He may be able to pursue areas of conversation with his protégée that he is unable to pursue with his wife, due to the latter's lack of knowledge or interest. It is easy to make too much of the concept of seduction, too. While some men and women prided themselves on their techniques and set out to make themselves endearing to the other, the growth of intimacy did not always come from a premeditated act. In some cases it was portrayed as 'taking advantage of a situation' when it presented itself. In others, it seemed that a gradual change in the nature of the relationship took place in which intimacy developed unexpectedly. Thus, the Career Woman generally professed affection for the man if not impassioned sexual attraction. While I would not suggest that every Career Woman eventually re-defines the nature of the relationship with her lover to such an extent that she becomes a Mistress type, the possibility exists. It may be difficult to express warmth and affection for someone of the opposite sex without the other defining it as a sexual overture or without becoming confused yourself about the emotions you feel for that person.

Fringe benefits at work also have their place in the life of the Career Woman. These can extend to living in a company flat, driving a company car and having the entertainment costs of the relationship put down to company expense accounts. The vulnerability of these women lies in their dispensability. Within a company this may result in transfers sideways – or even 'upstairs' – which leave the woman with a new, uncaptivated boss, office gossip, installation in a position whose demands she cannot satisfy and the subordination of the career to the relationship. Cary L. Cooper and Marilyn J. Davidson in their *High Pressure: Working Lives of Women Managers* have listed some of the potential difficulties a woman may face in forming a mentor–protégée relationship with a male sponsor:

> . . . having a male mentor can create enormous stress on the female manager concerned because (1) she feels she must constantly perform at her best to meet his expectations, (2) she becomes identified with him and suffers the whims and circumstances that befall him, (3) her own individual talents and abilities are not always recognized by 'significant others', but get fused with the boss's strengths and weaknesses, and (4) she is still playing out a 'dependent role', and not trying to make her mark on the basis of her own resources . . . In addition, this special relationship can cause resentment among the female manager's male peers, who cannot attain the same type of relationship with the high status male.

Forming a sexual relationship with a mentor is especially complicated when the partner works in the same office for here the public and private roles overlap. In contrast to the situation of Jenny (the subject of my second case history), one of my respondents, a former model, was funded by her mentor so that she could open a fashion house. However, her mentor plays an invisible role within her company itself. He introduces her to potential buyers, gives her introductions to others in related businesses, offers business advice and so on, but does not directly participate in the day-to-day management of her company. In these circumstances she is more easily able to separate her private life from her personal life than Jenny, who is directly employed alongside her mentor.

Recognizing the difficulties inherent in office romances, under the title 'The Woman's World Guide to Office Romance' *Woman's World* (November 1982) suggested 'Ten Tips to Help you Keep Your Secret':

1 Do continue to wear your old office clothes.

2 Do gain weight. Whoever heard of a person in love putting *on* weight?

3 Do ring in ill on the same day as he does . . . The very flagrancy of the act is sure to dispel any kind of suspicion.

4 Don't put your make-up on before you leave for work – habits of a lifetime mustn't be seen to change at such a time.

5 Do arrive at different times in the morning.

6 Don't send him looks in the canteen that are steamier than the treacle pudding.

7 Do wear different clothes each day – especially if you didn't go home the night before.

8 Don't play footsie with him over lunch – you may end up having an affair with a chair leg instead of the man of your dreams.

9 Don't play footsie at any time under a glass table.

10 Do ignore him in the lift.

Ridiculous as they may seem, these suggestions are not really bad advice. Strategies my respondents used include: recruiting ex-husbands or casual friends to act as their escorts to company functions (to suggest that they have a boyfriend and thus are not on the prowl for a man); the creation of a boyfriend (for example, placing the picture of a friend or an ex-boyfriend in a strategic position); not telling *anyone* about the true nature of their involvement with the man; maintaining an extremely formal pattern of behaviour with the man when others not wise to the relationship are present, and generally monitoring their behaviour and conversations with the man when in a public setting. The boyfriend of convenience or 'walker' allows the woman to appear in settings usually defined for couples, and to attend parties alongside the lover and his wife and create the impression that she has no desire to pursue anything other than a professional relationship with the man. However, because of the importance placed on the relationship even when it is conceived of as strictly a career-strategy, sexual fidelity to the man is thought important and women generally maintain that their other friendships with men are non-sexual. When they do pursue affairs at the same time as the kept relationship they still attempt to create the impression of fidelity.

The Career Woman who maintains that she views the man as simply a Sugar Daddy nevertheless seems to maintain patterns of behaviour with the man qualitatively similar to those assumed by the Mistress. If she intends to be manipulative or self-promoting, her role still requires that she present herself as other than egocentric. Women who acknowledge their duplicity suggest that career success requires hypocrisy. Success is seen to be achieved by being nice to people you do not like, and spending more time with people you do not like but who are potentially 'helpful' than with those you do like but who are simply good company. Since women believe that, by its nature, the business environment condones duplicity rather than condemns it, their strategy is thought logically consistent with that ethos.

In this chapter I have attempted to challenge three of the common presentations of the office affair. The first, the Casting Couch syndrome, suggests that women are inevitably transformed into suicide victims when they attempt to sleep their way to the top. It resembles the tale of Little Red Riding Hood, but in this version the wolf survives and future Red Riding Hoods are cautioned to remain at home, safe and secure. The second, Sexual Harassment, continues with the image of the woman as a 'victim', failing to acknowledge the woman who deliberately pursues the Casting Couch route to success. The third, the 'Love Among the Filing Cabinets' scenario, presents a maudlin version of the office affair. It ignores any suggestion of sexual politics in the workplace and patterns the woman's behaviour with a heart-shaped pastry-cutter. All these presentations, on their own, are unsatisfactory.

Forming a relationship with a powerful man may be a deliberate career strategy. It does not have to be in response to harassment or the conclusion to a love story. It may be part of a career-strategy of sexual sponsorship or it may arise out of intimacy fostered by working closely together in an office. The time spent in work relationships, the difficulty of maintaining social distance and the problem of negotiating male–female roles may all serve to promote the 'office marriage'. A manufactured affection may well develop into genuine affection. As such, the Career Woman role may be a bridging one between types of mistresses.

Chapter Three

THE PROFESSIONAL OPPORTUNIST

Being kept basically comes down to chasing him until he catches you. There's always the element of game-playing but all men/women relationships are like that. The golden rule is never to admit you're aware of the game. (*31-year-old woman, Toronto*)

The Professional Opportunist can be differentiated from the Mistress type not by the role that she plays but by her conception of it. In her relationship with the man, the Opportunist (as I will call her), unlike the Mistress, does not feel as if she were married to the man. It is this absence of emotional attachment that distinguishes the two types of kept women. The Opportunist may be as much of a self-professed romantic as the Mistress and she may be as idealistic in believing that a perfect marriage is tenable, but she does not feel that these concepts apply to her relationship with her lover. She is not necessarily an advocate of open marriage, adultery, or sexual liberation *per se* – in fact the majority of Opportunists are not. Nevertheless, her relationships are frequently presented as a type of esoteric experimentation, a growing experience. She generally depicts herself as a free spirit: independent, aware of her own worth and amoral rather than immoral. When the goal is neither marriage nor career success, it seems as if the relationship is envisaged as a game which is enjoyable, interesting and absorbing to an extent – but only a game. Unlike the Mistress who tends to be emotional about love and to rhapsodize about her affair, the Opportunist tends to be analytical or detached in presenting her relationship:

In fact my present relationship is in many ways a reflection of my first one. Tom likes opera, is well off, and twice my age. Although Tom's wife is dead, her ghost haunts us. When we met, his wife had just died and he doesn't want to remarry at his age [over 70]. The memories of his dead wife make me feel like Rachel [his wife]. My mother is dead and I have always had a close relationship with my father who is very generous. Perhaps I'm recreating this same situation all the time? Someone I can depend on because they have more experience of life and enough money, but I can never really have because of this ghost of another woman? (*43-year-old woman, London*)

In contrast to this woman who thought her participation in numerous kept relationships self-revealing, another of my contacts involved with an elderly man looked on the relationship as an opportunity to psychoanalyse him. She believed that he felt alienated from his daughter and sought a surrogate daughter with whom to enact his incestuous fantasies. Other women played less recondite games:

I'm in this purely for fun. I'm having more fun now than I ever had in my life. Giving your heart away to a guy you know you can't have makes no sense at all to me. It seems like some people just love to suffer. What is it – sado-masochism? Self-flagellation? They remind me of monks and their hair shirts – those undershirts that had this sharp hair interwoven into the cloth so that they'd feel un-comfortable. You see, they had to be uncomfortable, had to suffer continuously. Now the men who would have once become monks get married so they can suffer. Why should two women suffer because of one man? Faye [a close friend of the woman and also involved in a kept relationship] comes over to ask me what to take for acute depression . . . semi-depression . . . Marxist depression . . . and it's all related to being in love with someone she knows damn well is not going to marry her. She's either on top of the world because he gave her a diamond ring and she thinks it's an engagement ring or miserable because it's Christmas and she's all alone. You have to have the right attitude, it protects you from getting hurt. [*What is the right attitude?*] Accept it's just for fun and have a good time. (*53-year-old Canadian woman interviewed in London*)

I'm not the romantic school-girl type. I've been in love and I like men more than women as friends because they experience more things and lead more interesting lives. I'm not the sort who likes to organize jumble sales and spend the afternoon drinking tea with the ladies. Women lead boring lives and their conversation revolves around their children, their husbands and who is coming to visit. Men are better conversationalists because they live rather than exist. (*31-year-old woman, London*)

The Mistress in a love affair is addicted to 'love', but the fact that the Opportunist calls her relationship a 'fling' suggests that she can give up the habit any time she wishes to do so. She is likely to be straightforward about her emotional detachment from her man and to be rather nonchalant about the importance of any one particular relationship, generally looking upon it as vaguely rewarding or simply as an experience. One woman who has been involved in four kept relationships summarizes them thus:

> What's past is past and should be thought of as neither good nor bad but just an experience. During the relationship I usually enjoyed myself and grew as a person. And from there one just goes on. (*35-year-old woman, Los Angeles*)

It is not only women who take this attitude. A large number of men who kept women said that they were simply looking for a good time rather than emotion-laden liaisons. Approximately 68 per cent of my contacts felt it was possible to have a good sexual relationship without love and the absence of intense emotions is often claimed by the Opportunist to be desirable where the involvement is with a married man. In any event she maintains that the man would be threatened or scared off by a display of intense feelings:

> Men have a business attitude towards love. They want a goal to try for. He's never quite sure whether or not I'll be there for him and it adds to his excitement. I'm something that he wants but can't quite have. (*33-year-old woman, London*)

It is this emotional detachment from the man that authors have found objectionable when writing about kept women. While the Mistress proclaims that love conquers all and uses this argument to justify her affair, the Opportunist throws away the books on 'romance' and its protocol. The following detailed case histories will not only illuminate the lifestyle of the Opportunist and the way she attempts to present her role as respectable rather than disreputable, but also allow her to be seen as more than a mere predator.

The women in my Opportunist category had generally participated in their first kept relationship during their late twenties to early thirties, and about 75 per cent had been married, had children and subsequently been divorced. They were generally middle, or upper-middle, class and slightly over 60 per cent had attended an institution of higher learning. It was not uncommon for them to be self-styled intellectuals or cultural snobs, stressing what concerts they had been to or what high-flown conversation they had had with some highly placed person. Their marriages seem marked by at least one episode of extramarital sex, an event which they see as signifying a loss of respect for their husband and a lack of feeling for the marriage itself. They become emotionally detached from their marriage and their husband and seek sexual or emotional gratification elsewhere. On occasion a woman would say that her extramarital involvement is a form of retaliation against her husband's infidelity or an attempt to goad him into fighting for the marriage. More commonly, however, the extramarital affair is seen by the couple as marking time between their emotional divorce and taking legal action to terminate the marriage.

The Opportunist tends to have a somewhat exalted image of herself. Rather than admit to deviating from the norm, she is likely to see herself as astute, and superior to other women who do not know how to handle men, who cannot acquire her enigmatic mystique and who relinquish total control and power to a man in any relationship. The attitude of the Opportunist can be summarized as, 'Those who do not know the world get taken advantage of by it.' They pride themselves on knowing the way the world works and using their skills to make things profitable for themselves.

I introduce as my first case history a 40-year-old American woman, Irene, with whom I had several interviews while she was visiting London. She had contacted me after seeing the advertisement I had put in her local newspaper in America. She was of Irish/Polish descent and from a middle-class background. After high school she became a teacher's aide for a few years and then took up modelling, including nude photography, and has lived fairly well since her divorce in 1970. Her 22-year-old son and 18-year-old daughter have both left home, while she, Irene, shares her home with a girl friend. Irene was very articulate and self-confident and had obviously spent some time considering her 'life story', and its implications as far as my research was concerned, before we met. She even read out some parts from her notes. The following gives an idea of her unusual lifestyle:

> I've spent my leisure time – which is to say *most* of my time – in study, the arts (mainly music), volunteer activities and have elevated – by association – my social standing. That is to say I have attended symphony and opera balls, Governor's balls, and so called Gala events of press note. I have arrived – so to speak!
>
> There is another life being lived of course. It is difficult sometimes. What the neighbours think and *what is* are entirely two different things. Likewise the upper social strata I play in. It is thought by my neighbours that I am 'helped' by one man when in fact I am 'kept' by another. It is thought by those who only see me periodically that I am of independent means. It is known that I have travelled extensively (another man again) and enjoy the company of world-renowned classical musicians, doctors, the judiciary and so on. I am known for my taste in attire, I am a little envied for the time I have to devote to enjoying my record collection and literary library – which does receive most of my/his/their excess dollars . . .
>
> Men find me very 'up front'. They are intrigued and entrenched. Somewhere in all this there are degrees of altruism, idealism and no

small amount of audacity. But I think it is a fine game and no small work of art. In fact it's a full-time occupation.

In my home town we have our own small problem with prostitution and some few times as I have driven by one of our busier corners downtown I have wondered about the 'price' of their status *versus* mine. I live by my premise of never (only once a year it has laughingly been stated on Queen Victoria's birthday!) sleeping with the man whose money I am at pains to accept. A girl must eat. If I were willing to pay *that* price I would be on that street corner – perhaps earning more money but at a great cost. And that cost is my freedom. Also, I never live with a man. I should not say never of course for I would, for love, but not for recompense. I tried it once, however, but I soon saw the error of his ways and moved him into the rear bedroom and before the end of a trying year I had found him a 'cute' apartment and shipped him out. All this of course at extra cost. To *him*. I received an increase in my allowance. And please remember that I did not, after three times the first three months, nor do I now, go to bed with him.

I shall refer to the gentleman as H2 for there was – and is – a predecessor I call H1. Actually this was my second raise, the first being when H2 found out that H1 was in some small way making life easier for me. It was a simple matter of being absolutely firm in my resolve to not accept an allowance from (horrors!) two men! What kind of female would do that? One has one's principles and to accept money from two men both of whom wanted, expected, had enjoyed sex with me, well – I simply could not do such a thing. Ergo, H2 was delighted to be numero uno and generously offered to pick up the slack and he's ever since considered himself the better man. For this he left a dull marriage of twenty years (he is 55). He mows the grass, takes out the garbage for me . . . a new roof is needed. And to think he left his wife for a new-found excitement!. He remains my confidant and to a point thrives on my tales of adventure with other men. He supports me while I travel well, with another 'friend'. I have become for him the ultimate challenge – the one for whom he left his staid, dull wife and three children. I wish the money were better – but then I might have to pay the price of some of my freedom. And as both H1 and H2 are well aware – I can be 'had' but I cannot be bought!

Now perhaps you can see the intrigue here for a man. He's being 'had' to some degree and the audacity of the female to insist he be bright enough to see it for the 'honest' friendship it has to be and insist further he rise to this occasion, in his eyes can only elevate him to a stature that no other male (those to whom I've said 'no' to anything) can achieve. I ask you to remember one thing, these relationships are of some many years' duration and I cannot but owe a loyalty to the men involved with me. They ARE important and good people who I would defend against all.

In our next meeting I heard more of Irene's story:

My first affair was with my best friend's husband. It was a mutually satisfying relationship added to which was the companionship of his wife whom I'll call 'W'. I am sure it was the most wonderful time for all of us. We changed, independently and together. He and 'W' not so well. He and I splendidly. How selfish but how lovely and real. I orgasmed for the first time ever. We took 'retreats' as husband and wife. His wife and I were the best of friends. And ultimately, though we go our separate ways now, she and I, H1's and my relationship proved well for 'W' too. When after two years I could not stand any more deceit, I simply told 'W' what was going on. It seemed safe to assume – we all came to this realization – at least she and I did, we were never sure about him – that if I hadn't 'taken' him away and he hadn't left – well there was nothing to worry about was there? Until that ride to the hospital after she had taken something or other. He swore, when she demanded, that he would never see me again. So having left her overnight in the hospital he drove me back to her house and tried to make love to me in their bed . . .

Three years after his promise to her, 'W' walked into my garden one night and found us busy making dinner together via candlelight, moonlight, wine, etc. He couldn't take it and left to go home. She and I enjoyed the whole hilarious, silly scene for the farce it was and I realized that I missed her friendship during those years more than I enjoyed his. And we both told the 'Big I Am' to grow up, go make lots of money because he was going to need it and Heaven help him if we ever caught him with anyone else. And we proceeded to grow up ourselves.

None of us is dependent on the other now. We keep in touch, we care, but we care enough to stay removed. He helps me only when I ask. We have remained intact mentally and emotionally for which I thank God.

I asked Irene what she received by way of rent money, gifts or a regular allowance:

To be perfectly honest I accept all three, but remember, only if the gentleman is worthy, that is he must aspire to heights greater than his fellow man and be willing to descend to lows according to my list of priorities of which he may be one. Only then can I accept his offerings. After all I'm not just any woman.

These 'gifts' were all tax-free you must appreciate. These men being married could not in any way deduct me, so the degree to which my needs, wishes, wants, could be accommodated varied slightly. In between all these years, I have from time to time supplemented my income by renting to university students. One of these, I'll call him 'L', became another *dear* friend who, by his very proximity, could see the need to anticipate my monetary needs before the first of the month. Or the 15th. Or an opera I could not live without, or . . . whatever. From there it was a simple matter once again, as always of letting it be known to those concerned what a lovely fellow 'L' was. How thoughtful, how considerate, how *generous*!

'L' stayed with me for five years until H2 moved in. Then H2 moved out and as I said immediately increased my allowance. I do believe men have eyes much greener than any woman's, or more men have green eyes and I seem to meet them. To get back to 'L'. I went to bed with this lovely gentleman last about the same time I found a girlfriend for him. So, he is happy – which takes a weight from my shoulders. Now I only borrow.

When I get back home, H2 is going to drop around to clean the pool for me; I am going to find a birthday present for H1's wife for him because he is too busy and 'would I please?' and then I have a date with a judge.

Ah, to be a woman in a man's world!

At first glance this woman's attitude may seem a little mendacious or at least a case of self-deceit; how could a woman not care about cheating with her best friend's husband, or see something positive in a situation which drives her friend to attempt suicide? I believe it is true because it describes a situation and attitude which are consistently mirrored by other women in this category of kept women. It becomes a game to them and, as this woman accurately said, no small work of art.

A woman wrote to Irma Kurtz's agony column in the British edition of *Cosmopolitan* magazine (August 1982):

I am twenty-four and have never had an emotional involvement. However, as a student in my first year at college, I have just made the mistake of trusting a guy and going too far with him . . . I love this guy and care about him, but I don't know how to make him realise this . . . Please tell me how to use a woman's tactics. What can I do?

Ms Kurtz responded:

I'm afraid I know what you mean by a 'woman's tactics': outmoded ways of arousing jealousy, of flirting out of vanity, of pretending to unfelt emotions, of entrapping a mate in any way possible . . .

Despite Ms Kurtz's feeling that these mechanisms are outmoded, they represent the unconventional wisdom of the Opportunist that Irene herself is conscious of: 'Ah, to be a woman in a man's world.' She will be a caricature of the truly feminine female if need be, helpless, hapless and in need of a strong man around the house. With the Opportunist, fantasy enactment is a tool of the trade. The chameleon effect is very much in evidence here. To Irene, her behaviour is a parody of being a female within female–male interaction. In our next conversation she told me more about her background and the problems encountered through her attitude. At this point she also acknowledged her conscious use of flirtation as a means of attracting male attention:

> I was the eldest of three daughters, born out of wedlock – 'Father' an Irishman, mother born in Poland, but she moved to the States – to the west coast. I never knew my father and am convinced he never knew of my existence.
>
> When I was two years old I was sent to my maternal grandmother's in Ohio. I returned when I was four and a half to find a father and brand new sister whom I detested on sight. I was jealous – a perfectly normal reaction. I was a handful for 'Dad' (whom I adore now) who I hated, feared and resented then as an intrusion. My mother allowed Dad – '*that man*'! – a free hand with incorrigible little me to atone for her sin (that was me) and in gratitude that this 'good man' married *her* – who had committed the ultimate sin. All these feelings were all very real, very important as I was growing up.
>
> When I was 15 I found my mother's marriage certificate and confronted her with it. I knew he wasn't my real father – no one could hate me so much and be my *real father*! On the other hand – he was a gay, charming, sometimes incomprehensible, very Viennese and lovable man. He told the wildest, most romantic stories – our family name was, indeed, not a name at all, it was a *Title*. Stories about old Vienna, the Hapsburgs, Court, nobility, and most precious of all, stories about music. Viennese music, waltzes, Johann Strauss. And there was always music in our home one way or another. Dad could repair and recycle anything – an old accordion? – we listened to Strauss on it! A fiddle someone threw in the garbage? – Hungarian Czardas on three strings! I remember so well, he used to put me on top of his big workers' boots, and with a makeshift player and an old 78 of the 'Cuckoo Waltz' he'd turn the occasion into stardust dreams and teach me to dance – 'properly, so I should know how'. I love music, Vienna, dancing and my wonderful, wonderful Dad. In a sense, I became the first *son* – I am the only music lover and romantic in the family – and of we

three girls, I am the only one who has adopted his homeland and all that goes with it (perhaps my need was greater?). I am the one who has become a chef of some small note. My mother heats up tins of prepared food while I invite them to my place for schnitzels and tortes. My mother, unfortunately, has turned to the church. I say unfortunately, for she is no longer the happy person she used to be. She is still repenting. The family fought this thing for a few years but we have now quietly acquiesced . . .

Now about my sisters. Sister No. 1 is the one I adore now even though I wished to do away with her when I returned to my mother, I love her very much. She is two and a half years younger than I, a head shorter, very blonde and very beautiful – and of course 'the spitting image of Dad's mother!' Oh boy, did that line ever make me wince. There was no way *I* could look like his mother – and oh brother, did I want to!

Sister No. 2 is five years younger than I – she was a baby when I was young. She has become like a second mother – in the *worst* sense. I stay away from her for she has become in her mature years very strained, somewhat bitter re life. I believe she feels she has done everything one should do – *properly* and alas – 'Something is wrong', 'Something is missing'. She is a very uptight woman and no fun, no sense of humour. A dried-up prune married to a dried-up, stuck-up, proselytizing self-righteous prig of a fellow. Poor No. 2, for I think she knows this better than anyone.

There were no boys in this family – until I presented mine. Now for my kids. My son, whom I adore, is 22 years of age – very responsible and mature. At present he has a relationship with a 29-year-old female who tells me she loves and worships my son – and so on. He has, in his own words, learned a lot about relationships from me. I wonder if too much? He does not intend to marry for some years but he is *very* exacting in his friendships. Very self-confident and self-assured. Right now he cannot abide his sister for she is still immature and irresponsible. He has little patience with this. Me too, I'm afraid.

My daughter is an enigma. I do believe that she has had a trying time living with a person like me as her mother. Life with me can be at times exciting, even adventurous and fun but there are moments of intense emotions, melodrama at its best and worst – and indecision. As a mother I'm telling my children, on the one hand to conform to society because one must live within it, to do the right thing always, to say the proper things – and on the other, 'do your own thing', 'to thine own self be true' and all that. Doesn't matter what the world thinks. Be unique. Be YOURSELF!!

Can you imagine being brought up with this? Right now, she is living on her own and I am at odds with her. However, this will pass. I am trying to be patient whilst she gets on with maturing. Both my children are sensitive and can be easily emotionally overcome within our own circle where we can be secure. They are a little different from 'the kid up the street' but I think they are exciting to be with and interesting.

I asked Irene to tell me about her premarital dating:

I always gravitated to older men. I would flirt with my father's friends, the men he worked with. I worked in the cafeteria of a local firm. It was Mecca for me when I was 15 or 16. Hundreds of men! Certainly all older than I. I learned to flirt very well – and that was all. As far as it went.

I then got engaged to the fellow all the other girls wanted. He was older, had a nice car, dressed well and was oh so handsome! What a bore he was too – and I could twist him around my finger. So I walked next door one evening after returning another guy's ring and asked him if he still wanted to marry me. 'Are you pregnant?', he asked. Was this ALL men thought about re women? I was a virgin my wedding night and *he* was *surprised*! Respect goes when you have to sit up and take notice of the unintelligence of someone who is lying next to you in that situation.

Of course, there were many things and many trials in many years. We split, once, I had an extramarital affair, once, we reconciled, once. I conceived, had my daughter who remained in an incubator whilst we had a real bad hurricane, and one week before she was due home, his mother passed away suddenly. Papa (his father) invited us to move in with him. It was up to me, I was told by my then husband. I thought *not* and he kicked a hole in the wall.

So we moved in with our son to discover how little room there was in that house. I would have a bed and two cribs in a cupboard of a room while we would have papa's old room – he moving to the basement. Fine. Then he became sickly, with ulcers. A new lady friend – and her teenage kids – appeared. One evening we were out and came home to find her kids in my son's bed and my son in ours. Papa became worse. I had a teething baby, no washer or dryer. I had to go to the laundromat daily with over two dozen diapers. My father-in-law was on a special diet and there was this woman and her kids. Then my lecherous brother-in-law came home to his father's house from the airforce bringing his sleazy friend with him. I put signs on the fridge 'Please wash hands before handling food' and in the bathroom 'Please flush the toilet'. My husband was out drinking one evening. I was in bed and rolled over when he came in. Lo and behold, guess who thought he was coming to dinner? I have never said anything to my ex. Instead, sanity at stake, I sought a psychiatrist who told me point blank, if I wasn't crazy now and I was not, I soon would be. 'Get out of that house.'

Well, that at least turned the tide for me, mentally. Physically there were too many problems. Papa's ulcer was cancer and it had metasticized and he had to be watched constantly. So did my baby who was as wont to eat the teabags from the garbage under the sink as to chew the fringe off the blinds on the windows. The girlfriend disappeared with her new diamond ring, not to come upon the scene again until contesting that they were engaged and he *intended* to provide for her in his will. Guess who took care of her, the will, the funeral, sale of goods, etc.? My ex's mother never knew, thank God, that she was not legally married to his father. Upon his death, he had one legal wife (who had always been thought of as his mistress, one divorced wife, one deceased (but not legally tied in matrimony) and one fiancée. Quite a man! He was baby-faced in his late sixties, with a cigarette always hanging out of his mouth. He was slovenly and as tight with money as they come – but charming – obviously these women thought so!

I asked Irene what happened to her own life at this point:

> I took up modelling – not for long and only for fun at first. It never was too lucrative. There was money to be made, of course, should one be willing to move to the right places. I played at it more for vanity, interest, meeting men and ego and fun.
>
> Teaching came after my divorce and knowing myself I must admit, I do not know for how long I might have endured the work once the novelty wore off, for I was only a teacher's aide without much responsibility. The one regret I have is that I never went in for more qualifications when younger. I had already been through too much, relied on my own means, my intelligence, my fortitude to accept orders from someone higher up the teaching ladder who aside from being several years my junior, showed little intelligence, commonsense or discretion. About this time, of course, I still had two small children. The day I walked out with the kids my ex had been drunk and physically abusive and I walked out under police escort. This was the day my affair – the first – began and my new life.

Several points in this last conversation with Irene are worth noting. Freudians are likely to point to the woman's illegitimacy, and her subsequent feelings for her step-father (her wish to see herself like him in ways such as loving music and her envy of her sister who resembled his mother) as sublimated in her attraction for older men or her having an affair with one. Thus, they might argue, her early feelings of rejection propelled her into ego-gratifying flirtation, modelling, marrying the man all the other girls wanted and so on. With due deference to the Freudians I would argue that every daughter is likely to hate/love her mother/father and the danger in adopting this school of thought is that every later action in life is viewed as symptomatic of the individual's parental attachments. Thus, the woman who hates her father may really wish to (a) sleep with him or (b) castrate him because he 'steals' her mother; the argument goes on and on until all roads go back to the nursery. Undoubtedly the child is the embryo of the adult but prevailing circumstances may be as important as psychological motivation or predisposition.

I acknowledge that in the Opportunist category it was usual for a close attachment to the father and/or animosity to the mother to be expressed. Similarly, the father was often identified as being the first person with whom 'being his little girl' was thought to work to the woman's benefit. That is, women would reminisce about how being 'Daddy's favourite' or 'Daddy's pet' could result in his taking their side in battles with their mother, or giving them extra pocket money or sweets. Rather than see this as a sexually charged situation, it may simply be that earliest experiences socialize – induce – women into resuming their role of 'Daddy's little girl', being sweet, pretty and charming whenever they wish to gain a tactical advantage over other women when interacting with men to ingratiate themselves with them. The Freudians may see this as acting out a rivalry with the girl's mother; the rivalry may be with anyone who seems to intrude on the woman's desire for self-advancement. A woman's tactics for managing men may be based on early patterns of behaviour with her father.

The way Irene identifies her lovers is itself interesting. Although I changed the initials, the style itself remains as in her conversation. It is possible to conjecture that her use of H1 and H2 suggests that she views them as interchangeable. Not all of the women in the Opportunist category identified their lovers in this way but there were several who did and it seems consistent with viewing the relationship as a game and people as objects. For example, one woman referred to all her lovers as Willie. There was Willie 1, and Willie 2, and so on; the names women used differed but the style of identification was similar. It may have been no more than an attempt on the women's part to disguise the men they were, or had been, involved with, but it seems to mean more than that. It appears as part of the relationship-as-a-game structure.

Irene's justifications for her unconventional lifestyle are in interesting contrast to the conformist attitude she strikes when instructing her own children. It would seem that the woman does not refute social norms *en masse*; but she neglects ones which intrude on her way of life. It should not really be surprising that her relations with her daughter are more strained than those with her son as the moral and practical implications of her life-plan are perhaps more often realized by a man. That is, the double standard of society has managed to tolerate certain social boundaries being transgressed by men without censure, such as premarital sex, extramarital sex, paternity out of wedlock and so on.

Irene compares being kept to prostituting herself on a street corner, but she does not see herself as a prostitute. Indeed she emphasizes that her relationships with her gentlemen friends are not sexual – except at the start – and that they support her for the pleasure of her company and not for her sexual favours. Whatever the substance of this statement, it does suggest that the Opportunist type does not necessarily see herself or wish others to view her as sexually promiscuous.

The kept women in my research did not all have the same attitude towards sex. Some of them profess to have had upwards of a hundred lovers and say that they enjoy sex – even when they do not care at all for their partner – as long as the man is not a selfish lover. The general opinion of the sexually active woman is that sex is a pleasant way of forming a friendship, getting to know someone better, or simply 'getting it (sex) over with so you can really get to know him as a person'. Others maintain that sexual intimacy is not established quickly in their particular relationship and that they are indifferent, or at best tepid, in their feelings towards the sexual side of their relationship and/or sex in general. The Opportunist does not necessarily feel obliged to extend the hospitality of sex as payment for the man's support though it is unusual to find a woman such as Irene who categorically maintains that her relationships are fundamentally asexual or platonic. This is common only when the man is much older, say in his seventies or older, and even then there seems to be a ritual of suggestive comments, provocative dress and caresses to create a show for his friends on which to speculate. The Opportunist is noticeably relaxed in her attitude to sex but does not necessarily profess herself to be a tremendously enthusiastic participant – a fact she does not always bother to disguise from the man himself.

Many Opportunist women who had been married and divorced had been battered in their marriages, but they often blamed themselves for condoning this ill-treatment, thinking that they had in some way deserved it. Later they appear to reject this idea; Irene (my first case history) for example, was tremendously relieved when the psychiatrist identifying her father-in-law's house and not herself as the problem told her to leave it forthwith. Other women would say that as they are forced to make their own way in the world, living on their wits, they cannot be faulted for failing to live up to a society which does not come to their aid. Even so, they seem to bear little resentment about society's apathy towards the battered wife or the divorcee with young children, but have more of an acceptance of things the way they are. The women uniformly pride themselves on being survivors rather than defeatists. As an American woman wrote to me, she knows how to play the game to win.

For my second case history, I quote from another series of interviews over

a period of 18 months with a 31-year-old American, Norma, who was as
forthcoming with her information as was Irene:

> Although I am a kept woman, I did not look upon the relationship
> that way in the beginning but after a time, because I did accept help
> financially from this man. I suppose that I fit into your category. I
> am feeling very uncomfortable about talking this over with you.
> Since 1975, I have kept a journal, and every time that I felt
> particularly neurotic, I would record my feelings. The only
> information that I ever recorded about this man was the day our
> relationship began and the day that he died. By the time he died, I
> was trying to extricate myself from him because even though I had
> always liked the man and at one time even considered marrying
> him, I had always felt guilty about taking his money and wanted to
> be more independent.
>
> Tell me if I'm giving you too much background information but
> the whole thing appears to be so complex. In 1973 I married my
> husband Mark. In 1975 we moved into our first house, a small semi-
> detached house in a small country community with a population
> of under 2000. One of our neighbours was Fred. He had been
> married about 23 years with two children. He and Mark both
> worked for the same company and so they made arrangements to
> drive to work together. Because Fred was older and in a more
> established position than we were, he enjoyed coming over and
> helping us out – we were just a young couple and really struggling.
> In 1978, we moved to our second home, only two blocks away
> from the first one, but it was larger and in a nicer neighbourhood.
> By this time, Fred was in the habit of coming over to visit, especially
> on a Sunday morning. He liked our company and we liked his. He
> was quite a gruff man, and was known to call 'a spade, a spade'. For
> this reason, many people did not like him. He was also rather well
> off, and many people seemed to be quite jealous of this as well, even
> though he worked hard for everything that he owned.
>
> In the summer of 1979, I was working in an office in our small
> town, but made the decision to go back to school and subsequently
> got a better job. My husband was not happy with my decision
> because it meant my driving over 30 miles to school each morning
> and then 30 miles home again at night. Our part of the country is
> known for getting a lot of snow, and he was concerned that I would
> have problems on the road, since my schooling was going to be in
> the winter. In early spring 1980, I began getting a ride home from
> school with Fred on the one night of the week that my husband
> would be attending night school. Fred told me that he had always
> been interested in me sexually and would I consider having an affair

with him. I was quite taken aback at this but my marriage had always been one conflict after another, and so I gave it some thought. Finally, on April 1, 1980 he came over in the evening and we had our first sexual encounter. This particular date I recorded because I felt that it was momentous. Most of those early days were spent by taking the long route home on the nights that he drove me home from school and parking somewhere to talk or have sex. On Saturdays, I would give the excuse that I wanted to go to — to shop and we would meet.

In 1981, my marriage was breaking down completely, and my husband and I decided to split. I moved into a small apartment in —. Also by this time, I had been working as a travelling salesman for a year but had just been fired from that position. In my work as a salesman, I had spent every other week on out-of-town trips and Fred would drive to see me wherever I was and we would have dinner together. Also, he would always send me a bouquet of flowers to my hotel room, reasoning that they would personalize the room. Fred was always very attentive and loving. He wanted me to be a success and wanted to help me in any way that he could.

When I began living on my own, I was in a pretty mixed-up state of mind. I had the independence that I so desired, but I had had to give up quite a comfortable lifestyle to get it. My husband was keeping the children because he was more financially able to look after them. I think I am quite normal in saying that I love to be spoiled with attention and gifts, and Fred was willing and prepared to do those things for me. He asked me to marry him, but I told him that I felt it was too soon after one marriage break-up to go back to being married. At one point in the spring of 1982, I began dating a man that I felt quite strongly about, and told Fred this. I told him that if things became serious with this person, then my relationship would end with Fred. As it turned out, that boyfriend did not last and of course, Fred was still around.

From the time that I had been living on my own, I had never kept a steady full-time job, only a series of short terms of employment and felt that a change of scenery would do me good. Fred had given me money and of course there were always fresh flowers in my apartment. Holidays were fun for him and for me. I was the recipient of clothes and jewellery. Just a couple more details on what financial assistance Fred gave to me. One weekend, a long-time girlfriend was visiting me. She and I were out shopping and saw two expensive suits that neither of us had enough money to buy. I convinced Fred to buy both suits, so that I could give the one to my girlfriend as a Christmas present. There was also a time that she was in financial trouble, and Fred gave me $1,000.00 which I was in turn to lend to her. She never paid it back though, and Fred made the remark that he didn't really expect her to. The third example of his generosity was when I needed a car and as usual was not in any financial position to buy one on my own. If I ever got into a jam, Fred was there with moral support and his wallet to help me out. I remember thinking at one time, that I should not feel guilty about his giving me money because I was actually in a very lucky position. Here was someone who truly cared for me and was able to help me out financially as well, and do so without putting any conditions on the money.

After I moved to — and because I was so determined to begin a new and more satisfying life for myself, I tried to cut Fred out of my life. He realized this and tried to see me. He would call and try to arrange a weekend when he would come and visit me. I always found some excuse why he could not come. I think this saddened him very much. I was feeling quite selfish and even though I wanted to know that he was around, I did not want him to have any contact with me.

On October 23, 1982 Fred died in his sleep of a heart-attack. My ex-husband helped with the funeral and called me a couple of days later to give me the news. I was very sad and even to this day I remember little incidents every now and again. I was also concerned when Fred died, because he used to keep my picture in his wallet and other small things to remind him of me. He had always been the only one to touch his wallet, his wife had never been allowed, but now she would see these things and know for certain that we had had a relationship. I'm not sure when she began to suspect, but as the relationship with Fred and I increased, my friendship with her had decreased. I felt badly about that and talked about it with Fred but his own relationship with her had not been going smoothly for years, so he could not show much sympathy. So those are the facts.

I asked Norma about her present way of life.

I have grown up a lot this past year. I am now attending college full-time and will be for the next two years to become a social worker. I always used to be very concerned with portraying being the successful business person – driving a big car, eating in expensive restaurants, and having expensive clothes. I still have the closet full of clothes but those things aren't so important any more. I have developed my self awareness and see that it is possible to have personal happiness without being a success in the business world.

Although Norma spoke at great length with a stranger, her admitted hesitation in talking about a relationship that has ended and a partner who is dead, illuminates the extent to which people guard the secrecy of the kept relationship. Only on two occasions, for example, did she record anything about the man or by the relationship in her journal. The process by which she became involved (and then remained involved) with the man entailed gradual changes in the relationship; from being a family friend who worked with her husband, Fred became the woman's lover and then assumed the invisible role of provider. There is no attempt by Norma to disguise the relationship as a love affair. When she believed there was a possibility of having a relationship with a new boyfriend whom she did care about, she was ready to end her relationship with Fred. She seemed to view Fred as a passive provider – someone who courted her favour but whom she did not feel obliged to love. To the degree that he allowed her to live in comfort and impress her friends with magnificent presents, he was allowed to buy her favour. The Opportunist tolerates the man's patronage in order to realize her desired lifestyle. Norma recognizes Fred's willingness to help her but at no point identifies him as a beloved.

In a later interview I had with Norma she gave details of her family background, which in some ways parallels that of Irene. Both women conceive of their achievements as the result of a uniquely personal strategy, and attribute their success to determination and fortitude in overcoming disadvantages and misfortunes such as an unhappy childhood and broken homes and marriages. Norma told me:

> I was the eldest of two daughters. My parents were keen on their firstborn being a son but it was not to be. My father was raised by a very strict German father during the depression – so his attitude to raising a family was that he was the breadwinner and my mother was to stay at home and mind the children. He was a workaholic, he seemed unsure when he was around us as small children and did not easily express affection, he was autocratic, and he was emotionally devastated when he and my mother split up. When I was a child I was always very obedient. Probably because there was a fair amount of verbal abuse from my mother. Sometimes the physical punishment was too severe. They used a razor strap to hit us with. I was expected to achieve and do well in everything so that was mainly what I tried to do but no matter how much I tried my efforts were never good enough. During adolescence, I was also very obedient. I saw no reason not to be.

In reply to my questions about premarital dating, Norma said:

> Anything important as far as dating or social experiences goes comes from a collection of memories I have retained. My mother said I could not date until I was 16. I remember thinking on my 16th

birthday that boys would be banging down my door. Not so. I was
17 when I had my first date. That year I also had my second date,
with even a different boy. After that, dating became more natural
and routine. I did not go out again with boys who tried to get fresh
with me. I was more interested in intelligent conversation.

About my first marriage – he was a blind date who needed urging
by mutual friends to ask me out again. We began dating steadily.
One night about a month after I met him he proposed and I said yes.
So we left the party and spent the rest of the night talking about the
seriousness of such a matter. We were married exactly six months
from that night. I think we always got along well and suffered
through the usual 'young married' phases. He upgraded the type of
job he had and I got pregnant and left my work all within the first
year of marriage. We had not planned on having a family so quickly
but our first, a daughter, was an absolutely perfect baby. The
second child arrived two years later and he was terrific as well.

However, back to the marriage – I was very resentful after
six years of marriage of being tied down as a housewife, even
though I took evening courses and did some volunteer work. I
returned to work on a full-time basis and was expected by my
husband to still perform all 'housewife' duties. After a year working
I returned to college on a full-time basis. Immediately from there I
became a 'travelling saleswoman'. I was very happy with that
position but it produced an even greater strain on the marriage. My
husband resented the fact that I hired a woman who came one day
every two weeks to houseclean. He felt it was a waste of money and
that I should be doing the cleaning. Actually I still did the cleaning
and laundry every other week and grocery shopping every week, as
well as taking the kids to gymnastics class every Saturday morning.

We went to see a marriage counsellor but did not gain any
satisfaction there. When my ex and I decided to separate and live
apart, we tried to make several rational decisions concerning the
children's futures that we hoped were in their best interest. Since my
husband wanted very much to raise the children and I felt he would
do a competent job as well as being financially better placed to have
them, that was our first decision. The second decision was that they
would live together in our home in the small town the kids were
used to. One wanted to ensure that there was as little upset in the
kids' lives as possible.

My present relations with my ex have gone from good to
strained. I find it very difficult to keep in touch with the kids because
of his attitude. That, and the fact that I live approximately 750 miles
from them are not very conducive to keeping a consistent and
familiar relationship with them.

My children – are bright and wonderfully well-adjusted. I love my children very much and I miss not having them around me. I know I was a good mother and attempted to stimulate their development when I was at home with them. I will always be sorry that we are not having the opportunity to grow together but it was a decision that I made and intend to stick with. I have dreamed that one day when I am more settled that I will ask them if they want to live with me, but I am sure that that would not be fair to them, to ask them to choose between a father who has raised them and a mother who sees them once a year.

Several inferences can be drawn from this last conversation with Norma, the first from the fact that she strongly insists she was a good mother, and that the decision to remove herself from her children was an altruistic gesture done in their own best interests. Rather than deprecate an absence of maternal feelings she suggests that her leaving was not an act of abandonment but a selfless and/or self-sacrificing gesture. All my respondents with children stressed that they were good mothers whatever else they might be. One woman from Los Angeles wrote me pages wherein she admitted to everything short of patricide and incest, but when I asked her (in a letter) about her relationship with her children she wrote back in a very hostile manner as if my query had in some way dared to assume that she could be other than the most perfect of mothers:

> I have an *excellent* relationship with my children and grandchildren. There is no generation gap between *us*. We have never had a single fight and are best friends. My daughter phones me every week from New York to discuss everything in her life with me, just to talk or gossip, and values my opinion more than *anyone's*. I am her mentor, best friend and dearest confidante. She is the elixir of my life. To her I am her best friend and we have a wonderful relationship. (*55-year-old woman, Los Angeles*)

A woman can profess herself to be sexually emancipated, as this woman and others did, and still feel that motherhood is a morally definitive role. When asked the quetion in the neutral tones of 'Do you have any children? If so, could you describe your relationship with them?' women seem to become defensive.

Norma also reveals the change in lifestyle caused by a break-up. In our first interview she mentions that her divorce was financially debilitating and that to attain her freedom she had to give up quite a comfortable lifestyle. However, Fred's death was unexpected and no provisions were made for her in his will. While the kept relationship may allow for more freedom, a word that is continuously used by the Opportunist, there is also less security. She is in a 'Catch-22' situation of wanting financial security and yet wanting the freedom of not being married to her benefactor. Although Norma seems to strive towards a career, more often than not the Opportunist regards a job as something she plays at or interests herself in between relationships. This being so, a break-up often means going back to a less luxurious way of life, a smaller apartment and so on.

A recurrent theme in conversations or communications with the Opportunist type is her self-professed freedom and the importance she attaches to independence. She does not appear to consider the irony of having her independence conditional upon another person's positive assessment of her. Rather than being free, she is simply on a long lead held by her benefactor. The Opportunist is more of a petted lap dog than the free spirit she claims to be. One woman, who made a tremendous song and dance about her freedom and only omitted singing 'My Way' as a grand finale, was in fact totally dependent on her lover to finance her independence. At best, many of the women in this Opportunist category are like the rebellious child who runs away from home with her father's credit cards. The kept relationship offers only as much freedom as can be had in a close relationship with any person upon whom you are financially and/or emotionally dependent. Nevertheless, the Opportunist makes a conceptual leap when she equates money with freedom, neglecting the fact that her possessing money is dependent on a relationship which intrinsically limits independence and freedom.

Judging from my London contacts, the particular appeal of any Opportunist (or for that matter any kept woman) varies enormously and must be a purely subjective assessment. The appeal of one of the women in this category who has had an extremely lucrative career of being kept by various men is unusual. Almost six feet tall, built like Brunhilde, she has a voice loud and shrill enough to summon the cattle back from the pasture. When I interviewed her with her present lover she was, in my estimation, rude and abrasive to him. However, he terms her 'vivacious' and 'lively'. On one occasion, a friend and I met them and as she proceeded to insult and ridicule the man to his face, we both exchanged uneasy glances, expecting the man to resent her manner and tell her so in no uncertain terms. The result, however, was that the man said no one else dared be so honest with him and wasn't-she-a-wonderful-girl?

Each Opportunist seems to be aware of what the man wants from their particular relationship and claims to meet his expectations in that respect. Starry-eyed adoration is apparently not the only thing that men desire.

It is difficult to capture the enigmatic quality which makes the Opportunist so successful. When her allure for a particular man has waned she can apparently charm the wallet off another. As if in preparation, she does consciously tend to mix with men and flirt as if unattached. Even when already involved in a relationship, she is never really out of circulation. To illustrate, one woman continuously seeks to meet new men and when one of her friends mentions a man's name, she asks for details about him. If he meets her specifications, she discusses with her friend how she can arrange to meet him. Similarly, if a woman has ended a relationship with her lover or has been dropped, her friends will cue her to their various male friends' preferences in women and likes and dislikes in general. Thus, when the introduction takes place, she will appear tailor-made to the man's specifications. She knows what topics of conversation to pursue, how to dress and so on. Generally the Opportunist is well-versed in a variety of subjects. Even if her knowledge is superficial rather than deep, she can interject an appropriate comment to make you believe that she is at least interested. She generally has a stock of parlour tricks to inject some levity into a conversation such as astrology, palmistry or graphology which are occasionally brought into the conversation as openings or as stop-gaps:

> I'm not really an expert at palmistry but if things get really quiet or dull when I first meet a man I ask him to let me read his hand and then trace with my nails the lines in his hand . . . You're holding his hand in yours and really caressing it in a subtle way . . . You really haven't done anything but the man sees you as sensual because you've got him excited just by touching his hand. Sex should be something that is just hinted at – you always let him think that he is the one who is seducing you. (*34-year-old woman, London*)

Compared to women in London, the case histories of Irene and Norma (Americans whom I interviewed while they were visiting London) are examples of a somewhat financially restricted lifestyle. London, on the other hand, seems to be one of a series of watering-holes where the wealthy congregate for periods of time and to which women seeking to maximize their opportunities for meeting wealthy men are drawn. Some Opportunists from the group interviewed based in Great Britain deliberately chose to live in London in the belief that it is a territorial stomping ground for the rich and powerful. In addition, since the 1970s London has attracted a very large number of Arabs whose extraordinary wealth is reflected, amongst other things, in the opulent lifestyle they provide for their kept women.

The slang for prostitutes who come into London for a profitable day's 'work' on a cheap day-return ticket is 'Away-a-dayers'. Both the Opportunist who is London-based, and the Smart Set type, regard London as an advantageous place in which to make their living.

Unlike the Career Woman, the Opportunist does not appear manifestly to want a career. She may be as intelligent or capable as the Career Woman but her career consists of being kept by interchangeable partners or, upon meeting a suitable man, retiring to marry. Unlike the Mistress type who tends to see her relationship as special and a preoccupying thought and factor in her life, the Opportunist thinks in terms of a series of relationships – although she might become absorbed in one of them and turn into a

Mistress type. Although she might envisage herself married at some future time the Opportunist views the bonds of any particular relationship as intrinsically weaker and more frail than does the Mistress. When the Opportunist maintains that she prefers long-term monogamous relationships she does not necessarily mean marriage to her present lover but rather a relationship that lasts several years but is interchangeable with others in her past and presumably in her future. One woman describes her life as weeding a garden of eligible suitors and thinks that through a process of elimination she will be left with the most suitable man. Other women are similarly blasé about their numerous involvements and phrases such as 'You have to kiss of lot of frogs before you find a prince' describe their idea that involvements with many men are the best guarantee of finding and capturing the most suitable one.

The Opportunist often seems to have a conscious plan by which she can meet eligible men and encourage them to assume financial support for her. For example, one woman maintains that she always travels on Concorde or first class, although it is more expensive, because that way she is certain to meet wealthy men. She feels the situation provides the opportunity for a lengthy chat and to establish contact with men who ordinarily would be inaccessible. Being kept is dependent upon establishing yourself in a network of men who can afford to keep a woman in the style to which she wishes to become accustomed. This is generally secured on the basis of her past relationships. The period during which she becomes kept for the first time will be a working apprenticeship in which social skills are acquired; during the second her refinement of those skills earns her the diploma – she knows how to dress, how to behave, where to go, who is important and who is not.

Although the Opportunist can resemble the typical dumb blonde, she may be consciously performing a role, and may feel proud of her ability to carry off a convincing performance that results in lavish rewards. If the man believes that women are helpless creatures and prides himself on understanding them, the woman may find satisfaction in playing the dumb blonde. Doing so mocks the man and his opinion of women as childlike and not very bright. The woman may look upon the man's willingness to provide financial support for her as a sign that he deserves to be conned. For example, one woman manipulated her lover into a top boutique – Chloë – in Switzerland, selected several outfits, and feigned astonishment when the bill came to slightly over £11,000. She had calculated that, while the man was likely to recognize a Dior or Chanel boutique as costly and discourage mass purchases, Chloë was a designer label less likely to be familiar to him, and once items had been selected and a bill presented, the man would not wish to lose face by cancelling the order. Engineering such situations is simply part of the game. What defines the Opportunist type of kept woman is the consciousness of the requirements of her role, not her past role or number of previous relationships. Although she is more likely than the Mistress or the Career Woman to have had a number of kept relationships, promiscuity is not a necessary quality. Rather, she seeks to maximize her profits in this area, is acutely aware of the qualities she needs to exercise attraction and knows how to engineer a profitable relationship. One such Opportunist noted:

> The first date doesn't really show much because most men will be trying to impress you and will spend money fairly easily. Little things do tell: what wine he orders, how he tips . . . If he asks you what you'd like to drink or just orders for you you can see he's not afraid that he's wasting his money. Then, you just see how easy he is about picking up a few things on his way over. After that, when you're together in a store lead him to something you-really-want-but-just-can't-afford-but-still-would-love-to-have. Sales girls usually make this really easy because they'll be hovering about just waiting to make the sale. Generally I'll not press the issue and let her do the sale. By the time it's bought it's the greatest bargain in the store, the only one left, the last day at the low price . . . If you can tell the man to meet you there for lunch or nearby you can just vaguely wander in. The man won't want to seem cheap in front of you and the saleswoman. (*27-year-old woman, London*)

One of the favoured strategies of this woman when she is uncertain of a man's attraction to her is to meet him for afternoon tea at Harrods. She says that if he fails to buy her something from the vast assortment featured there he is definitely not attracted enough to be worth her while. Other women use the more tried and tested means of saying that they are short of their month's rent, household maintenance bills, or whatever and wait expectantly for the man to help them out. Going clothes-shopping with him is another common ploy. On occasion I'd run into respondents in fashionable and expensive shopping districts of London with their man in tow, looking as if they had completed their Christmas shopping in May.

Another skill on which the Opportunist prides herself is being able to detect what role the man wishes her to play, knowing just how to dress and present herself. The convincing performance of a kept woman, like that of an actress who can portray a fine lady in one play and a psychopathic killer in the next, is dependent on costume, tutelage and imitation. Her audience is the man and his social circle and the success of her performance is reflected in the length of her engagement. Like the professional drama critics, the group will react and let the woman know whether her performance deserves applause or if she resembles Miss Piggy. Clothes are particularly important; if the woman starts out with a hopelessly inappropriate idea of fashion, she will soon notice – if she hopes to prosper – that the women surrounding her lover and his friends are dressed rather differently. She will learn how to dress and where to shop. In the same way, behaving like a lady, not a gift bestowed on all women, can be learned through imitation. The woman's ability to blend into the group and establish herself as an in-member, who can be taken anywhere and counted on not to be an embarrassment, will be important if she wishes to remain in that particular network after the relationship itself ends and use it to furnish new patrons.

Financial support will start by covering anything from day-to-day expenses to help with the rent. The Opportunist stresses the desirability of encouraging the man to give her her own place rather than rent accommodation predominantly for two reasons. First, much of the financing of the kept relationship is given in terms of monthly support; should the relationship cease the woman may be left with little in terms of convertible assets. A dress costing £1000 may be worth a negligible amount in resale value. Second, if her residence is her own there may be less desperate urgency in finding a replacement for the man at the termination of the relationship, so she can be more selective.

The strategies of these women are often imaginative. One woman who lives in a flat bought for her by a previous lover told her present lover that it is rented and accepts his monthly cheques for its imaginary rent. Being given a home is generally dependent on a strong attachment between the woman and her lover and the majority of kept women are unlikely to receive a freehold lease. Even when the flat is purchased specifically to accommodate the man's mistress, it often remains in the man's name.

Women in the Opportunist group have various attitudes towards love and marriage. Some of them have rather fantastic ideas about finding a man who fulfils all their desires, some look upon marriage as an institution for the deranged, while others with a practical outlook see it solely in terms of finding the most eligible suitor, with their love for the man a non-issue. The general attitude is that love is a leisure-time activity and that marriage is better founded upon something more concrete. They think it relatively easier to love a rich man than a poor one and that marriage to a wealthy man has the definite advantage of enabling a woman to loosen the harness of domestic servitude, cooking, cleaning and so on. As Groucho Marx once remarked, while money cannot buy happiness, all things being equal, it is lovely to have some around the house. Even the most romantic women in the Opportunist category do not neglect the man's financial position. One such woman said:

> I don't see why I should settle for a guy about whom I don't feel anything really special. It's not as though there were some reason why I should feel I have to compromise. I can go out with Tony and enjoy the relationship as long as I like him and want to, but why force myself to carry the relationship one step further than I feel

whole about? I don't see why I should have to go through life without joy, which is what getting married to someone you don't love very much is. The first time I married I found someone who was wealthy, lived well. But those alone are not good enough reasons for me to get married again. Compatibility and attraction, in my opinion, are absolutely essential, and if you don't feel a truly special feeling towards the guy, don't let it go further than you feel you can live with for a long, long time. It's very nice when a guy is nice to you and makes you feel that he's crazy about you and can afford to provide you with a good life and I don't think a woman should settle for anyone who doesn't under any circumstances.

But just think about all the wonderful things that one can do in life and share with that one special guy and think how hollow those much-looked-forward and dreamed-about experiences would be if the guy you share them with you don't feel that genuine warmth and tenderness about. I was really distressed at my first wedding, I felt trapped and miserable, trapped with someone I didn't love and what was the whole point of it. Even the wedding itself, how I do regret that I wasted my chance on someone I didn't feel good about. It's meaningless, even at the time it's happening, unless you feel that love, which is what makes all the experiences so special and deeply felt and without which you begin to feel disassociated from what's happening to you in your own life, since the joy, the meaningfulness isn't there because you don't love your partner. Choosing someone who is good and treats you right, of course, is a prerequisite. But beyond that, it's a subjective thing, and to thine own self be true. (25-year-old woman, London)

'To thine own self be true' may only have been one in a series of platitudes uttered by Shakespeare's Polonius but the Opportunist still manages to get tremendous mileage out of it. It is the motto central to her chosen career.

There is a tendency among the Opportunist category to equate money with freedom, and to see marriage as imposing limits on freedom. By extension, there is a reluctance to marry unless substantial rewards are on offer. However, making a career out of being kept means that the Opportunist is continuously channelling her energies into establishing and maintaining her various relationships. Rather than refute the conventional female role of being a wife, it seems that the role of wife is repeatedly adopted. A relationship which allows the woman to leave it when and if she chooses to has disadvantages as well. There is an interesting ambivalence expressed about the role of wife by my kept women contacts. Some view the wife as more oppressed because she is married, others think her more secure – the benefits of security are double-edged.

Making a career out of being kept by a series of different men may be the only one in which previous experience works against the job aspirant. While there is a certain cachet attached to having a Famous Person's former girlfriend as your present one, there also seems to be an invisible meridian beyond which additional known affiliations result in the woman being labelled a groupie, a slag or a whore. One man with whom I talked commented that a certain dilettante's girlfriend was second-hand goods. She was thought rather too experienced or too well-known in her role as 'professional girlfriend' still to be thought an eligible candidate for girlfriend or desirable lover. This problem may mean that while previous experience makes the woman more astute in her role, at the same time, it makes her less eligible for it. This situation is particularly likely to occur in my Smart Set classification. A 20-year-old girl may have been involved with several dozen men and be regarded as a has-been a year later. The moral divide between her role and the role of a prostitute is crossed when and if she is thought to be randomly promiscuous or used goods. It is not surprising that women deny the extent to which their relationships are sexual and prefer to maintain that they are platonic companions to their men.

The role of 'companion' suggests itself as a shadow one, a person who draws upon another for strength, definition and status. The Opportunist acquires status by being the personal affiliate of a highly placed man. Firmly established next to him, she is vicariously elevated. Some of the women in my research knowingly derive their social identity from a series of relationships with men. On more than one occasion I would see a picture of a woman I had interviewed, or see her name mentioned in a Sunday newspaper in which her claim to fame and/or notoriety is based solely on being (quoting from one such caption) 'the former constant companion of —, the millionaire and intimate of —' or, (from another) '—'s long-time companion and mistress to —, — and —'. 'Companion' may be the polite equivalent to 'fancy bit', but the role itself may simply be a parody of what Thorstein Veblen in *The Theory of the Leisure Class* portrayed as the companion role of the wife. That is, the wife, as the silent, glamorous adjunct of a man well placed in society, has no social identity apart from him.

For the Opportunist, selecting a male partner is a form of conspicuous consumption. When, on occasion, I would visit an Opportunist at her home, photo albums would invariably be brought out so that I could properly appreciate her having been to parties with Famous Person X, Y and Z or gone on a yacht trip with the esteemed Mr So-and-So, and her being great friends with this, that and the other celebrity. It is rare for any Opportunist not to indulge in a fair amount of name-dropping and some seemed distressed that I had not brushed up on my knowledge of Burke's Peerage or a *Who's Who* guide to the wealthy and powerful, especially when they mentioned European political figures or minor luminaries and I would admit that I did not have the foggiest idea who they were talking about. My ignorance propelled them into offering life-histories of their associates, undertaken with considerable attention to detail so that I could fully appreciate their splendour and hence the glory of the association. While they were frustrated that I did not immediately display awe-struck admiration, I was amazed that secrecy, discretion and reticence were thrown to the wind while they elaborated on who the man was, how he was socially placed, his influential friends and who his girlfriends were. Since her identity is shaped from the reflected glory emanating from her lover, it seemed that my failure to appreciate his importance threatened the validity of her social status. It may be that in all heterosexual relationships there is a tendency for the woman's social status to be dependent on that of her male partner. Certainly, the Opportunist's concern that I should appreciate her lover's status suggests her dependency on a man despite her claims to the contrary. She believes she betters herself through him. The paradox is that while the Opportunist prides herself on her free-form approach to life her interactions with men in particular reveal that in fact she is more traditional and reactionary than may be superficially apparent.

Maxine, a 43-year-old British fashion designer, is the focus of my third case history in the Opportunist group. She has been kept by three men in the last ten years and is presently being kept by a man 11 years younger than herself. She is very attractive, usually wears her hair in a chignon and is stylishly dressed. Despite a relatively successful career of her own she emphasizes the high status of her past lovers, who include a European ambassador and a corporate president of a multinational firm, as if to establish her worth on the basis of her affiliation with them rather than of her creative talent. She often neglects her work during the course of a relationship and takes it up again as a bridging role between episodes of being kept. Although she appears talented, there is no doubt that her professional career comes second to the vicissitudes of her social life. When her lover wishes her to devote her time exclusively to him, this is perfectly acceptable to her.

When I first met Maxine in 1980 she was rather half-heartedly trying to extricate herself from a relationship with an Italian man who apparently had a violent temper. The woman who first introduced me to Maxine mentioned that he had recently beaten Maxine because he thought she had been over-flirtatious with another man. The woman said that Maxine had telephoned her to take her to the hospital after the incident happened. Maxine had been fearful that the man's passport might be revoked or his career jeopardized if she phoned the police and if the episode became public knowledge. During 1980 and 1981 Maxine, her friend Charlotte and I had numerous conversations revolving around Maxine's indecision about whether to end the relationship. Whenever Maxine grew wistful or commented that she did not want to give up his company, the lifestyle he provided or the social advantages attached to being his girlfriend, Charlotte would admonish her, saying that she would soon find someone even more suitable. These little pep talks lasted for several months but I noted that a more effective anti-depressant for Maxine was being able to attract any man's admiration. While she would play down the importance of men in her life apart from their financial usefulness, her actions often belied her words. She could switch off her melancholia at the drop of a man's compliment, although Charlotte and I together were often unable to lift her spirits even after hours of flattery and sympathetic noises. While the Opportunist type disavows her attachment to any particular lover, she nevertheless places great importance on appearing physically attractive to men and winning their favourable opinion.

I had known Maxine for a year when I met her one day in the company of her new lover, Brian. The way she acted with him was a complete surprise to me. I had not met him before and she had boasted to Charlotte and me that she had him well-trained to dance attendance on her. Contrary to expectations, she acted the typical geisha, solicitous of his comforts, ending each sentence with 'dear' or 'darling' and acting in a manner befitting a newly-wed bride. I have no way of knowing how many fiercely independent Opportunists turn into blushing debutantes when they deal with men but it seems that the way they act with women is often utterly different. For the majority of London-based Opportunists, flirtation, coquetry and effusive compliments are ingrained patterns of behaviour when dealing with men. On the occasions when I observed an Opportunist when both men and women were present it was obvious that she was a man's woman. In the presence of men, other women are deemed unworthy of attention and she concentrates largely on making herself agreeable to the men.

Being a man's woman, being coquettish, becoming good friends with those men who are thought important and seeking to establish camaraderie with men whether you like them or not, reveals the subordinate status of the Opportunist. A man who has status or power of his own does not automatically have to adopt synthetic, sycophantic ways with others: he may straightforwardly express himself. The female adjunct can only utter banal remarks and mime others' opinions precisely because of her subsidiary position. This means that in the presence of the man and his friends, she often plays the obsequious and fawning girlfriend – not only as an appeal to the man's vanity, but also to gain recognition from others that she is a worthy person who truly cares about the man and deserves to continue to be at his side.

The role of the Opportunist as a social adjunct can be likened to that played by women whose husbands hold public office. The Governor or the Ambassador's wife, for example, may well in private behave in a way that does not conform to the public image required – but in public, those requirements must be met. The official's wife is not supposed to give her personal viewpoint on matters of national importance, or to cause vexation by engaging in independent thought. Whether or not the woman dislikes her husband, the reigning political party platform or being on display, she must publicly appear to be the man's staunchest supporter. She may privately give vent to her grievances, plan various intrigues or console herself with mass purchases. While she may occasionally be excused her ill-temper or bad mood, if her private attitude interferes with the performance of her public role, the woman will be seen as a social liability. The Opportunist who acts as her lover's hostess is required to play a role similar to that of the dutiful political wife. Unlike her lover's wife, however, she has no guarantee against a curt dismissal. As such, her behaviour, if calculated and insincere, may be all the more convincing precisely because it is a performance.

The discrepancy between what the Opportunist professes to be her attitude towards men and the way she actually behaves with them makes her rather unpopular with women who know what she is doing. Since the Opportunist thinks of men as toy-like objects that could not possibly be the focus of anyone else's life, or at least uses this as her *modus operandi* when talking with women, she is quick to note and point out signs of sexual interest in her from her girlfriends' male companions, manoeuvre her way between them and still expect her friends to remain unconcerned at her behaviour. Irene, my first case history in this category, felt it was her honest friendship that made her confront her best friend with the news that her husband was having an affair with her. The woman was apparently supposed to welcome this show of camaraderie in a women against men campaign. Among the women in my research, the word friendship seems to cover relationships of cordial animosity. Maxine and her friend Charlotte, for example, have a curious relationship. Charlotte told me on more than one occasion that she would prefer to have Maxine as a friend than as an enemy. Maxine had a way of denigrating Charlotte with remarks which may have been honest but were more obviously cruel and she freely joked about Charlotte's relationship with her lover. Theirs seemed to be a friendship of the Brutus–Cassius variety, each hoping the other would fall off her pedestal of comfort. Charlotte said of Maxine:

> I feel sorry for Brian because he really thinks he's got the treasure of a lifetime. She's very good at manipulating situations so that she looks the martyr, trying so hard and so unselfish and he's giving her more and more . . . I could throttle her at times because she won't even admit what she's doing. [*What do you mean?*] She lives so much with play-acting I don't think she knows what the truth is any more. She's started to believe her own stories and feels sorry for herself. She's never wrong and she's always put upon . . . He's intoxicated with her and can't see what she's doing to him.

Although analysis of the Opportunist may make her difficult to like, yet in her encounters with men her sublime self-confidence and perceived self-attractiveness are infectious. Mistress of the back-handed compliment she may be, but it is always flattering to hear compliments and the Opportunist dispenses them freely. By making other women conspirators in her games, whether her friends think her charades amusing or irritating, they believe that they themselves are not being conned. Given that people do not like to think of themselves as gullible fools, other women are often ready to accept that the Opportunist is not intentionally hurtful but just thoughtless. Among women who play similar games, the Opportunist type is a heroine. If one such woman intrudes on another's terrain there is a certain resentment but still a grudging admiration for someone who knows so precisely what she wants and goes after it. Moreover, because the Opportunist is likely to be materialistic and acquisitive, she seems to benefit financially to a greater degree than other categories of kept women. This makes her a success story to other women who similarly attempt to engineer profitable relationships.

The following two examples show how women deliberately try to play the game to win. I interviewed a girl of 19 whom I shall call Judith. Although she is the youngest in my Opportunist category she has an extremely polished style. At the time of our interview she was being kept by a lawyer in his mid-forties named Guy and she played him like a violin. By nagging in velvet tones she acquired a yellow Porsche, a full-length mink coat and a cupboard full of clothes. However, through Guy she met Scott and decided that he was more aesthetically pleasing to her. Unfortunately, Scott was a close friend of Guy and also married. Not discouraged, she became close friends with Scott and his wife Jacqui, though better friends with Scott. She encouraged Guy to invite Scott along on their outings, dropped in to Scott's office en route to see him, and made herself generally agreeable. After a while, she broke up with Guy, used Scott as a sympathetic shoulder and invited herself along to his weekend house where she had previously been welcomed as Guy's date. In time, Scott's wife grew to resent her presence but Judith had foreseen this. She told me that Scott would rally to her defence: she had always praised Jacqui to Scott and she felt that he was bound to notice the difference between her loyalty and Jacqui's nagging suspicions and hostility. His apology for his wife's unreasonable accusations grew into an affair. Watching from the sidelines Judith's game of enticement had been obvious and its conclusion somewhat predictable.

A second case of game-playing involved Barbara, a 32-year-old Londoner, who believed herself to be pregnant with her lover's child. She confronted her lover Maurice and when he reacted defensively, protesting that he had a family to think of, questioning her whether or not she was sure it was his, Barbara packed her bags in what she described to me as the perfect exit and moved out of the flat he had provided for her. She accepted a substantial amount of money from him for a hotel to stay in until she got her affairs in order but declined to live in the flat, given his attitude. She did, however, intend to be reinstated. She deliberately sought out a semi-squalid room and called up a girlfriend José (who incidentally was being kept by a friend of Maurice) on whom to unburden her sad tale about how she had been abandoned in her hour of need. A few days later Barbara found out that she was not in fact pregnant. By this time, Maurice, chastened and embarrassed by his friend's admonitions for his unchivalrous behaviour – duly passed on from José to her benefactor – obtained Barbara's phone number and arranged to meet her.

> He asked if he could see my room and I told him I really didn't want him to, there was nothing to see. He came up, took one look and packed my bags for me and said 'You're coming home'. [*Did you tell him you're not pregnant?*] No, he didn't ask. He acted like a real bastard when I told him I was pregnant and I want him to suffer. But he's bound to find out the fact. I've already thought of that and it's not really that complicated. I can tell him I had an abortion in time – for him, you see. Or, if he doesn't want to act like a mature man [divorce his wife and marry her] I can move and tell him I'm going to disappear and that he'll never see his child. Or, I can just get pregnant. It's not very hard.

The final decision was to tell Maurice that she had sacrificed their love child to make life easier for him. Barbara maintains that he was properly appreciative – which fact I am sure she exploited as fully as possible.

The contrast between the Mistress and the Opportunist in describing their role emerges clearly in their discussions of each other. Apart from acknowledging the fact that each is kept, both disown identification with the other. The Mistress denigrates the calculated way in which the Opportunist spins her fantasies and the Opportunist undoubtedly views with suspicion the Mistress's professions of love for her male partner. However, if the behaviour of the Opportunist involves deliberately misleading the man as to the nature of her motives, her behaviour in her chosen role and that of the Mistress do not seem to be substantially different. This is not surprising. After all, the woman who marries for love and the woman who marries for money both become a wife and the woman who becomes kept for whatever reason is a kept woman still.

A relationship which is devoid of love may exist quietly and prosaically alongside more emotion-laden unions. Even when the reasons for the relationship are purely lucrative, there are contributory factors involved such as loyalty, lethargy in the face of change, cynicism about the very possibility of ideal relationships, and the idea that whatever amount of emotional and financial security the relationship offers it should not be discarded lightly. In addition, the kept relationship may be valued simply for allowing the woman access to a preferred lifestyle. If miscast in the role of a woman in love, the woman may nevertheless value the elaborate wardrobe and the glorious set design of the performance. Moreover, it is a mistake to think that the Opportunist is indifferent to the unfavourable opinion of others. Rather, the contrary is true. She is inordinately concerned with making a good impression. To illustrate, I need only refer back to the triumphant announcement of Irene in my first case history who maintains she 'has arrived'. She believes that she has been admirably clever and that she is respected and admired. Why? Because she can elicit not only admiration but envy on the basis of her wardrobe, the time she has to devote to her record collection and library and her attendance at social functions where she mingles with world-famous men. She values the freedom of a relationship which allows her to pursue such pleasures as going to the opera and becoming a gourmet chef. She plays the role of the rich man's wife and expects others to be impressed and envious.

The Opportunist bases the success of her role on the perceived admiration of others. She is likely to feel that she is accepted by the people whose opinions count. She can deal with the criticisms of others; if the neighbours do talk, it will most likely be dismissed as gossip inspired by envy. All the same, she is unlikely to do anything that would invite castigation. Her attitude may be unusual, but her life, while deviating from the norm, escapes social censure. The ethos of narcissism and relative morality need not be manifestly offensive. Indeed, the symbols of success accrued by a 'Me-first' philosophy may be deemed admirable. The Opportunist may simply be seen as an admirably feminine woman. As Susan Sontag noted in her feature 'The Double Standard of Aging' in the *Saturday Review* (September 23, 1972):

> To be born a woman is to be an actress. Being feminine is a kind of theatre, with its appropriate costume, decor, lighting and stylized gestures. Indeed a woman who is not narcissistic is considered unfeminine. And a woman who spends literally most of her time caring for and making purchases to flatter her physical appearance is not regarded in this society for what she is: a kind of moral idiot.

The Opportunist has an extensive network: she will be a capable tour guide to the right clubs and restaurants; claim access to the right groups that host the right parties, and be generally knowledgeable about the ins-and-outs of social climbing – who it is fashionable to include or exclude from your guest list, where it is *de rigueur* to have your hair done, buy your clothes, take your holidays and so on. Some of the London-based women in my research live according to the rules of an unwritten guide of social snobbery. I was never quite sure whether they really liked their friends, holidays or clothes or chose them because they were eminently fashionable. There is a strong emphasis on conspicuous consumption. On one occasion I met one of these women for coffee and noted that she wore a rather nice striped-cotton blouse and skirt. It was not especially unusual – orange, red and yellow stripes on a white background – but when I remarked that it was attractive the woman speedily informed me that it was by Dior, that she had bought it in the designer room of Harrods, and that it had cost £465. As an appendix she informed me with somewhat theatrical despondency that her lover had just given her £1000 for clothes and that she had already run through it by buying a single day dress, handbag and shoes. At times the Opportunist's shopping sprees signified little more than her attempt to circumvent boredom, and the expenditure on clothes simply represented mindless extravagance. However, the tendency to flaunt designer labels is marked and brand names are often used to establish her social indentity.

Identifying herself with a brand label may be one way in which the Opportunist attempts to gain recognition in a society that is increasingly anonymous. That is, the designer label in itself has become a recognizable symbol of wealth and/or success. Similarly, surrounding herself with fashionable human accessories and claiming attendance at equally fashionable gatherings may be ways in which the anonymous adjunct seeks to establish a social identity. Without the grand settings, the costumes and the supporting cast, the woman herself is nothing. She enters the limelight only when in costume and in the company of famous players. In this too, she follows the conventional role of women. There is little radical about the role played by the Opportunist kept woman. Unlike the Career Woman, who at least goes through the motions of seeking to establish an independent identity based on a professional role, she plays the age-old game of finding a wealthy husband or surrogate figure to provide for her and furnish her with an identity. Her freedom is illusory; her role is intrinsically a dependent one.

If a culture or sub-culture's heroes are symbols of what its members admire, then marrying well is what calls forth praise from the Opportunist rather than achieving success in independent work in the way someone like Marie Curie did. Shortly after the Royal Wedding, one woman commented to me:

> Did you hear Lady Di's remark when they [newspaper reporters] asked her what she thought of marriage so far? [No, *what did she say?*] 'I highly recommend it'. I highly recommend it!! I bet she does! (*25-year-old woman, London*)

The Royal Wedding became to this woman, the classic example of the importance of knowing the right people and marrying well and the Princess of Wales was a folk heroine. She was thought of as someone who had done all right for herself. My respondent was not swayed by the romance of the event but admired the Princess of Wales as someone who now had a life of comfort and ease guaranteed. She viewed it as the latter-day equivalent of the Cinderella story, the female equivalent of the Horatio Alger – or self-made man – myth which every girl seems to be subjected to at some time or another in her childhood. The rags-to-riches fantasy has a handsome prince thrown in for good measure as well as the obligatory happily-ever-after ending. It conditions the female reader to seek escape from drudgery by finding a man who will make her his princess. It suggests that the woman need not set off on her own to seek her fortune and independent success, but that by relying on a kindly benefactor (the fairy godmother in the story) a handsome prince will assuredly catch sight of her, fall madly in love with her and whisk her away, glass slippers and all. She will ride behind him on a white horse to his splendid kingdom where a life of opulence awaits. End of story.

In *The Cinderella Complex: Women's Hidden Fear of Independence* Colette Dowling enlarges on the theme:

> It is the thesis of this book that personal, psychological dependency – the deep wish to be taken care of by others – is the chief force holding women down today. I call this 'The Cinderella Complex' – a network of largely repressed attitudes and fears that keeps women in a kind of half-light, retreating from the full use of their minds and creativity. Like Cinderella, women today are still waiting for something external to transform their lives.

The Cinderella story-line is the youthful predecessor to a book by Tracy Tanner called *How to Find a Man . . . And Make him Keep You*. It promulgates the very same idea – a woman should concentrate on finding a wealthy man and capitalize on his successful position.

The ideology of the narcissistic Opportunist is highly receptive to the ethos of conspicuous consumption. She may adopt her particular lifestyle because it offers her a token membership in the social worlds of the wealthy and powerful. I suggest that the role of the Opportunist is adopted not only because it gives easy access to money but because it fulfils the Cinderella rationale – the consort of a wealthy man can look forward to living happily-ever-after like Cinderella and her prince. More than rent money, it offers a place in society which is enhanced with the mystique of being one of the 'beautiful people' and in which, as a spectator or participant, she can mingle with people of high status. Terms such as 'quality of life' and 'self-realization' become debased clichés used to describe a situation in which, because the woman can claim access to a Jaguar and a cupboard full of expensive clothes, she thinks she is in a worldly paradise.

There are strong links between the Opportunist category and the Smart Set which are summarized at the end of the next chapter.

Chapter Four
THE SMART SET

I tell men I am an artist. I always ask for change for the ladies room. If I don't get at least £50 to begin with – I just vanish . . . My dates also buy my clothes and usually pay my rent. I say that I'm a 'starving artist' and have dates take me back to my studio – there's a bedroom there. Evidently most men like to think they're supporting an artist or a student and not just a hooker. (*27-year-old woman, London*)

A case of facts in the 1980s bearing out fiction of the 1950s? In *Breakfast at Tiffany's*, Truman Capote's seminal short story first published in the *New Yorker* magazine in 1956, the central character is a Hollywood starlet and highly publicized girl-about-New-York, a playgirl or glamour girl named Holly Golightly. She is not quite 19 years old although on the basis of her appearance the narrator originally places her age at 'anywhere between 16 and 30'. He writes that 'one might have thought her a photographer's model, perhaps a young actress, except that it was obvious, judging from her hours, she hadn't time to be either'. It is Holly's full name 'Holiday Golightly' (changed from Lulamae Barnes) that gives the clue to her occupation. She is a 'party girl', a woman who receives $50 from her dates when she goes to the powder room and another $50 for taxi fares, who makes her living by dating various men. In the story one of her friends describes her lifestyle as 'living off tips'. Although Holly describes the men she dates as 'rats' and, strictly speaking, earns her living through prostitution, she does not think of herself as a prostitute:

Really, though, I toted up the other night, and I've only had eleven lovers – not counting anything that happened before I was thirteen because, after all, that just doesn't count. Eleven. Does that make me a whore? Look at Mag Wildwood. Or Honey Tucker. Or Rose Ellen Ward. They've had the old clap-yo'-hands so many times it amounts to applause. Of course I haven't anything against whores. Except this: some of them may have an honest tongue but they all have dishonest hearts. I mean, you can't bang the guy and cash his cheques and at least not try to believe you love him. I never have. Even Benny Shacklett and all those rodents. I sort of hypnotized myself into thinking their sheer rattiness had a certain allure.

Like Holly, the women in what I have classified as the Smart Set were often on the periphery of prostitution. For some, prostitution took place while the women were involved in a kept relationship; others engaged in prostitution as a bridging role between episodes of being kept. However, the party girl cannot simply be called a prostitute or a call girl even though she may be a 'professional' enthusiastic amateur. The way in which she earns her living is more than an occupation – it is a way of life, a social role, not simply an occupational one. Her dates do not only provide her with money for services rendered; they allow her to move among the 'beautiful people' in the world of glamour.

The girls in the Smart Set category are generally younger than those in any other group, often as young as 16. Their lifestyle is characterized by short periods of affiliation with one man, frequent resumptions of the role of being kept and generally living life in the fast lane. They are glorified groupies, often forming part of an entourage surrounding a man and his friends. It is rare for a woman to remain in this group past her mid-twenties. She generally tends to graduate to the longer-term affiliations of the Opportunist category, to drop out voluntarily to get married or otherwise burn out in a self-destructive process involving drugs, alcohol and the pursuit of a nocturnal, time-warped existence. My respondents in this category did not all belong to one single network group, as for instance a specific man's harem. Girls who were affiliated predominantly with men from the Middle East would sometimes wind up in a group of largely British businessmen. There is only a limited amount of intermingling of groups. A woman who becomes a pop star's mistress is more likely to become another pop star's mistress than switch to a sheik or an oil magnate.

Women in the Smart Set are fundamentally night people. When they do have a job it offers erratic employment and/or middling levels of salary. The girl who parties all night is incapable of working at a nine-to-five job. Her daylight hours are most often spent sleeping or recovering from the previous night's fun and games or preparing for the forthcoming night's work, or shopping. In some instances, a novice in the Smart Set would have a job and attempt to integrate the two sides of her life, but the lifestyle does not allow for dual careers. These women view paid employment as something to be grudgingly sought when they are between patrons and not unhappily discarded when their social situation improves. The roles of actress, model, dancer are common covers between engagements because they are not utterly incongruous with facets of the girl herself, and she also derives satisfaction from successfully passing as a person in a glamorous profession and thinking that men find her attractive enough to be a model or an actress:

> I say I'm a model and they're convinced that they've seen my picture. It's not like he's going to go through every old issue and you can always find a girl who looks enough like you so that they'll think it's the lighting or the makeup that makes you look a bit different. (*20-year-old woman, London*)

Among the Smart Set, to boast of bogus jobs and embroider on biographical histories is routine and it sometimes remains unclear what are the real career ambitions or attainments. Amy, a 26-year-old London respondent, is a regular at a Mayfair club and was introduced to me as a clothes designer. When I asked her whether she made the clothes as well as designed them she haltingly answered that she did not know how to sew and that a friend did the sewing for her. Her friend Donna referred to herself as a translator and stated that both she and Amy were fluent in French and had studied at an upper-class private school from which their friendship dated. When I attempted to speak to her in French she answered in English 'Yes, I speak French.' The club owner (who had introduced them by referring to their superior education) then admonished her, 'that's not how you speak French', at which Donna grudgingly obliged with a form of schoolboy Franglais. I met 'actresses' who had never acted, 'models' who had never modelled, non-productive girls doing something vague in the creative arts, and self-professed upper-class debs who clanged their teaspoons around their cups when stirring their tea in a decidedly Non-U manner or who had a forced attentiveness to etiquette directly out of Emily Post which, when forgotten, made the contrast extremely noticeable.

One of my respondents originally maintained that she was an American and affected a Dashiell Hammett-style way of talking – not a very good imitation of Sam Spade – but about five months after my first meeting with her she admitted that she had never been further west than South Wales. Precisely why she thought a mass-infusion of 'yeah' and 'man' added to her charm escapes me but she felt there was some charisma attached to being thought an American. Some women had got the con game down to a formula, with a sad tale designed to tug at the heartstrings of potentially critical people or those who asked the well-worn question, 'What's a nice girl like you . . .?' Amy's particular sad tale revolved around the child conceived out of wedlock for whom she struggled to provide. Unfortunately, neither Amy nor her close friends seemed to agree on the gender of the infant – her best friend Donna told me that Amy's child was a boy and the spitting image of Amy's departed lover (a fact which of course would have made it especially heart-breaking if Amy had not previously told me that her child was a 'darling little girl').

The typical Mistress type either finds herself in an isolated position and with somewhat limited contacts because of her illicit relationship, or with an apportioned network of friendships, the man providing the nucleus for this network – and demolishing it if, or when, the relationship collapses. But for the Smart Set girl (and to a lesser degree for the Opportunist type) there is an extended friendship network made up of women in similar roles and those with whom she has dealings. In the world of glamour, the party girl is as common as an athlete at the Olympics. She is in her element and may be more at home, more comfortable in her surroundings, and better-known than her male companion. By and large, the world of glamour (as defined by magazines such as *Tatler*, *Harpers and Queen*, and *Ritz* newspaper) is an insular, self-congratulatory little world where the inhabitants pride themselves on being fashionable and knowing everyone else, or at least everyone worth knowing. Although it prides itself on its insularity, the party girl, during her season, may become a fashionable in-member of this glamour group. Since the Smart Set member can claim to be the past girlfriend of a large number of fashionable men and organizes her life around parties, devoting most of her time to perfecting her appearance, she is tailor-made to embrace the prevailing ethos of conspicuous consumption. Andy Warhol, in *Andy Warhol's Exposures*, calls this way of living 'Social Disease':

> The symptoms of Social Disease: You want to go out every night because you're afraid if you stay home you might miss something. You choose your friends according to whether or not they have a limousine. You prefer exhilaration to conversation unless the subject is gossip. You judge a party by how many celebrities are there – if they serve caviar they don't have to have celebrities. When you wake up in the morning, the first thing you do is read the society columns. If your name is actually mentioned your day is made. Publicity is the ultimate symptom of Social Disease.
>
> But you know it's really fatal when you don't want to get rid of it. You couldn't anyway.
>
> How do you catch Social Disease? By kissing someone on both cheeks . . .

In the world of glamour, women gravitate to other women of the same age or life-cycle stage and engage in reciprocal exchanges of support, knowledge and confidences. Just as a man will be more likely to disclose information of his affair to another man known also to be maintaining a girlfriend on the side, these women converge as a group because of their similar circumstances. They occasionally band together to provide support groups for each other. Several women I met had deliberately sought out other women who would act as their mentor in teaching them the ropes, or provide an example on which to pattern their behaviour. Others had been taken under the wing of a more experienced woman and became that woman's protégée or star pupil.

Unlike the Opportunist who welcomes the chance to tell someone her life story and the various ways in which she cons the man, the world of the Smart Set is more self-contained. These women draw support for their actions from other women in their network; they do not seek outsiders in whom to confide. For example, Arab women who are part of small harems accompanying a man and his friends are extremely difficult to interview; they are reticent and somewhat taciturn even when the most powerful man in the network would introduce me to the group and tell them to talk to me. Their relations with other women in the group are much warmer and seem based on their perception that 'one hand washes the other'. Thus, the woman who is the favourite of the most powerful man is likely to be the most popular, but as well she is expected to be magnanimous and to share her good fortune with the other women in the group. On one occasion, six or seven Moroccan girls affiliated with a Saudi Prince went on a shopping spree chaperoned by one of the Prince's aides who acted as their human 'charge card'. The favourite of the moment selected numerous items and the other women simply heaped the goods they desired on the counter along with those the woman selected and waited for the man's aide to pay for them all. This scenario repeated itself several times that afternoon in various shops until the expedition had cost the Prince approximately £10,500.

The game of one-upmanship played by women in this world of glamour is not very difficult or new. Essentially, being an expert games player depends on proper packaging, that is having a wardrobe sufficiently extensive to look admirably fashionable. Women in the Smart Set do not have to be sparkling wits, scintillating conversationalists or profound thinkers; they are simply required to be eye-catching and stylish. The following quotation, also from *Andy Warhol's Exposures*, is written in the gossipy tones favoured by social columnists and although not describing the Smart Set woman of this chapter it does suggest that the standard of comparison for women is their packaging:

> Halston is still all in black, but he's no longer in the corner. He sits in the middle of his huge house on a big Ultrasuede pouf, spooning out caviar. And all the glamour girls perform for him. Bianca Jagger always stays at Halston's house when she's in town. One night Marisa Berenson arrived in a really sexy low-cut Halston. When Bianca saw Marisa she ran upstairs and changed into

something sexier. Meanwhile Marisa asked Halston if her dress was on backwards. He said yes, to keep the game going. Just as Bianca came walking down the stairs Marisa was turning her dress around. Bianca ran back up and grabbed a few jewels. Then Barbara Allen arrived in tight black pants and a black T-shirt and stole the show from both of them.

Simone de Beauvoir in *The Second Sex* suggests that from childhood women are made acutely aware of the importance of dressing to fit a role or an image:

> Even if each woman dresses in conformity with her status, a game is still being played: artifice, like art, belongs to the world of the imaginary. It is not only that girdle, brassiere, hair-dye, make-up disguise body and face; but that the least sophisticated of women, once she is 'dressed' does not present herself to observation; she is, like the picture or the statue, or the actor on the stage, an agent through whom is suggested someone not there – that is, the character she represents but is not. It is this identification with something unreal, fixed, perfect as the hero of a novel, as a portrait or a bust, that gratifies her; she strives to identify with this figure and thus to seem to herself to be stabilized, justified in her splendour.

Women in the Smart Set category often fit the garish stereotype of the kept woman bedecked in an over-the-top display of jewellery and designer-labels. Dressing-to-kill is a form of over-compensation, or the deliberate attempt by the woman to establish her right to be included in a high-status group and/or establish herself as acceptable rather than disreputable. I noted several occasions when a woman from this category sought confirmation for this image. If I asked a woman respondent the time she would often take the opportunity to tell me that she had an Ebel or Rolex watch; and on only a slightly breezy day in May I interviewed a woman who thought it cold enough to wear a white mink jacket. My first interview with the Smart Set woman would be the one when she flaunted her most ostentatious jewellery. Sometimes the weight of gold hanging around the woman's neck looked like horse-brasses for a ceremonial ride. It was important to these women that I should appreciate their exalted position, outwardly expressed in their style of dressing.

Rather than see their preoccupation with beauty and finery as narcissism, it may be that the importance of being beautiful to women who make a career of being kept magnifies the traditional emphasis placed on all women to be beautiful. Throughout my research all the female respondents were vastly more concerned with their appearance than were the men. It was not uncommon for women to ask me about the attractiveness of other women I interviewed, get me to compare their looks to those of their friends, badger me for compliments, or themselves denigrate their appearance and wait expectantly for me to disagree. Among those women who made a career out of being kept by interchangeable men, the emphasis on beauty was especially marked. These women consciously defined youth and beauty or their appearance as essential qualities for their chosen role. Even the most tawdry of escort agencies contacted in London prided themselves on rejecting those they termed 'scrubbers' – the unattractive, the gauche, or the socially unpresentable. Selling yourself is possible only if there is a market for the commodity, and beauty and youth are defined as marketable assets.

The Smart Set woman was frequently recruited from professions such as modelling and acting (or girls aspiring to such professions) which stress physical beauty, deportment and the necessity of maximizing your physical attributes. One of my respondents, currently being kept by a minister of a West African country, was a former house model for Dior. Another, coached in the establishment of the notorious Madame Claude (of Paris brothel fame), spoke of a period of apprenticeship in which she was sent to beauty salons and specified designer houses to be groomed by them for her debut as one of Madame Claude's natural beauties. Her training also entailed lessons in etiquette and social graces so that she could mingle with the desirable men in the most elevated circles. Her 'coming out' crowned an intensive period of 'finishing' similar in method and intent to that of the society debutante. Both pursue the end of increasing their attractiveness and eligibility to men.

There are several reasons why these women seek to be thought of as beautiful and desire to be flattered. First, they identify physical attractiveness as instrumental in attracting a patron. The more beautiful the woman is or thinks herself to be, the more she feels able to compete with other women for the most eligible men. If she is identified by herself and/or by her friends as beautiful she is likely to allow herself to be more selective in choosing a male benefactor. One woman remarked that while her friend's lover was wealthier than her own, she herself was not as young as her friend and thus could not hope to attract men as easily. Although the woman is in her early thirties an eavesdropper just hearing her speak would have estimated her age as well over twice this figure. Vigilance in maintaining diet and exercise regimes is in deference to their role requirements. If she becomes old or frumpy she will be thought to have negligible choice, if any, in selecting a lover. Beauty is an indispensable asset because men will seek out girls who have it and yield to their requests. Women who make a profession of being kept are apt to credit their beauty as important in successfully negotiating for favours, gifts and 'perks' of the relationship. Moreover, in the Smart Set where there are groups or 'harems' of girls the best-looking is likely to be viewed as the leader or the figurehead of the group. By clustering around a beautiful representative, the group attempts to capitalize on the woman's ability to focus and hold male attention, and her behaviour in her relationship with her lover is thought to set a standard for conduct within the group. For example, if she can get her lover to spend money freely on her it is thought that other men will be encouraged to follow suit and bestow members of the group with gifts as well. In this way the woman's beauty gives her power within the group as well as in dealing with men. Beauty becomes star quality and just as a theatrical producer may assume that a famous actress will have a drawing-power upon an audience, the beautiful woman is thought to exert a drawing-power upon a man and his friends. By being attractive and well-groomed, these women are aware that they convey an image of being economically and emotionally secure. They feel it is important that they do not look as if they need someone to support them. On the contrary, the man should think it a privilege to support such a splendid being. It is also important for the ambitious kept woman to present an image of splendour so that the financial rewards given are correspondingly grand. To fit in with the tableaux of impressive hotels, restaurants, clubs and so on, the woman has to be suitably dressed. It is difficult to convey the social world of these women without taking into account the settings in which they operate. The environment of the Smart Set is fundamentally a world where money, although worshipped, is often spent as if it were Monopoly paper notes. An evening out can easily add up to several hundreds of pounds, and the cost of the woman's costume may represent several months' salary of, say, the average schoolteacher. Looking the part is essential and entails meticulous attention to hair, make-up and clothes. Since any one relationship is ephemeral and not guaranteed by a contract of employment or marriage, the Smart Set woman cannot allow herself to neglect any detail of her appearance. If she cannot maintain the present man's interest, she must be ready to attract another.

For the woman herself to be satisfied that she succeeds in looking good may depend on her feeling that everyone else thinks she does too. Since she can never be absolutely sure about this, she may resort to using the props of beauty as a measure of her self-worth. In groups of kept women, the clothes and jewellery of an individual are taken to indicate how clever she is in attracting gifts from her partner.

Training in the art of manufacturing glamour is often provided through the network of associates, and may be direct or indirect. The man with whom the woman is involved, or other women in her group may instruct her and suggest ways to dress and behave, but unless the woman is dreadfully gauche, it seems that most often she adjusts to her position by imitating those around her. However, the novice is often over-concerned with the socially correct way to handle a chicken bone even when the people around her have the social graces of a group of starving hooligans. Precisely because her status is still in the process of negotiation, the Smart Set woman tries too hard to be agreeable, to drink – or take drugs – as much as the rest of the group, to flaunt her designer-labels, in the attempt to penetrate the group and establish herself as an in-member of it. It is the classic behaviour of the 'marginal man', the person who is barely tolerated by the larger group, like the Jew in pre-War Germany and the Black in the present-day American South. In his study, *Hell's Angels*, Hunter Thompson notes that women attempting to penetrate the all-male clubs as equals (rather than as 'mommas' or girlfriends) are often exploited; their eagerness to ingratiate themselves with the group means that they will willingly suffer degrading treatment (allowing themselves to be gang-banged, for example) specifically to impress and please others. In the Smart Set newcomers can be distinguished by their tendency to accept without question that whatever the group thinks fashionable is something wonderful and worthy of imitation. This applies not only to personal appearance but to ways of behaving with others and acting the part of the glamorous woman.

Howard Becker in his *The Outsiders* suggests that becoming a marijuana smoker is dependent upon participation in a social network. It would appear that marijuana is not the only drug whose enjoyment is learned in a group context. One of my respondents, when I asked her if she took drugs, offered the following account of her experience:

> . . . [I take them] all – PCP, coke, amyl nitrates, peyote buttons, LSD – everything but heroin because that's addicting. [*What do you prefer?*] LSD. I love it. [*But isn't that addicting?*] No, I don't think so. [*How did you first try it?*] I was going with a guy and he gave me some. I thought I was going to die. I didn't know what was happening to me. He must have taken less because he fell asleep and I was by myself. You can't fall asleep when you're tripping and it lasts about twelve hours so you start thinking you're never going to sleep or that you're going crazy. I didn't touch it for a year because of that but it was hard because everyone would be taking it and that would make me feel like I'm different. Then I just said yes, and it was great. I knew what to expect and I saw that what made me not like it the first time was that I was with a stranger. Now I'm with friends and it's very good . . . I never get it myself – it's always there just to take if you want it. [*Do most of your friends do drugs?*] The ones who are smart do. It's there for us to enjoy ourselves. (*20-year-old woman, London*)

The most frequent drug noted is cocaine and, among Arab networks, hashish. There is considerable complacency in certain London clubs about transactions in the drug trade. In one case, in a predominantly Middle Eastern club restaurant, a man came in and made a slow tour of various tables, generally consulting a single man at each table as to whether or not he wanted to purchase any cocaine. If the customer did not, he merely shrugged his shoulders and the man moved on. In another highly exclusive private disco it is possible to get virtually any drug from the staff itself.

Using drugs is generally treated nonchalantly, like alcohol, as an accompaniment to enjoying yourself and having a good time. Because it is thought fashionable to be open to new experiences and clever to be avaricious and take advantage of all the fringe benefits the situation offers, addiction may often be the final result. This equates high consumption with high worth. Conspicuous consumption in drugs, as well as in material paraphernalia, is seen to coincide with high social status and self-esteem. This view, combined with the fact that the woman cannot be assured that her membership of the group will be renewed or indefinitely extended, gives rise to a last meal mentality about activities. Gorging themselves, whether on clothes or drugs, is common, and these women tend to be indifferent to the consequences of their behaviour.

Sex and sexuality become yet another commodity. Indeed, the women themselves are objects of consumption. Certain parties are patterned on Greek orgies or scenes from a soft-porn best-seller. One man, who has an incredible house in Hertfordshire decorated like the set of a blue movie – replete with mirrors, tacky nude sculptures, a heated indoor pool and a jacuzzi – gave a party largely consisting of call girls, party girls, hero-worshipping dumb 'bunnies' and an assortment of male and female hangers-on. The host was indifferent to who appeared at his parties or to the escapades of his weird collection of exhibitionists and voyeurs, hell-bent as they all were on having a good time. A rather worn-out pop singer from the 1960s strutted about with two partially-clad teenagers in search of others who wished to join them in watching some pornographic movies in one of the rooms. The girls themselves appeared inordinately pleased to be pawed by this minor celebrity and clung close to him all evening.

The tactics of ingratiation are not simple; it would be wrong to say that sex is offered in straight exchange for a party invitation or that these women simply place so little importance on the sexual act that they are indifferent to the men with whom they perform it. In the 1970s a group calling themselves the 'Plaster Casters' emerged who congratulated themselves on, and sought publicity by, making phallic impressions of the various men they had either slept with, or at least gained intimate physical access to. The ideology of this group throws some light on the way in which some of the women I encountered viewed sex with a famous person. The sexual act becomes symbolic, conferring a certain degree of celebrity upon the woman herself. She may be likened to the avid autograph-seeker or fan club member who, by possessing a scrap of paper with her hero's name scribbled on it or a rubber-stamped glossy photograph, feels herself entitled to identify with this hero or seek identification through spectator-participation in his life. Nor is this star worship confined to women. I found a man in his fifties who prided himself on owning one of Monroe's costumes, in which he made various lady friends dress up, later displaying pictures of them so attired.

Perhaps this celebrity reverence is best illustrated by a woman I met, now in her late forties, who had a bit part in one of Elvis Presley's early films. She took pains to drive home to me the fact that she had actually slept with Presley and moreover that he had admired her small and elegant feet. The belief that they have in some way gained possession of a part of their hero and their awe at having done so, seem to transfix these women with a kind of reverential wonder. Whether or not the claim by my woman correspondent is true, sleeping with Presley was not considered simply an act of fornication, it was the highlight of her life, something she recounted with pride. 'Doing what it takes' to gain access to the famous and celebrated may be rationalized as a type of divine sacrifice which is justified in the belief that the famous are worthy of worship and adoration. I should emphasize that here I am only referring to one sub-group of the Smart Set population, in which the woman bows to the power of the man.

Society has chosen for its heroes people who are glamorous and famous. A cult of adoration rises around them and newspapers employ gossip columnists to trace their every move – they are the chosen few. The intrinsic worship of money and/or power is manifested in the great value placed on the symbols of celebrity – the big house, the fast cars and the extravagance – but it is the hero, the figurehead of conspicuous consumption, who becomes the object of adoration. Especially for young girls who latch on to pop singers, sex with a famous person acquires a symbolic value. It is thought that by affiliation they, too, have become superior. This can lead some women to become haughty and arrogant. One woman who has been with her rock star lover for less than a year is sanctimoniously derogatory about the female hangers-on who attach themselves to her lover's entourage. In her ascent to glory she has developed a severe case of amnesia as to her own humbler origins and neglects the fact that the man has a wife and she is merely his personal aide. The men themselves seem like minor gods, accepting the worship of their subjects, allowing the women their moments of grandeur through association and then rather unceremoniously discarding them when they see fit to do so. It is not precisely a slave–master association because a slave may not recognize the legitimacy of his 'master's' hold upon him. These relationships are characterized by the woman's need to identify with the man and her willingness to accept his hold over her. To a lesser degree, however, other women may derive satisfaction from the status of their partner.

When I interviewed professional call girls they unfailingly spoke of two cost sheets: one for non-Arab men and another, usually twice the fee otherwise charged, for Arab men. This practice may be attributable largely to the awareness that the Arab man is likely to have a large amount of money to spend. It may also be influenced, however, by the fact that the Arab is not considered a high-status partner. If the call girl prides herself on only going with the 'best' clientele she may regard the inflated price as compensation. This is speculative but the comments these women made suggest that there are distinctions in this area and that Arabs are not looked on as legitimate members of the elite.

In his psychoanalytic study, *The Elegant Prostitute*, Harold Greenwald confirms this attitude:

> The type of clientele to which a girl caters is another factor in establishing her status. Girls will often boast that they see only the 'nicest type of men': businessmen, professionals and people from the theatrical world. Many of the girls during the interview managed to mention that they had had business relations with leading television or movie stars at one time or another but usually remained true to their code by not mentioning names.

Alongside women who hero-worship their male partners exist others who worship not the man but the symbols of his success. They may be called prostitutes or call girls but the name itself is of little importance. Although various writers have suggested that there are differences between the amateur (who retains her amateur status for the extra thrill of self-degradation it gives her) and the professional (who is a distinct social and psychological type), I find such discriminations obtuse. The women I interviewed in this group pamper themselves, enjoy lavish lifestyles, and appear well satisfied to spend their time reading the latest edition of fashion or gossip magazines, shopping, and dining or dancing in 'smart' clubs. They view sex as simply the nexus which connects them to the lifestyle they desire. One woman said that she only found the kept lifestyle offensive when the man did not know how properly to keep a woman. That is, if the relationship resulted in surroundings of high aesthetic value, she found it completely satisfactory. She contrasted her own situation with that of her friend who was kept by an Arab man. She commented that while her friend had dozens of pairs of shoes, none of them was hand-made and while her friend's lover had bought her a house in a fashionable London mews street, it was not really a very nice mews house. Put succinctly, her attitude is 'It's not what you do but the way that you do it.' Some of these women have become so well-known by being the girlfriend of a famous man or men (although the press obliges them by identifying them with desirable labels such as starlet or model) that even when they are self-acknowledged prostitutes they regard themselves as celebrities. Of one such, another woman commented, 'they say all roads lead to Rome, well, all roads lead to Alison'. If Alison wrote a resumé of her affiliations it would read like a gossip listing of well-known men. She is frequently pictured in various magazines and newspapers, always exquisitely groomed and stylishly dressed; she regards herself as a success story. Alison was disappointed that I did not follow through on her suggestion that I identify her previous lovers by name as she seemed to fancy herself the star of my respondents.

Moreover, when I contacted her about appearing on a British Broadcasting Corporation television documentary being prepared on mistresses, she was not at all upset when I warned her that the producer would not consent to film respondents in shadow. Other women had immediately recoiled from the idea of having their situation made known but Alison was unperturbed as long as the programme made no mention of her receiving economic support from her lovers. Her only concern and questions were: (1) how much would BBC Television pay, and (2) who were the other celebrities appearing?

The difference between the party girl and the call girls I met in my research is somewhat vague, reflecting the movement from one category to another. Harold Greenwald (in his *The Elegant Prostitute*) has sought to distinguish the two and defines the party girl as:

> . . . the girl who goes out on no more than one date per evening and where the question of fee is not made explicit. That is, the girl never discusses fee with clients, but it is understood, usually by arrangement with the person making the introduction, that at the end of the evening the man will unobtrusively slip her an envelope containing anywhere from a hundred dollars up . . . Also, most girls in the 'party girl' category will occasionally refuse their favours to a man who does not appeal to them. 'Party girls' are very careful to keep the prerogative of refusal as a means of denying that they are engaged in prostitution.

These distinctions do not fit the women in my Smart Set research. Greenwald's suggestion that the party girl receives an unobtrusive envelope at the end of the evening suggests a delicacy which is not always observed and leads to the assumption that the call girl receives her money in some abrasive manner such as the man flinging her money at her. While his suggestion that the party girl sees only one man a night may have some truth in it he ignores the fact that she may also have lunch or teatime dates, and that the call girl may act as a man's companion for an entire evening. Admittedly some call girls are whisked from one hotel to another by a mini-car firm to accommodate a large number of clients but other high-class call girls have a fairly exclusive clientele. There is a greater degree of movement between the two categories than Greenwald's statement would suggest.

Neither the party girl nor the call girl is welded into her role. There is no retirement home for aged party girls and after a while some of them do become professional prostitutes. Moreover, the suggestion of implicit or prior arrangement of fees applies as much to the call girl as for the party girl. Although the call girl generally receives her payment prior to the sexual act when she is specifically sent for that purpose, in situations where she acts as the man's 'date' the manner of payment does not have to be abrasive. For example, with Arab men, the man himself does not usually negotiate with the woman; this is done by an underling or by prior arrangement with the girl or the agency, madame or ponce for whom she works. The man will give her a 'tip' but the payment of fees will be handled by someone else. The party girl, however, does not always graciously accept whatever fee the man gives or thinks suitable; women mentioned haggling over fees or threatening to cause scenes over what was thought to be an insufficient amount of payment.

The party girl appears to acquire gifts more often than cash but it may be that she gives this impression because she wishes to present herself as other than a prostitute. One of my party girl respondents originally identified herself as a model but over the two and a half years I have known her, she has never had more than half a dozen modelling jobs. She travels around the world with her various gentlemen friends, spends her time night-clubbing and partying rather than modelling, and she has a flat, car and wardrobe that could not possibly have been independently acquired. She does not claim that she is self-supporting, and even if her possessions were all gifts it does not explain how she gets her spending money, money for petrol, shopping and so on. Additionally, both the party girl and the call girl are excitement-seekers. They changed men frequently, not simply because they themselves are discarded, but because they feel any long-term relationship to be boring. If they do consent to be kept and maintain the kept relationship over a long period of time, they are unlikely to remain faithful to the man, especially if he is older. They feel that cheating on their partner adds to the excitement of the situation. Unlike the Opportunist category who paradoxically find 'freedom' best achieved in a stable, luxurious lifestyle, the women in the Smart Set seem restless and in a never-ending pursuit of excitement.

I have previously noted that the women in my Smart Set category are generally younger as a group than any other of my types of kept women and that their affiliations tend to be relatively short-lived. These women are youthful not merely because young women are preferred by the men. The work of these women – and work it is, both in terms of furnishing an income and taking up a large section of their time – requires considerable emotional and physical stamina. It was not cattiness that made me think an 18-year-old girl looked as if she was in her middle-thirties – she did, in fact, look prematurely aged.

Whether to anaesthetize themselves, or simply as a by-product of conspicuous consumption, or as a supposed mechanism to retain a slim figure and increase their energy, women seem to abuse drugs and/or alcohol. These women also use alcohol or drugs to combat boredom in the same way that they changed partners, as a method of providing additional excitement. Life in the fast lane may sound eminently glamorous, but it also appears to be somewhat monotonous. An average day for a typical kept woman would be to get up around noon after a late night out, spend the afternoon sipping alcohol either at home or at a wine bar after shopping, and pass the early evening preparing to go out and resume partying with virtually the same people she had last seen the night before. Some women will go to bizarre lengths to combat boredom. For example, some women would take a trip to Paris every four weeks to have their hair trimmed; others make a tour of every European airport simply for something to do. However, as the sixteenth-century French moralist Montaigne suggested, the traveller takes himself wherever he goes. No matter where they go, these women always seem to find yet another fashionable party or nightclub or have the telephone number of someone whom their friends suggest would be just their type.

Holly, a 21-year-old Londoner, is representative of a Smart Set party girl. She currently lives in St John's Wood in an apartment bought for her by her previous lover, a sheikh in his sixties, who recently died. A month or so after his death Holly had already found another sheikh from Oman to keep her. When I first met her in 1981, she was seeing half a dozen clients in France and an additional half dozen in the Middle East, in addition to being kept by the sheikh. Among her clients were four brothers, one of whom was 'keeping' her, unaware of her simultaneous patronage by the sheikh and her business relationship with his brothers. There is nothing special about Holly's physical appearance that would distinguish her from other young women. Unlike the women in Xaviera Hollander's books who are always described as gorgeous creatures with massive mammaries, long legs and flowing hair, Holly has shoulder-length blonde hair, is of average height and is attractive rather than beautiful. She maintains that all her relationships with the various men are fundamentally business relationships and that she is emotionally loyal to an English boyfriend working at the time with the boat people in Hong Kong.

Holly attended a rather grand finishing school. She comes from an upper-middle-class home and although her parents have remained married, her mother has been involved with an unmarried government minister for the past eight years while her father is keeping his secretary in a company-held flat. Her brother, two years younger than herself, is a homosexual who periodically asks Holly to find him a girl who will convert him to heterosexuality. When asked if she practises birth control, Holly said that she had been anorexic during her late teens and was told she had become sterile as a result. She said that she herself had been untroubled when she ceased to menstruate for two years and that her mother had thought having an anorexic daughter fashionable; it was, Holly said, an upper-class disease. Holly herself felt it a faddish, teenage preoccupation that she grew out of. She does not really mind being sterile as she has no particular desire to have children and is glad to be spared the monthly inconvenience of menstruation.

Holly met the sheikh through his nephew, a 21-year-old university student she dated when she was 19. She said that after meeting the sheikh his aide telephoned numerous times, attempting to arrange a dinner date on his behalf. This intermediary approach is very common among Arab men. They would never approach a girl directly but enlist an aide or an intermediary such as a club manager or head waiter to intercede for them, conveying their requests to a girl they find attractive or want to meet. I asked Holly if the sheikh's nephew had minded being usurped by his uncle and Holly said that she did not think so; because of the sheikh's age and position he had his nephew's unequivocal support to do whatever he wished to do. At the time of her first meeting with the sheikh, Holly was not a professional call girl, neither was she a virgin. She ascribes little importance to the state of virginity and admits that she and her female friends had had few qualms about going to bed with boyfriends by the time they were 15 or 16 years old. The sheikh's liberality in bestowing gifts upon her made his company pleasant and compensated for any absence of physical attraction she felt towards him as a man. The sexual side of their relationship, she maintained, was minimal and she felt that he supported her because he wanted companionship rather than sex. When I asked Holly for her thoughts on what men want most in a relationship she answered 'loyalty'. It may seem an ironic reply considering the other relationships she conducted during her association with the sheikh, but even if she was not loyal in practice to the sheikh, she took care to convey that image to him.

Holly saw the sheikh the three months of the year he lived in London and flew to the Middle East every ten to twelve weeks during the course of their relationship to be with him. There she stayed in one of his houses; she selected which one she preferred and he simply uprooted any hangers-on that occupied the house prior to her arrival. His wife and family, the youngest of whom was three years old, knew of her existence but were uncritical because they were completely dependent on the sheikh who had absolute power over them. She said that she had met all the members of his immediate family, including his wife, and had photographs of herself with his 40-year-old son and his youngest child. When in the Middle East, a car and driver were specially provided for her so that she could tour about and her chauffeur was expected to guard the sheikh's proprietorial rights over her in his absence. The chauffeur acted as a rather large symbolic wedding ring, warning other men to stay away. In London, she made weekly checks to see that the sheikh's apartment was safe and attended to her business, unmonitored by him or his agents. Through the sheikh she had met a large number of other men, and on her own or through other women she also associates with Middle Eastern men. On one occasion when I interviewed her at her apartment our conversation was interrupted by a telephone call. A member of Middle Eastern royalty, greeted upon arrival by British royalty and whose visit to London had generated substantial media coverage, had enlisted an underling to request Holly's presence at an Embassy dinner.

Holly, at the time, identified herself as having two roles: that of the call girl and that of the mistress. Both were thought of as professional roles but there were differences in the way she enacted them. Of the four brothers she attended she told me:

I met 'No. One' in the lift of the building my mother's friend lives in. I noticed him because he was very good-looking – tall and dark. We went down in the lift together. It was raining outside and there was a cab I had phoned for. He motioned for it and I told him it was my cab and went off. About a month later I saw him again in the lift and he said hello and asked if I lived there too. I said no and in the lobby he asked for my phone number. I was in a wicked mood – it seemed so obvious that he had such a lot of money and he was just a young guy. [*How did you know he was rich?*] Just him living there and the way he dressed . . . Anyhow, I told him that I was really hard up and if he wanted to go out with me he'd have to pay me. He seemed to think this was perfectly ordinary and asked if £500 would be enough. I just was shocked and told him, oh no, I meant £50 or so. Stupid fool! [Making a face and referring to herself.] That was the first time I ever took money – it was different with the sheikh. [*How?*] The sheikh pays all my bills but I mean, with 'One' it really felt like buying my time. [*How did you meet the other brothers?*] In France . . . I thought he was French but he isn't. He took me with him to Paris for a fortnight and the second night we were there we both got totally drunk. He went to the loo and his passport and wallet were sitting on the table. I'd never seen a red passport so I picked it up and it says 'Prince —'. When he came back I started screaming at him that he had lied to me and threw an ashtray at him . . . The ashtray got him on the face and cut his lip and it started bleeding . . . I ran out and he ran out after me – the people there must have thought we were both crazy. [*Why were you so mad?*] I don't know – we had been fighting on and off and his lying just bothered me. We made up and since I already knew who he was he introduced me to his family. I knew right off that one of his brothers fancied me and he asked me that evening when 'One' wasn't there, to give him my number in London. I told him I didn't want 'One' to know and he swore he wouldn't tell him. Actually, aside from one brother I have fucked all of them. [*How do you feel sleeping with them? Is it attractive at all to you?*] With 'One' he's very attractive so I like sleeping with him. His brothers, well, two I don't mind – it's not as if they want to go on and on. Sometimes they get so excited just seeing me lay down on the bed they come without me doing anything or touching them. The fourth brother is a real slob, fat and hairy but he pays enough – actually he pays more than any of his brothers. [*Do they know that their other brothers see you?*]

Two, Three and Four know but I don't think they know what the others pay.

[*How do you decide on a price?*] It depends. One time, I was coming back from seeing the sheikh and had to stop overnight because I missed the connection to London. I was staying in a Hilton hotel and there were some others (people from England) and they invited me with them to go to this reception. It was a horrible party and I decided I wanted to go back. I asked a waiter to phone me a cab but he said there were none. This middle-aged guy who had been staring at me all evening said he'd give me a lift back to the hotel. We get in his car and we're in the middle of the desert and he stops the car and starts trying to rape me. I said 'Look darling, if you want to fuck me, wait until we get back to my hotel, we can be more comfortable there.' I thought once I get back to the hotel, he's a minister right?, he won't make a scene and I can just tell him to get lost. Anyhow, he takes out a gun! [*What did you do?*] I was wearing tight jeans so I told him just to hold on a bit and I let him rape me. After, he just drove me to the hotel. In the morning I got a phone call from reception – he's inviting me for breakfast. I went down – I think he wanted to see how I was and if I was going to make a fuss, call the Embassy or the police – that sort of thing. I just told him he owed me £1 000 for the previous night – that was what I charged. He paid. If men know you're a professional they find it easier because they know you'll just take the money and not make a fuss or look for publicity. [*Do you have a set price?*] A lot!! [*Is sex enjoyable for you?*] I don't know what you mean – I don't think it's particularly important, or think you have to be in love with someone to have good sex with them . . . With the sheikh I probably have sex a couple of times a year – that's not much is it? With the others, it's just an hour or so and then you go and do whatever you want and have the money to do it with. [*Why do you see these men?*] That's obvious, the money.

Holly's relationship with the sheikh, however, seems to be different from her relationships with her other men, even in the way she labels the others clients while she refers to the sheikh as her boyfriend. Although she is not loyal to him physically she was loyal to him in seeking to protect his interests:

He is constantly surrounded by relatives and people who are always trying to cheat him . . . He has a flat about a mile from here – six bedrooms, really massive. He asked me to decorate it so I phoned up a company to send someone to measure for drapes. I answered the door myself because if the workmen see an Arab they just raise the price incredibly. He came in and was measuring the windows and one of the Sheikh's friends came in and asked where the Sheikh was – I just saw the look on the workman's face and knew the price would go right up.

The relationship with the first sheikh lasted approximately five years but intensified in its third year when the man developed cancer and was hospitalized for over seven months. Holly said that during that time she lived at the hospital and that a section was bought up so that his entourage could be accommodated. She said she was disgusted to see that his companions treated the hospital as a substitute hotel and carried on partying without regard for the sheikh's serious condition. Many call girls deliberately select accommodation around London's 'Arab hospitals'. It seemed as if the reason the man entered hospital was insignificant to his hangers-on so long as the accommodation was comfortable and equivalent to a hotel in providing service. Holly mentioned that she had been irritated with her brother because after she requested that he visit the sheikh to offer get-well wishes, her brother found the living arrangements so comfortable that he simply stayed and joined the party for a few weeks. Holly does not believe she exploited the sheikh and sees herself more as having protected him as a companion and friend would.

When the sheikh went abroad they kept in touch by telephone and Holly attributed the longevity of their relationship to her ability to distract him from problems by being lighthearted and refusing to take anything too seriously. The one conversation between Holly and her lover that I heard was frequently punctuated with girlish giggles and amusing vignettes of daily life. This was unlike her. The Holly I had known was rather serious and sombre. I asked her later if she realized she seemed different with the sheikh and she laughed and said yes, but he relied upon her to be cheerful and so she made sure she fulfilled this desire. Additionally, Holly had read various books on the Middle East and had a working knowledge of Arabic so that she could speak with the sheikh on topics that interested him and exchange at least rudimentary pleasantries with his friends. She told me that her attempt to speak in Arabic both amused and pleased the sheikh.

At one point I asked Holly if she ever envisaged herself getting married. She answered that she intended to marry her boyfriend when he returned from Hong Kong. Although she feels that marriage would not allow her to retain a kept relationship she does not see why it would be impossible to continue as call girl. When I asked her if she desired an open marriage she strongly rejected the idea and said she would kill her husband if she found out he was unfaithful. Since she thinks of her call girl activities as 'work tasks' she apparently does not identify them as potentially unfaithful behaviour. However, her answers do reveal the somewhat foggy, conventional/unconventional notions that she had of what is acceptable behaviour. Holly seems to be unaware of the incongruity of saying she wishes to marry her boyfriend, while constructing her social life around other men. A month after the sheikh died, she had found another to support her; she did not attempt to join her boyfriend in Hong Kong. Having a remote boyfriend whom she intends to marry at some future point is characteristic of the vague way in which both the professional and the amateur party girl regard the future.

Women in the Smart Set seem to be tremendously vague about their goals in life even when they acknowledge that they cannot go on living in the same manner indefinitely. None of my women thought a 40-year-old could successfully perform their role. Reality for these women is firmly based in the here and now. Some of my respondents find the idea of ageing utterly repulsive. It is as if they totally ignore the certainty that they, too, will grow old. While these women often dress and apply make-up with remarkable sophistication, they are markedly childish and uninformed about the social facts of life. For example, Holly has never been to a gynaecologist and does not see the need to be concerned about the possibility of venereal disease for she claimed that she only makes love with 'respectable married men'. Other women apparently think the man's 'celebrity' status provides him with immunity from venereal disease; they maintain that they could not get pregnant if they made love with two or more different men in succession (asserting that one cancelled out the other); they argue that LSD is not addictive; that alcohol has no calories; that you could not become an alcoholic if you only drink wine – in no matter what quantities. It may be attributable to their age or to their philosophy of living for the moment, but as a group, the women in the Smart Set are naive if not innocent and extremely short-sighted about the consequences of their way of living.

Women in the Smart Set category regard being kept as a continual vacation but it can also be seen as a vacationless career. Life in the fast lane is something of a roller-coaster ride from which you can't just walk away. To mingle with the jet set crowd requires that a large amount of cash and time is channelled into clothes, travel and cultivating the friendship of others in the network. To get into the crowd takes money, and once you're in, a high standard of living has to be kept up. Unless a woman is able to coax her lover into providing her with a cash allowance, she may get only possessions and gifts which have a negligible re-sale value. If comfortable surroundings are a high priority – and for the Smart Set they are – there may be no alternative method (to being kept) by which they can so readily enjoy gracious living. For example, after Holly's first lover died, she accompanied his body for burial back to the United Arab Emirates and then took a month's vacation in India as she felt rather depressed. While she had the apartment and the other gifts he had given her during his lifetime, she was used to a grand scale of living and felt her financial position somewhat shaky.

When women become call girls to make fast money, the original target set before they would be prepared to quit the life will, over a period of time, be no longer thought of as sufficient. Since Holly viewed her call girl fees as 'spending money', with the sheikh's support financing her standard of living, she decided to enter into another kept relationship when the occasion arose. Thanks to friends and contacts met while in her relationship with the sheikh, the period in which she was required to finance herself independently – or strictly as a call girl – was very short.

It often seems as if those women who are on the game or who actively participate in the 'night life' are part of an extended family relationship; there is mention of favours given and favours owed, long-standing relationships, an informal system of mutual benefits dependent upon co-operation, of protection. In the Smart Set, initial introductions to any particular man are often the by-product of inclusion in a network group. For the majority of the Smart Set and the Opportunist categories, getting involved to start with and forming an association with any one particular man is often brought about through an introduction by mutual friends or by going along in a group to a party. Invitations to parties must be very loosely extended, with the result that parties group together a random assortment of people who scarcely know the host, much less each other. Instead of bringing along a bottle of wine for the host or flowers for the hostess, guests bring along additional guests . . . especially young, attractive women. One of my respondents, originally from Nigeria, elaborated on her introduction to her first kept relationship and the party where her introduction to the man took place:

> It was about five years ago – I was invited to a party by a girl I met at work along with another girl and the girl's boyfriend. My uncle was away on holiday so I had his BMW and thought I'd drive myself but they came to pick me up. There was a Rolls Royce outside and I asked them where their car was. The girl's boyfriend just pointed to the Rolls – I had felt such a rich lady with my uncle's BMW! We went to St John's Wood . . . it was pretty late at night for a party to start – about 11.30 and five years ago parties tended to start earlier. We drove up and past the gates was a long drive and there wasn't a sound. Absolutely still. The house was gorgeous – I never found out who owned it but they definitely had taste. Around the back was a heated swimming pool and around it were sitting about fifteen to thirty people at any time. The first thing I saw was a girl and two guys sitting on a stair when you came out of the house towards the pool. They had nothing on. I couldn't believe what I saw – I kept thinking to myself – 'Did I see THAT? – and just tried to be the big liberated lady. Later I saw a couple in front of everyone making love . . . they had just thrown a towel down on the cement and were making love in front of everyone. A group were playing some kind

of children's game and the winner got to make love with the loser's wife – in the meantime there's these butlers walking around serving drinks with black bow ties on and everything and I kept thinking that the police would come and find everyone naked and smoking hashish and I'd be saying I came with friends and didn't even know whose party it was. I was nervous and ate myself sick to keep occupied. I didn't even have a car so I could leave and the people I came with are sitting naked around the pool!

Then one of the men who still had something on asked me if I wanted to see the house. It was a marvellous place. The master bedroom was all in off-white with off-white carpets a couple of inches thick, the bed had a canopy and there was a *chaise longue* with white satin buttons. In the bathroom between the carpet and the bath there were marble floors and these two were making love in the bath. There were champagne bottles lying on the carpets and I felt sorry for the carpet because it was a room you really don't want to live in, just look at. After, he asked me if I lived in London and we started talking. That's how I got to know him. (*22-year-old woman, London*)

Although my respondent was originally shocked by the scene which confronted her on her arrival she now laughs at her naivety and believes that there was little reason to be shocked. She prides herself on her 'sophistication'; those who might have a more puritan attitude or feel uncomfortable in such surroundings are ridiculed as gauche and unsophisticated. Her comments explain how a woman may simply drift into situations which facilitate her entrance into the world of glamour. It seems that the middle- or upper-class woman is more likely to become part of the Smart Set simply because she is more apt to receive invitations to parties or functions where wealthy men are present. Although a lower-class woman might become an escort and be recruited to enlarge the women–men ratio at a party on the assumption that she will be willing to entertain guests, unless a woman knows someone who can extend an invitation, she may never gain entrance to elite circles. Her class origins may make the possibility of her entrance into the Smart Set and the people within it more remote.

In contrast to 'drifting' into the Smart Set, women may enter the world of glamour by engaging in occupations, including, but not limited to, prostitution, which allow them to mix with people connected with elite circles. The croupier in a gambling club, the club hostess and the *Bureau de Change* teller in a smart hotel may all perform the roles which allow them to meet men who may facilitate their introduction and incorporation into an elite network. Stewardesses working on flights to and from the Middle East gain access to men with Arab oil money. The women are required by the nature of their occupational role to be charming and courteous to their customers and in some cases, are required to present themselves as sexy or at least well-groomed and attractive. Moreover, in certain cases, the host organization for which the woman works has a vested interest in prostitution. For example, although some of London's four-star hotels have a reputation of being clean of call girls, others simply sweep out stray girls while their staff members work hand-in-glove with club girls, agency escorts and the entrepreneurial professional. While certain hotels have developed fairly stringent security measures (such as television monitors and intercoms identifying the girls to security personnel) to deter the un-affiliated girl from loitering about their premises with the aim of soliciting their customers, the hotels which had the most elaborate security systems in London were not the ones with the fewest links with prostitution, either directly or in its subsidiary forms.

Of the hotel security staff members I interviewed, most did not look upon prostitution chiefly as a moral offence but as a security risk because of the woman's real or supposed links with crimes of theft. It was generally felt by these security officers (always male) that the professional prostitute's network included thieves or that stealing was a sideline of the woman herself. It was suggested that the woman kept the thieves informed about who kept large sums of money or expensive goods in the hotel. There were some hotel security officers who saw themselves as moral vigilantes and prided themselves on the second sight which enabled them to spot the hookers:

> If a girl comes in off the street and goes straight to the lifts we'll stop her and ask her which room she's going to and what the person's name is. If we have seen her before or if she looks 14 years old we'll call the man down. Sometimes you can tell by the way the woman looks, there's something about these girls you get to recognize. If they're sent for we usually don't bother stopping them or if they come in with a guy and he makes a fuss. You can't tell a guy in a £100 a night room 'Your "girlfriend" is one of our regular guests'.

Recognizing the hooker type seemed to be based on processing stereotypes and it often took the form of treating every woman as guilty until proven innocent. Circulated among the security personnel of various hotels is a file of known prostitutes who had been stopped by them, with their photos, names (generally acknowledged as aliases) and physical characteristics. These security officers, often former members of the police force, claim that their previous training, experience and affiliation with others still in the force, make them wise to the characteristics of the prostitute. However, their instinct seems to me unsound at times: they would simply home in on any unattached young woman unless her outfit indicated wealth, in which case she was deferentially bypassed. While having coffee with the head of one hotel's security force, I witnessed his subordinates evicting two women while he casually pointed out two other women as high-class call girls but made no attempt whatsoever to have them removed.

In addition to being tolerant of those women whose clothes are considered fitting for an elegant hotel, being 'wise' to the undesirable type includes acceptance of those women and their representatives who have previously proved themselves to be co-operative team players. Girls whose past credentials indicate that they are not thieves, or whose affiliations are impeccable, are deferentially treated. Moreover, some security officers benefit financially from being tolerant – they accept money for being courteous to girls associated with certain clubs or they are awarded free membership at those clubs. One club owner told me of his cordial relationship with the manager of one large international hotel:

> One of my girls had been with a man at the X hotel and when she was coming out of the elevator on the way down two security guards stopped her and took her into their office. They took her money and made her screw them for free. When I heard about this I called up the manager who was vacationing in France and told him what his bastards had done. He was really apologetic and when he got back to London they were fired.

The convenient connection between taxi and minicab drivers, hotels and clubs is obvious. One evening I had scheduled a meeting with the hall porter of a London hotel. Shortly after I arrived he received a telephone call from a dinner club about the non-arrival of two Arab clients for whom he had placed a reservation for that evening. He became livid and loudly complained to me that some cabbie had probably redirected the men to a club from which the cabbie would benefit. He was extremely annoyed that he would lose his commission for sending the men to his particular club. In this example the cabbie and the hall porter were on opposing teams but both seemed to be playing according to the same rules. Although the prostitute is not the only person who benefits financially from this sort of set-up, she is seen to be the central figure.

The links between clubs and specific hotels are very evident in the practice of providing temporary memberships. Although certain establishments capitalize on the snob appeal of their exclusive membership, the eager tourist or would-be patron can often penetrate the membership-only club with the help of a solicitous hall-porter or hotel manager. Through their help I was able to gain entrance to a number of clubs and even to one which congratulates itself on restricting its membership to what it considers high society. Once again, by entering a network of 'the right people' the inaccessible becomes accessible. The mobility of club and hotel staff personnel also oils the wheels of these linked networks. For example, during my research I met a club manager who had previously managed two other clubs and acted as a public relations officer for a third, a hall porter who had free memberships in several exclusive membership clubs with normally high membership fees, bartenders in clubs who used to work in hotels and vice versa, hotel managers who rose through the ranks from menial positions in restaurant/lounge dining rooms and call girls who had started out as hotel gift-shop sales girls. This cross-fertilization of staff illustrates the informal structure of prostitution and its related activities.

The international call girl deliberately seeks out the best hotels because they are thought to house the most eligible men. A sub-group of my Smart Set category consists of nine international call girls who seem to know each other quite well, and one of my women contacts referred to this group as the 'international white trash'. To ask these women 'where have you been hiding yourself?' elicits a response that sounds like a travel brochure for a round-the-world trip. It is part of these women's professional routine to gain access to the best hotels, if not as paying guests, then through the good graces of the hotel staff. Although I did not have the chance to observe their dealings with hotel staff in other countries, they have acquired remarkably amiable relationships with certain staff in four-star hotels in London. One respondent regularly drapes herself decoratively alongside the pool of one hotel although she is not a resident there. She did this because she said the number of single men staying at the hotel was far greater than the number of single women.

The women tend to seek out large international-chain hotels rather than those establishments which may be grander, but are thought largely to accommodate dowagers up from the country, debutantes with their mothers on shopping sprees and 'hooray Henry' types likely to be too slow and dull to suit their purposes. Although my respondents have their regulars in each city in their particular circuit – San Francisco–Los Angeles –New York–London–Paris–Rome–Switzerland–Marbella–the United Arab Emirates – and so on, with variable routes between cities and top resort spots, there is a sense of urgency about making the trip financially profitable. Their tour package and the hotels they select are scheduled with an eye to attaching themselves to a man in the shortest amount of time possible. Escort agencies or individual madames who regularly provide a planeload full of girls and/or assorted entertainers, not unnaturally have the idea that the women should arrive in style – at the man's expense – on the basis that if you believe you pay for what you get, the higher the cost of the commodity, the more it will be prized and evaluated as something to be treasured.

The intrinsic value of a commodity is as nothing compared to its ostentatious exterior. The symbolic value of the hotel, or of the women, lies not only in the service that she or it provides. To paraphrase Gertrude Stein, 'A girl is a girl is a girl', the significant difference between an £8 streetwalker and the £1000 call girl is in the 'packaging' of the commodity. It is the difference between shopping at Harrods and shopping at the local high street store. You pay for the privilege of spending money in luxurious surroundings and not solely for the quality of the goods themselves. The items you buy may fulfil similar functions but there is a snobbery affixed to selecting a fashionable label and doing it among people who can afford to indulge themselves in the same way. The men are catered for by women who, among an assortment of objects of conspicuous consumption, have become commodities themselves.

In Michael Thompson's *Rubbish Theory: the Creation and Destruction of Value* it is argued that what people discard and retain is an indirect way of presenting their status to others. If a man pays his female companion £1000 it is not simply a sign of his gullibility or her worth, it is equally a hidden form of conspicuous consumption showing that he can afford to be parted from his money any way he wishes.

In his *Prostitutes: Portraits of People in the Sexploitation Business* Jeremy Sandford calls businesses which pander to titillation – pornography, strip clubs, hostess clubs and so on – 'sexploitation' businesses and provides clear evidence of the drift of women into prostitution because of their job situation. He gives one example of a club hostess who nonchalantly discusses how a club patron came to keep her for several months and took her on holidays, and how prostitution was therefore indirectly encouraged by her professional role.

The very presence of people in certain situations may in itself lead to conclusions being drawn about what type of person they are and their receptivity to being propositioned. The brothel is, of course, the primary example but there are other places where you would not expect to find the stereotypical pure and innocent maiden. Men who would not as a rule ask their 'dates' to sleep with them for cash may feel little reticence about approaching a club hostess with the same request. An escort may be hired from an agency with a knowing leer in the expectation that the woman is a prostitute. In this way, there is an occupational drift into prostitution which may be recognized by the woman when she enters the role of club hostess or escort, but may also be reinforced by the expectations of clients and become a self-fulfilling prophecy.

The patterns of recruitment and the role prerequisites for hostesses and escorts underline the importance of the woman forming a network with others. Unlike the TV horror stories where the young innocent becomes ensnared by a villainous pimp who commandeers her salary and beats her daily, the hostess and the escort tend to enter their profession independently, or on the suggestion of a female friend already involved in the profession, as an easy way to earn some money. Whether or not escort agencies are basically mobile brothels, they are in the type of business which does not appear to suffer from the vagaries of the economic climate, and does not practise the 'closed shop' hiring policy. Advertisements for 'young attractive woman' are frequently displayed by escort agencies and you can always find advertisements reading 'hostess required' in the employment section of London newspapers. The reasons women give for entering such professions include: to earn money in a profession which requires little in the way of formal job training or experience other than good looks and a nice figure; to meet men of a 'better class' who can afford the cost of the club or agency; for excitement, that is, the chance to mingle with people who have a large amount of money; to cross the class-system and to better themselves by affiliation; to pursue an occupation which is thought not to be 'boring' or over-taxing and possibly to form friendships with others who are thought desirable as friends.

In Arabella Jedburgh's article 'High-Class Hostesses' (in Jeremy Sandford's *Prostitutes*), one such suggested how her role can lead not only to prostitution, but to the 'kept' relationship:

> . . . After about a month you might be going away together (the hostess and the john) on holiday to Majorca or somewhere like that and then if they get on well it's all, you know, 'I know you've got lots of money but I really do love you anyway. It's not the money.' And that is probably true and untrue. The answer is probably something to do with not being able to see the woods for the trees. Anyway, this particular girl I'm thinking of didn't marry him, but she did get a car out of it. An E-type.

Jedburgh suggests that the hostess who can earn £1000 for a couple of weeks' work being 'kept', is not likely to question whether such behaviour is desirable. For the woman in my Smart Set category who entered the kept relationship for material gain, the term promiscuity was reserved for women who gave it (sex) away. For the single evening the standard price range of the girls I interviewed ranged from £175 to £400. The highest price I heard of was £1000 and while the women may have upped their salary scale to impress me, because a higher price confers higher status, prices were consistently in the range of £200 to £400 and were corroborated by those who were in the know. The single girl who is successful can make a lot of money although the girl who is not 'kept' may have heavy overhead costs – clothing, tipping to attract attention, kickbacks to cabbies and club personnel, club membership fees (though these are often waived when and if the club recognizes an individual girl's drawing-power and her ability to attract a man who would be good for it).

Despite the large fees many of my respondents command, they rarely seem to have enough money to satisfy their needs. While their complaints may be part of the standard dialogue used to seek the financial sponsorship of male patrons, these women are often tremendous spendthrifts and act as if the money was burning a hole in their pockets. Much of their money is spent on flashy purchases – the zippy sports car, gold jewellery, and mountains of clothes. Knowingly or not, they subscribe to Oscar Wilde's dictum: 'Take care of the luxuries and the necessities will take care of themselves.' By and large, these girls tend to buy on impulse. One afternoon in London, after I had met one of these women for coffee, within three hours she had spent approximately £150 by wandering vaguely into shops and selecting several items. She started at Bond Street and drifted into one shop after the other, acquiring something at each. None of the purchases she made was very costly but the total soon added up. It was the sort of regular spending spree that encourages bankruptcy. Similarly, since these women tend to be label-conscious, a hair-cut and perm would often cost in the region of £100 for it is important that it be seen to be done at the very best Mayfair salon, where prices are correspondingly high. As a result, it becomes a necessity for the woman to continue with her professional role; her occupation and her lifestyle are mutually supportive.

In her occupational setting, the woman may be encouraged to continue in her unconventional profession. The intimate network provides reinforcement by offering support to the individual despite her sometimes discreditable pursuits. The idea that 'We'll stand behind you (no matter what)' serves not only to reaffirm the person's acceptance as a valuable member of the social group but to suggest that perhaps her behaviour is not really quite as blameworthy as she might originally have thought. If others accept her behaviour and are engaged in similar activities, then she may come to see her own behaviour as normal rather than exceptional. If 'everybody's doing it' then nobody's crazy, and neither is she. People such as the escort-agency operator and the club manager are wise to the woman's activities and supportive of her. As they may well benefit financially from her activities, and thus be disposed to view her role favourably and extend support to her, the woman profits from these complaisant contacts, and she feels comfortable just being herself with them. If you can't con a con there is no need for pretence.

The manager of an escort agency treats negotiations for an escort as a straightforward business deal. A man who is uncomfortable about being a 'john' can feel more at ease by thinking of himself as a sober businessman selecting a product for its quality – blonde, brunette, black, white, tall or short. By disclaiming interest in what might go on during the date, the woman does not blatantly have to identify herself as a prostitute. One of the managers I interviewed said that the day after one of his escorts had a date he telephoned and asked the escort 'Did everything go all right?' He did not wish to know the details of what took place. If the reality was taken for granted, not knowing the facts provided a safety valve whereby he could deny culpability for the behaviour of his escorts. His role, however, lends support to the acts of both the escort and the patron. The operation of such businesses makes it clear that both supply and demand exist and as the product is formally requested and provided, the unconventional nature of the transaction is glossed over.

One respondent, who manages an escort agency which has over three times as many homosexual male escorts as heterosexual female ones told me:

> The meeting is kept totally confidential. If the man wants, I'll go with him to — [restaurant] and introduce them myself. The boy doesn't even have to know the customer's surname if he doesn't wish to give it. I'd say that 75 per cent of our customers are regulars and the rest tourists who want a girl for the evening. We have boys throughout England and Scotland, a few in Wales. [*How do you find your escorts?*] Some just come in off the street, others see our ad in the gay newspapers or the entertainment guides. We ask them to come in and give us a picture, a large recent one preferably.
>
> [*What are the qualities of a good escort?*] They're attractive of course and they don't ask a lot of questions. I'll have girls come in and lots will be real scrubbers that I know no one will ever book anyway and they're the ones who will ask a million questions: 'What do I have to do?'; 'How much do I get?'. . . You accept their pictures but when no one asks for them anyhow, you just take it out of the book. The professional knows how to dress. Of course it doesn't matter if the client is just by himself but if they're out for dinner, you want the escort to be dressed conservatively but well.
>
> I call after a date and ask 'Did everything go all right?' All I want is a 'yes' or 'no'. On the employment form you saw that the contract is only for a date. That's why we get the fee first and they pay the escort on their own. Once we introduce them, we don't get involved. We tell our escorts that they're not supposed to get in touch with them (the patrons) again on their own but I know this happens quite often. We protect both the man and our escort. If anything goes wrong we're here. So far it's never happened.

The terms of contract for this agency were that the man paid the agency separately for the introduction and then 'tipped' the escort as he saw fit. The particular agency fee was between £30 and £40 for the introduction alone and it was suggested that the escort was to receive considerably more than this, depending on whether the man liked her, and if she spent money travelling a long distance and so on. If convivial wining and dining were on the agenda, it was supposed to compensate somewhat for any inconveniences that had to be reimbursed. Nevertheless, the attitude of the agency was that a good company stands behind its products. While the manager professed himself uninterested in what went on during the date itself, he acted in a manner similar to that of a solicitous sales assistant, trying to assess the needs or desires of the client in making a purchase. He recommended certain girls or men to patrons as especially warm and friendly and dispassionately asked the man if there was anything special he was looking for in his selection of an escort.

The club manager similarly can be identified as a professional intermediary whose role supports, and is supported by, the success of his hostesses in accommodating patrons. The interdependence between a successfully operating club and the effectiveness of its hostesses was attested to in one owner's comment that 'You can't run a club without girls.' At this particular club the owner-manager stated that the girls were not affiliated to him and he only tolerated them; 'As long as the girls play fair with me I play fair with them.' However, despite his comment that he was fundamentally uninterested in the activities of the girls in his club he admonished one of his women for failing to appear the previous night. He asked her where she had been and she smiled and said 'fucking'. While she had not been at his club, she had still been at work.

It was harder to interview a club call girl or hostess when the manager or owner was present because he often tried to take over the interview by prompting the girl or asking leading questions of her, such as 'I don't take your money, do I?', 'I've helped you out, haven't I?', 'You were hooking before you came to work for me, weren't you?'. The girls were guarded when the owner was around and while they could not refuse his prodding questions one woman later told me that she had resented being put on display so that the club owner could feel grand. The woman, however, did not refuse to be interviewed when the man summoned her and this suggests that she was dependent on him to an extent and anxious to retain favour with him.

The greatest benefit of my being in the good graces of the manager, or interviewing such women with the consent of the club, was making contact with the woman and being able to arrange for a second interview outside the club. However, there was ample evidence of the business relationship between the manager and the hostesses he employed, the women he allowed to decorate his lounge. The woman is considered as just another salaried performer on his staff whose function is to contribute to the smooth running and success of his business. Like any other employee, she may be fired if she is thought to be inefficient or unco-operative. If she has misgivings about her role, she must swallow them or leave. She is expected to order an expensive bottle of alcohol when seated with a customer or order an expensive drink which the man would then pay for (even if she only received soda or tonic water when she ordered champagne or gin). She must encourage the man to spend his money as freely as possible. This game was played with especial enthusiasm when tourists and out-of-towners visited the club. These men are regarded as prime candidates for being conned. It is generally believed that tourists have large amounts of money to spend or can chalk it up to entertaining or travelling expenses. Additionally, even if the man comes to realize he is being played for a sucker and proceeded to create a fuss, he would most probably be leaving the country very soon. The tourist is thought unlikely to press criminal charges against the club and involve himself in a court case or lawsuit. Moreover, the transient visitor was unlikely to do any damage to the club by making known his bad experiences there because it would show his friends how stupid he had been. The staff think that men who patronize their clubs are simply asking to be conned.

When the women call a man a punter it means they think of him as someone who deserves to be conned. The man who makes the mistake of thinking the club girl is running a charitable service when he propositions her may get a surprise when she quotes her price. It would be insulting and fruitless to suggest to the professional that she engage in free sex with a punter. A woman who fails to con a punter would be thought a greater fool than he. To 'give it away' would cause the woman to lose status among her workmates. If she can justify not demanding payment immediately in the belief that she will get more later they might give her the benefit of the doubt; but to refuse payment or not demand it would be considered a bad business tactic. Moreover, while the woman may find it acceptable to have sex with a man for payment, to have sex with a man for whom she feels little attraction, and without money, would be degrading. It could also be that not to offer payment is to fail to acknowledge the woman's professional status, and so make her feel affronted. The punter is a figure of fun, a man who is not really respected by the staff of the club. If the woman prides herself on her ability to engineer profitable encounters or relationships, it would be self-demeaning and ultimately self-defeating for her to empathize or feel sorry for the man. It would interfere with her performance in her work-role, and would also mark her as a loser, someone who is too stupid and soft-hearted for her own good.

Although the party girl and the professional prostitute may know many of the same people, attend the same parties and exchange roles at various times there is some difference between the way they represent themselves and their role image. The difference is easily explained by using the anaology of bacon and eggs, where the chicken is involved, but the pig is committed. When the 'involved' party girl becomes a prostitute or frequently subsidizes herself through prostitution, she becomes 'committed'and no longer looks upon her behaviour as simply having fun. What was a pleasant lifestyle has become an occupation, something that is engaged in not for the pleasure of the moment but in anticipation of something else. There is total commitment rather than a limited involvement. Women tend to become more cynical as they participate in a greater number of kept relationships or become more committed to prostitution as an occupation. The 'whore with a heart of gold' would appear to be an invention of the novelist for the process of 'burn out' does not refer solely to physical wear and tear. The woman tends to become jaded and more likely to define her goals within her relationship or in any anticipated relationship in either pragmatic or rather fantastic terms. One of my respondents described her ideal man as a cross between J. Paul Getty, Robert Redford and Dr Kildare. With this vision of the ideal man hovering in front of her, she justified her many relationships as passing time before he appeared. She was 'involved' with the man, but 'committed' to being kept.

There are several similarities between women in the Smart Set and Opportunist categories. Both are more enamoured of the lifestyle that goes with being kept than of any particular man, and both tend to have a large number of past relationships and the expectation of more in the future. There are also several noteworthy differences. First, the link with prostitution tends to be much clearer in the Smart Set category, where prostitution is more often taken up as a bridging role between men than it is in the Opportunist category. Secondly, the lifestyle of the Smart Set women tends to be characterized by frantic socializing. If I scheduled an interview with a woman in the Smart Set, I could give myself 50:50 odds that she would not show up, for various reasons ranging from her flying off to the continent with someone who had decided it was an opportune time for a holiday to her simply not realizing what day it was. In contrast, the Opportunist tends to have a more stable lifestyle, since she maintains a longer relationship with her lover and her position is relatively more secure. Third, the women in the Smart Set who have this frenetic social life are much younger than the women in the Opportunist category. All of my Smart Set respondents were under 30, and over half of them under 20, whereas most of the Opportunists were in the 30 to 39 age bracket. Fourth, women in the Smart Set have more liberated attitudes towards sex than is the case in the Opportunist category. Smart Set women use the supposed existence of the sexual revolution to argue that their behaviour is not disreputable but rather the norm. In contrast, the Opportunist would play down the image of herself as a woman who participates in sexual relationships for profit, preferring to concentrate on those refinements of conduct which, she supposes, make her way of life acceptable, even enviable. One woman, for example, stressed that she always had fresh, real linen sheets between lovers. Such details seem to mean a lot to women in the Opportunist category, while for women in the Smart Set, such distinctions are somewhat superfluous. Nevertheless, one category can lead to another.

Chapter Five
'SUGAR DADDIES'

It's gratifying sexually but I would never marry her. She'd just never fit in. I rather think a man will do things with his mistress that he wouldn't do with his wife, but then I'm from another generation which tended to pedestal the wife and mother. I've no experience with call girls or prostitutes but I expect the same exists. (*49-year-old man, London*)

There is an assumption that the kept relationship is a contractual scheme which guarantees the man the sexual favours of a woman he finds attractive in a setting which he finds agreeable. The motivation for his adoption of the role of patron or 'Sugar Daddy' is thought to be strictly sexual and the man becomes an anonymous figure whose role is presumed to be interchangeable with other men who pay a prostitute for sex. Studies of prostitution are curiously lacking in any serious analysis of the male role. The implicit assumption is since men have a higher sex-drive than women, when paired with a sexually unresponsive wife or denied a regular sexual partner, they will turn to a prostitute as a palliative for sexual frustration. If the sex drive is beyond a man's control because of his innate physiological imbalance, can he bear much blame for the behaviour which results? Men are forgiven their sexual adventures when they are deemed to be driven by a biological force beyond their rational control. The drive-reduction theory of rape (that is, that by raping his victim the man is relieved of his overwhelming sexual urge) depends on the idea that the male is unable to control his sexual drive. The woman is thought to court aggression if she dresses provocatively or hitch-hikes after dusk. Her complicity in arousing the male is salient in determining whether or not the male's act can be excused or made understandable.

My Secret Life by 'Walter', written in about 1882, is the anonymous autobiography of a man who regarded his obsessive quest for sexual adventure as a sign of a natural and laudable voluptuousness. Pausing in his adventures only long enough to recover from his latest bout of venereal disease, 'Walter' proceeds to document his sexual adventures with some 1500 girls and women and rather smugly reports:

> I have tasted the sexual treasures of all these fair creatures . . . I have sought abroad variety in races and breeds . . . They may differ in face, form and colour, but their endearments, tricks and vices are nearly the same, yet I found great charm in the variety, and always voluptuous delight in offering the homage of my priapus to a woman of a type or nationality unknown to me.

Seducing pre-adolescents, aged house servants, prostitutes and friends' mistresses, 'Walter' embarks on a mission to experience sexual variety. His marriage is mentioned only obliquely but with considerable acrimony:

> There was that about me now which brought sorrow over to me. The instant that I saw her, she checked my smile, sneered at my past, moaned over my future, was a nightmare to me, a very spectre. I tried to like, to love her. It was impossible. Hateful in day, she was loathsome to me in bed. Long I strove to do my duty, and be faithful . . . I, loving women and naturally kind and affectionate to them, ready to be kind and loving to her, was driven to avoid her as I would a corpse.

Having a wife who is anathema to him, Walter's natural voluptuousness finds recourse in extramarital sex. He fights against his sex drive, seeks 'relief from misery' in reminiscences of times past, but finally seeks out a prostitute and sobs with relief at 'the entrancement of the carnal pleasure'.

My Secret Life is not simply erotica. Such works bear latent testimony to society's belief in a natural order of sexuality. Although the sex drive was a source of alarm to moral reformers in the nineteenth century, only to be glorified in the twentieth as a self-ennobling liberator, both points of view set it apart from individual control, so that sexuality becomes intrinsically distinct from the responsible self.

Although the importance of sex in the kept relationship is not to be ignored, it is not the be-all and end-all of the relationship. It is important to note that a mistress does not exist merely for coitus. If the relationship is seen as solely sexual, this would fail to account for the relationship which is consummated infrequently if at all. When asked about the sexual side of his relationship, one man laconically remarked, 'If I didn't have to use the toilet I wouldn't know that I had one.' The importance of sex varies greatly, from sex as it would be in marriage to sex in a 'one-night stand'. The French term *'cinq à sept'* is an accepted reference to the supposed daily time – from five to seven in the evening – spent with a mistress but the kept relationship in the British and North American context excludes any idea of circumscribed times. Although one of my kept women contacts has met her lover every lunchtime for the past 26 years, others meet only occasionally or at sporadic intervals. In one instance, a relationship which has lasted for over 12 years consists of weekends four times a year at a London hotel. For the annual eight days spent together, the man, presently in his early sixties, travels from Hertfordshire to London and supports his lover at a cost of roughly £20,000 per year. Even if you suppose that the man's mistress is superlative in bed, this does not explain why a man, wealthy or not, seeks to establish a relationship with a mistress rather than with a prostitute or enthusiastic amateur every time he feels the need for sexual variety. The kept relationship therefore cannot be explained as strictly sexual.

One of the earliest differences I noted between male and female representations of relationships was in the importance attached to it as a 'sexual' liaison. Men are much more likely to claim that their appeal to their partner is personal virility while women tend to play down the sexual side of the relationship. Moreover, men tend to portray the extramarital affair or fling as simply the result of being naturally more lascivious than women. This may be not so much a result of real biological differences as an adherence to conventional male and female sexual roles wherein the man is typecast as a virile 'he-man' while sexual voraciousness in women is discouraged as unseemly. Just as male and female attitudes to sexuality are not identical, so claims to sexual activity also differ.

In one of my cases, the man took especial pains to emphasize that he was a great lover. He went on and on about his inordinate sexual capacity, anatomical dimensions, propositioned me and became hostile and offensive when I tried to ask him about any facet of his relationship which was non-sexual. This view of sexual fun and gaaes was utterly discordant with his mistress's presentation of the relationship as a love affair. It may be that neither the man nor his mistress was deliberately misrepresenting the nature of the relationship but simply that there was little overlap in what they privately felt to be its *raison d'être*. It may also be that the sexual behaviour society encourages us to exhibit reinforces the presentation of relationships in this way. So men are encouraged breezily to portray them as a manifestation of sexual appetite or, as one man termed it, 'the ongoing leg-over situation' and women as *Sturm und Drang* – a romance of storm and stress.

In Thomas S. Szasz's *Sex: Facts, Frauds and Follies*, the author argues that the work of Masters and Johnson, the noted 'sex researchers', though it purports to be scientific can be seen to have moral or religious overtones. An underlying morality suggests that the sexually active are not only the most desirable but also the most conscientious. Sex becomes a duty instead of a right or desire. The elect in the secular religion of performance sex are heterosexual and seek to maintain or deliberately cultivate their sex appeal. The aesthetically unpleasing, the unsexy and the sexually uninterested are cast out.

While the theorists of respectable sexuality base their model on biology and the superimposition of the Bible's tenets ('And he shall take a wife in her virginity'. . . 'Thou shalt not commit adultery') the religion of contortionist sex adopts the epistles of the sex manuals. Charts which set out 'appropriate' age/sex schedules for intercourse seek to establish a scientifically based 'natural order' of sexuality. Given that X percentage admit to behaviour Y, deviance is rated by a majority statistic. The creed of the new sexuality nullifies the ideal of marital fidelity and making love, replacing it with the importance of having a good sex life. Sex appeal becomes a commodity, marketed, packaged and saleable to those with the resources of money, time and the combination of a good plastic surgeon and health spa.

Although feminists may bemoan the double standard as a psychologically repressive force which makes women deny their sexuality, the freedom of men to do as they please may also be curtailed by the injunction on them to prove their masculinity by being promiscuous. If the adult female virgin is a supposedly rare species, you would expect the adult male virgin to qualify for his own glass case at the Natural History Museum. For the 'real' man, sexual activity is the essential norm and sexual prowess becomes a technical skill. The proliferation of sex manuals from ancient to modern times similarly extols a course of sexual acrobatics. From *The Jade Door* and the *Kama Sutra* to *The Joy of Sex* and beyond, sexual technique is championed. While 'Walter's' *My Secret Life* discusses sexual desire and intercourse as personal inclination and preference, *The Sensuous Man* by 'M' reads like an Emily Post manual on sexual protocol. Its format resembles the step-by-step instructions given in a mail-order dancing course, suggesting that by putting your hands and feet in marked-out sequences, you can become the Fred Astaire of the bedroom. Sexual technique becomes a deadly serious concern insofar as real men are supposed to be knowledgeable and competent in the mechanics of love-making. The Letters to the Editor column of *Penthouse* magazine reads like pure pornography but suggests that the 'ordinary' male student, plumber, window-cleaner, dentist can have a riotous sex life so-what's-wrong-with-you? In male fantasies of contortionist sex, 'masculinity' is calculated by assessing how often and how well he performs. If men are thought to have affairs because they have a high sex-drive, the result could be that men themselves will find ego-gratifying support for their behaviour in the belief that it proves their true masculinity.

An example of how an individual may find ways of justifying his actions by looking at how they improve his image of himself is seen in the varying interpretations of the term Sugar Daddy itself. Sugar Daddy is an idiom popularly used to describe a man who supports a generally younger woman in an extramarital or non-marital relationship. Eric Partridge's *A Dictionary of the Underworld* defines a Sugar Daddy as:

> . . . a fatuous, elderly man supporting, or contributing to the support of a 'gold digger' or other loose girl or woman . . . perhaps common until circa 1925 and then slang, but probably always slang.

When the term was used by people I interviewed, it was sometimes part of a deprecating description of the male by the woman. It was also used by outsiders to the relationship such as hotel staff, club personnel, knowing friends and others who viewed the role with a mixture of amusement and incredulity. It expressed disbelief that the male could allow himself to be conned or exploited by the woman involved. When a man identified himself as a Sugar Daddy, however, it was with jocularity and it became apparent that he did not use it of himself in at all an unfavourable or self-demeaning way. While others may find the man's liaison unseemly or embarrassing and employ the term pejoratively, the man himself may welcome being called a Sugar Daddy. It often appeared to support his idea of himself as a sport, cutting a dashing figure, a ladies' man. Even when the term 'tin soldier' is used synonymously with Sugar Daddy by some women to suggest a man who dances attendance on their whims and acts as a general 'dogsbody', the man for his part will still see himself as the dominant figure in the relationship. Supporting the woman does not mean that the man will regard himself as less of a man. As Virginia Woolf wrote, 'Money dignifies what is frivolous if unpaid for.' Thus, men stress that they do not buy their lover but follow their honourable instincts by assuming financial responsibility for her.

The idea that the fatuous, elderly male is especially susceptible to the calculating caprices of a manipulative gold digger reappears in the notion of the male menopause. This refers to a supposed mid-life crisis in males which is marked by sexual anxiety, morbid concern with the diminution of physical attraction and mental depression. 'Agony Aunts' blame the male menopause for middle-aged men having affairs, dyeing their hair, taking up hang-gliding and/or investing in chest-hair wigs. As a quasi-medical term, the male menopause serves as an umbrella term to cover a variety of behaviour which can then be seen as no more than a collection of quirks. It also stresses the involuntary nature of the behaviour for which the man, who is the victim of his physiology, is blameless.

A review of the literature on the male menopause makes it apparent that the May/December romance has been considered a symptom of the condition ever since the inception of the term. *The Climacteric: The Critical Age*, the 1929 work of the gynaecologist Gregorio Marañón, is representative of others underwritten with dogmatic loyalty to the model of respectable sexuality. Marañón, a firm champion of male dominance, saw the man involved with a younger woman as one who courted disaster. He warns the older man that he will be unable to keep up with the sexual demands of a younger woman and will be mortified by his sexual failures. The man's situation will also cause chagrin for other men as they watch him become what Marañón called 'a slave of the woman' of whom he is enamoured in his state of social and sexual disequilibrium. Forewarned that no normal man would willingly accept a state of subservience, the reader is exhorted to adjust to the sexual neutrality of advancing age by a course of serious exercise, the pursuit of an innocuous hobby such as philately or golf, and most importantly, spiritual contemplation. The ideal is to grow old with tranquillity, unruffled by bestial impulses.

Some of the men I interviewed justify their behaviour on the ground that their wives had lost interest in sex since experiencing the change of life. It was not a criticism but rather a statement used by these men to furnish their wives with an understandable excuse for lack of sexual interest. Paradoxically, they certainly do not define middle-age as a period of asexuality for themselves. The affair itself is used as a denial of this. Even when the men's mistresses and friends privately ridicule them as suffering from the menopause, they see the affair as disproving the presence of the condition. The relationship is thought to deter others from thinking them past it or no longer sexually active. The idea of being sexually active, being man enough to satisfy both women – wife and mistress – economically and sexually, appears to be important. It was clear that they equate 'masculinity' with virility and the relationship is believed to attest to their personal virility and sexual desirability.

My women respondents for their part do not always support their lover's claims to an inordinate or insatiable sex-drive. Moreover, women who are dispassionate about the nature of their involvement with the man, regarding the relationship not as a love affair but as a fling or an activity undertaken strictly for self-gain, often invoked the male menopause to account for the man's behaviour:

> He was going through a mid-life crisis and wanted a young girl so that he'd feel he's not past it. Men around 50 start to worry that their life is over and get scared that they're in a rut and can't get out . . . Going with a young girl makes a guy feel younger . . . he'll start looking after himself, doing exercises, dressing better so that he'll look good to his girlfriend . . . it's probably the first time in years any woman is looking at him so he'll make the effort. (*28-year-old woman, San Diego*)

> I rather got the impression that he was a good husband but he was going through a middle-aged problem. (*43-year-old woman, London – referring to her first kept relationship some 20 years earlier*)

There is a certain pathos in a situation where men describe themselves as Don Juans while their partners privately describe them as suffering from the menopause. However, while the phrase male menopause may seem innocuous enough, there is an admitted danger that its application will define the man's behaviour as out of his control. The popular press often describes the May/December romance with faintly concealed mirth, suggesting that the man is something of a bemused figure of fun and the affair self-destructive.

Any theory which seeks to answer conclusively why people enter kept relationships will create caricatures. For example, Lewis Yablonsky, in his book on extra-marital affairs called *The Extra Sex Factor: Why Over Half of America's Men Play Around* attempts armchair psychoanalysis with his 'supermomma launching pad' syndrome. He puts forward the idea that some men have affairs because they marry women who resemble their mothers and since 'no self-respecting son of a supermomma is really a good boy' the extramarital affair is therefore an act of rebellion against their mothers. When the question of why people form kept relationships is answered by theories of the menopause, ungovernable sexual desires or *post hoc* psychoanalytic explanations, the individual is seen as the victim of his physiology.

Although the majority of the men I interviewed were aged between 45 and 60, the positive correlation between maturer age in men and the keeping of a mistress could be spurious. The association between age and the attainment of wealth and/or positions of power may be more significant.

In 1952 C. Wright Mills discussed the chief executives in America in his work *The Power Elite*. He found that only two and a half per cent were under 60 years of age. More recently (1981) John Fidler's *The British Business Elite* revealed that the average age of the men was 56 and that 60 per cent of their ages fell within six years of this age. What stops people from having affairs is not merely antipathy to the idea or lack of desire, but lack of opportunity – and the wherewithal – to do so. Moreover, personal 'desire' is not exclusively sexual. Keeping a mistress provides the man not only with a sexual partner but a social prop as well.

Keeping a woman can be likened to possessing a status-trapping such as a second car or holiday home. Like them, the kept woman becomes a disposable commodity designed to impress. Above all, keeping a woman signifies a standard of wealth and power great enough to bring interested women into the man's circle of acquaintances. That King Solomon had many wives was thought to show how rich and powerful he was, not merely his sexual appetite. It may be that the ability of a man to attract women is in itself important and not simply the sexual act *per se*.

In a study made in 1976 by the psychologists D. Bar-Tal and L. Saxe, students were asked to give their impressions of attractive and unattractive persons after looking at slides in which the man and woman were depicted as a married couple. Their findings showed that a man paired with an attractive woman vicariously acquired desirable characteristics. An unattractive man paired with an attractive spouse was judged as likely to have the highest income and professional status. They termed this effect 'radiating beauty'. If men can acquire socially desirable qualities by affiliation, binding themselves to an attractive woman may be a technique whereby they attempt to persuade other people to make a favourable evaluation of them.

Phrases identifying the woman as a 'feather in his cap' or a 'rose in his lapel' suggest that she can be a decorative adornment. If the concept of 'radiating beauty' is accurate, it suggests that a man may be judged a 'better man' for his association with a beautiful woman. The attempt to create a positive impression in this manner is suggested in the following gossip story about a popular singer which appeared in the London *Standard* in 1982:

> Is [Mr X] really the great bird-puller he'd like us to believe he is? I have discovered that this crooner's obsession for being surrounded by beautiful women has led his record company [Y] to extraordinary lengths to round up luscious ladies. Last week, while [X] was in London to play the Albert Hall, [Y] telephoned top model agencies asking for girls to escort him. Naturally, the record company are reluctant to admit this and thereby dent [X's great] . . . lover image.

The psychologist Hans Zetterberg's concept of 'secret ranking' is constructed along similar lines. Secret ranking is a somewhat amorphous concept in which an individual's erotic ranking is defined as 'the secretly kept probability that he can induce an emotional overcomeness among persons of the opposite sex'. Zetterberg suggests that erotic ranking is only partially based on visible attractiveness; it is not precisely a theory of sex appeal as used to describe the allure of the aesthetically beautiful. He suggests that an unattractive man could have as high an erotic ranking as a top film star. Thus, a wealthy or successful man who is only marginally better-looking than a gorilla need not be rebuffed by a beautiful woman. Basically, Zetterberg's theory is one of matching or similarity. It justifies the attribution of desirable qualities to a man who is paired with an attractive woman (as forwarded in the theory of 'radiating beauty'). It presumes that partners in a relationship will be of a similar status or erotic ranking and that some subtle evaluation of suitability has been made.

If both these concepts appear rather tenuous, my own examples elaborate on how the kept woman can serve as a social prop, a variation on the need that drives adolescent boys to seek sexual partners in order to boast of their success to their peers. This locker-room mentality is similarly demonstrated by those who are somewhat older. Adult males appeared to think that their friends (and myself as interviewer) would find it remarkable and awe-inspiring to hear how many times they had made love the previous night or the sum total of women they had slept with. At times, my interview discussions with a group of men sounded like a sports commentator interviewing athletes on their track records after a competition. Their anecdotes tended to be quasi-pornographic, only mildly entertaining and thoroughly anaesthetizing. The most original attitude came from a man who compared himself to vintage wine. This man, in his mid-sixties, stated that sexual desirability in men improved, like wine, with age. He argued that the potency of a wine of a good vintage made the quality rather than the quantity the aspect that was important. Aside from this analogy, comments from other men followed a formula which stressed personal ability, the ravishing beauty of the women they had been involved with (models were apparently beating down their doors) and so on. One man proudly told me that his mistress had been the former lover of a black singer. When I stated that I was unfamiliar with the singer and asked what type of songs he sang, the man got rather irritated, abruptly informing me that I was missing the point, which was that he could satisfy a woman as well as a black man could. He said that his mistress had been involved with the singer simply because he was so great in bed but now she was completely bowled over with his own remarkable capabilities. Men would also proudly point out that their lover had been the girlfriend of so-and-so and/or that their own previous lover was now Mr Famous Person's girlfriend or his wife. Sometimes involvement in a kept relationship and the status of the woman would serve as a way of keeping up with the Joneses.

Another way in which the kept woman can act as a social prop is shown by the man's attempt to make her a walking advertisement for his wealth by wearing the luxuries he can afford to lavish on her. Within groups, especially in Middle-Eastern circles, I came across many men making energetic efforts to outdo each other. One woman would be given a ring; suddenly bigger and more garish rings would be given to others until someone had the originality to produce a new type of gift. One woman was given a Cartier watch but this was speedily replaced with a Rolex. The reason for the rapid substitution, she informed me, was that her lover had been told that Cartiers were *passé*. Incidentally, since the Rolex – inlaid with diamonds – was one of a limited edition attempts to copy his choice of gift would be difficult. It is a case of bigger, better and more powerful *ad nauseam*. Similarly, selecting a car for your mistress is not affected by concern for efficient performance or petrol mileage. It is a pawn in the game of one-up-manship among the men themselves.

In their article 'Human Sexuality In A Cross-Cultural Perspective' in *The Bases of Human Sexual Attraction* P. Rosenblatt and R. Anderson state:

The role of gifts in sexual relationships may vary greatly from one society to another, but the apparent commonness of such gifts is intriguing. The gifts may be a symbol of male power, a sign that is common around the world to define male sexual need as somehow greater than female, or a symbol of relative control of goods cross-culturally (if males control more goods, they have more goods to give). Gifts may also indicate who is more actively involved, and the initiator of the relationship may feel the greater obligation to provide compensation.

It may also be that giving gifts enhances the giver in his own eyes, making him seem generous and considerate, and at least superficially able to afford it. The tendency is to see the kept woman as avaricious and the man supporting her as exploited; but a cat wearing a jewelled choker does no more than reflect glory on the owner, and the bestowing of gifts need not be seen as exploitation of the man. Such men pride themselves on their generosity and there is a subtle difference between others describing a gift as extravagant and the men themselves defining it as generous. The former suggests a superfluous expenditure, the latter a thoughtful gesture.

The role of the kept woman depends on the existence of a male partner who assumes financial support. It is the financial element that has often encouraged authors to link the role of the kept woman with that of the prostitute, but part of the etiquette of the Sugar Daddy role is based on the ability of the man to provide for his mistress, a more substantial undertaking than paying for occasional sexual favours. Just as a man may refrain from getting married until he feels financially able to do so, men in the kept relationship use criteria other than a pulsating libido when they think about keeping a mistress. One 56-year-old man wrote to me from San Francisco:

> Let me give you some suggestions about the conditions about keeping a woman, assuming that the man is married.
>
> 1 He, and preferably both, should live in a metropolitan area where discreetness is available, which it isn't in Little Rock or Paducah and where there is available a variety of things to do, such as opera, ballet, symphony, funky shops and good restaurants. In this, San Francisco is ideal.
>
> 2 The man must have discretionary income to spend without depriving his family of much of anything and for which he account to no one except the tax authorities.
>
> 3 The man must have available free time, particularly in the evenings, and frequently overnight.
>
> 4 The man's family must not be deprived of anything, including if possible, private schooling for his children, a good home, furnishings, clothing, interesting vacations, etc.

5 A non-possessive attitude: after all, he's not bought either his wife or his mistress (this is not advocacy for 'open marriages', but more on the side of the double standard). I know it sounds unfair, but who, in his or her right mind, should believe that the world is fair? Of course, things have changed with the Pill, but the old traditions, beliefs and shibboleths persist.

By stressing that they seek to ensure the comfort of both their families and their mistresses, gift-giving is not portrayed as extravagance leading to less expenditure on the family, but more of a praiseworthy ability to support two households simultaneously.

Comments made by my male respondents suggest that their behaviour is ruled by a code of conduct which allows them to conceive of it as honourable rather than otherwise. Although the concept of 'the gentleman' is fundamentally elitist in its origins, in a broader sense it can help to describe the etiquette of the Sugar Daddy role.

Although acting the perfect gentleman may be an antiquated ideal, gentlemanly conduct was an implicit concern of the men I interviewed. In its strictest sense the concept of the gentleman refers to a well-bred man and suggests that ancestry and pedigree are all-important to the determination of moral and social character. However, while Dr Johnson defined the gentleman as 'a man of ancestry . . . all other dimensions seem to be whimsical', since the time of Chaucer and his depiction of the 'very parfit gentle knight' and perhaps before, other qualities have been thought equally important. In *The Four Georges* Thackeray wrote:

What is it to be a gentleman? Is it to have lofty aims, to lead a pure life, to keep your honour virgin, to have the esteem of your fellow-citizens, and the love of your fireside; to bear good fortune meekly; to suffer evil with constancy; and through evil or good to maintain truth always . . . ?

If the answer to these questions is yes, there is an acknowledgment that the term stands for an ideal of social morality which need not be identical with social rank. A 'gentleman' then, has more than ancestry to recommend him; indeed, the man of noble birth whose conduct is boorish, irresponsible or without honour is no gentleman. Strictly on the basis of social rank, the men I interviewed could not, by and large, claim to be gentlemen. The majority of them were part of what can be termed the working leisure-class and unlike P.G. Wodehouse's mockery of the English gentleman, Bertie Wooster, they could not – or did not wish to – neglect gainful employment. If historically the term gentleman denotes a man of leisure, the men I interviewed, with the possible exception of the Arab aristocracy, do not appear as an idle elite. They wish to establish themselves as responsible. They stress that the affair is not financially debilitating to their families or socially an embarrassment. And, whether true or not, they maintain that their marriages are not adversely affected by their extra-marital relationships. One man rather pompously proclaimed that he had been 'happily married for 37 years' and did not seem to find any irony in going on to describe his present kept relationship of 15 years' standing or others he had had before. Commitment to marriage may not be the same thing as commitment to duty, and a man's idea of himself as a dutiful husband may be only partially based on conventional assumptions.

My contacts presented themselves as being good husbands and fathers primarily by drawing attention to their willingness and ability to provide financial support. They would point out what good schools their children were attending or had been enrolled in, the conveniences their wives had in terms of creature comforts, and tended to equate the trappings of wealth with symbols of family devotion. In satisfactorily fulfilling the role of provider it seemed as if they thought they had performed their family duties well. Similarly, having an affair was not construed as being a transgression inasmuch as it was considered irrelevant to, or not intrusive upon, their being a good husband or father. Occasionally a man would speak of the sacrifices he had made for his family and portray the affair as a compensatory self-indulgence.

The vernacular for the 'other woman' in an extramarital affair is the home-wrecker, conveying the idea that she exercises a catastrophic effect on the man's marriage. My research tends to challenge that assertion, however. Although the term brings to mind broken homes and disbanded marriages and suggests that the mistress acts as the catalyst to a divorce, academic studies have found that extramarital sex is not irreconcilable with a happy marriage and may paradoxically contribute to marital satisfaction.

The affair is not conducted solely to satisfy sexual needs, but for other desires which may be unfulfilled in the marital union. Even if a marriage has become an aching void there are reasons why men may remain married. Although keeping a woman may be an economic burden, my male contacts generally remarked that it made more economic sense than going through a divorce. Beyond the financial consideration, men spoke of wives threatening to alienate them from their children, for example by speaking disparagingly of them and restricting access. Since in the majority of custody cases, care and control of children if not jointly awarded is generally given to the mother, the great difference in the amount of time spent with the mother and the father is thought to expose the children more to interpretations of behaviour given by their mothers. Similarly, men with adult children thought a divorce could result in their offspring's ill-feeling towards them. One man felt his children would think of him as 'senile' were he to divorce and/or remarry. Another did not wish to divorce because he did not want his estate to be shared with his mistress (or potential new wife). In effect, there may be a division of labour between the wife and the mistress. While the extramarital affair may not promote marital bliss it may allow for the stability of the legal marriage. The unhappily married man need not divorce to allay his matrimonial discontent.

The Sugar Daddies tended to pride themselves on how well they treated women and tell me that they understood women and what women wanted or needed. Women, they suggested with monotonous regularity, needed to feel loved. When I asked them if this was really exclusively a feminine need rather than a human desire they would stress that, for example, a man would not particularly appreciate flowers but that women attach great significance to such gestures. When the men stated they understood what women needed, it often meant that they were acquainted with the uses of the props of love. In a way, the culture of romance allows for a certain amount of fraud since the flowers, perfume and glittering trinkets are seldom unique to a particular relationship. Although the tendency may be to keep emotions private, gestures of 'love' can become clichés of romance. There is no test to determine the truth of a statement or the sincerity of a gesture in a 'love affair' and if red roses are thought to signify love the cost of sending them is hardly a deterrent to the man feigning love. Many of my women respondents did, in fact, attach importance to loving gestures such as gifts, flowers, and being told 'I love you', but in spite of their automatic protestations to the contrary, men did as well.

The most marked example of the use of romantic gestures as artifice was illustrated by the behaviour of one couple I interviewed, each of whom privately professed emotional indifference to the other. The woman, a 19-year-old New Zealander, was convinced that her Arab lover truly loved her because he had bought her a £20,000 full-length fur coat. He was equally convinced that she 'loved' him because she tended to kiss and embrace him frequently and had once gone on a shopping spree and instead of buying something for herself, returned with a £90 jumper which she gave him as a gift. The gift of the jumper was, in fact, a ploy which the woman consciously used to convey the idea of concern for the man. The woman and one of her female friends told me rather proudly that they regularly employed this strategy on the assumption that everyone liked to receive a gift and the man would ignore the fact that it was bought with his own money. The strategy itself formed the basis of a private competition between the two women. They would buy gifts for their respective lovers and see whose gift would be the most generously appreciated. Apparently one good turn was thought to deserve another and the women themselves anticipated that their lovers would reciprocate in a 'thank you' gift. When I told the first woman's lover that I had seen the coat he gave her and thought it lovely, he made light of the cost and significance of his gift. He said that he could afford to be generous to a woman so obviously devoted to him but gave no support to the woman's idea that he loved her. It was simply presented as a sign of his largesse. In this situation and others, the symbols of romance and love were emotionally empty gestures.

If gift-giving is facilitated by wealth it is also an opportunity to display a sense of style. Given that style is connected to what is currently fashionable, stylistic differences may still be possible. Although the quality common to all my respondents was wealth or the access to it, I found extreme variations in the personal wealth of the men who kept women. To describe all the men simply as rich obscures the extreme variations possible, including differences in style. J. Paul Getty once remarked that no man is really rich who can count his money and Aristotle Onassis rather haughtily described a millionaire as a 'heavy borrower'. Networks among the rich exist and are differentiated. One man's comment to me that 'Out of every ten kept relationships, five are women keeping women, three are men keeping men and two are men keeping women' says little about the nature of the kept relationship in general circles but does suggest that his particular network is characterized by more homosexual than heterosexual liaisons.

It is difficult to give any precise information on the wealth of the men I interviewed for a variety of reasons. First, the currencies are not identical, and then certain men make use of their positions rather than their bank balances to provide for their mistresses. Access to company expense accounts, company flats and company cars may not constitute real income or personal wealth but still allows the man certain facilities for luxurious living. Second, the richer the man the less precise he is likely to be in assessing his total wealth. A variety of factors may be involved here, including reticence to appear a braggart, suspicion at having his financial position made public and a simple lack of knowledge. It may be relatively easier for a man with £100 in a building society and a yearly income of £6000 to be fairly precise. Men who own businesses and invest in a variety of enterprises are uncertain or loath to assess their total wealth. Finally, cultural background appears to be an important factor in whether or not a man is likely to present himself as wealthy. The American lawyer earning $60,000 a year is likely to say so, and casually work in some reference to his $250,000 home and $18,000 car. When wealth is not inherited the man is likely to discuss his rags-to-riches story at considerable length. If success is the American Dream the man who achieves it may not see anything unsophisticated in calling others' attention to it. The British aristocrat, on the other hand, is much more likely to hedge about his personal fortune and to portray himself as the caretaker of his family's wealth. This may, of course, be the case, but whereas studied indifference to wealth is part of the English gentleman's style, it is not an important concern of the Arab. While it is common for an Arab to flaunt his wealth or estimate his fortune in tens of millions of pounds, the British man talks about taxes and the way in which wealth is usurped by government agencies.

As to appearance, among the men I saw it was common to wear a well-cut suit, have an expensive watch, a neat hair-cut and manicured nails; by and large the wealthy man does not parade his wealth in ostentatious dress. He tends to profess himself uninterested in clothes and generally says that he is a functional rather than fashion-conscious dresser. There is an absence of jewellery; men tend to sneer at other members of their sex who wear it or otherwise affect the appearance of a dandy. It is, they suggested, a middle-class affectation, a sign of vulgarity, or a sign of suspicious effeminacy. Generally speaking, dress was so unremarkable that the only men I can clearly remember were those who tended to be over-generous in their use of after-shave or cologne.

The settings in which I interviewed these men tended to be formal. They might take to brightly coloured dinner jackets elsewhere but I doubt it. While women's clothes are chosen to set them apart from the crowd, men's dress in the world I am writing about is selected more on the lines of camouflage to make them blend in among other men. If he wants to display his wealth a man is more likely to drive a bright red sports car than wear flashy clothes. The kept woman can be seen as an extension of the man's personal space insofar as her finery testifies to his wealth. She becomes an indirect way for the man to present his status while he appears to be inconspicuously conspicuous.

In general, the toys of wealthy men represent a more sizeable investment than those of women. Indeed the kept woman may herself be one of his toys. Like the big fish swallowing the little fish, relative power is shown in the scale of conspicuous consumption.

Cars, planes, yachts and summer or multiple residences may all be seen as extensions of personal space. A man can view his possessions as an extension or representation of himself and the image he wishes to present to others. For example, being the owner of a Ferrari or a yacht summons up the idea of luxury that would not be invoked by driving a Volkswagen. Holiday homes that are seldom visited, planes that remain in the hangar and sailing vessels that spend long periods in dry dock nevertheless serve as a source of pride for their owners. In one instance a man referred to his yacht in tones of such affection and tenderness that I was unable to distinguish the exact point at which the 'she' in the conversation switched focus from the boat to his mistress. Owning costly possessions can be a source of enjoyment but also an opportunity to present a certain image and to display the mark of success. In *Mirrors and Masks: the Search for Identity*, Anselm Strauss suggests:

> Self-regard is linked with what is owned, with what is one's own. A man's possessions are a fair index of what he is . . . It is no accident that men mark their symbolic movements – into social class, for instance – by discarding and by acquiring clothes, houses, furnishings, friends, even wives.

The kept relationship has a style which identifies its strong association with wealth. The playgrounds of the rich such as Gstaad, St Moritz, Cannes or Las Vegas, which provide a setting where people may deliberately seek to be known as rich, are common holiday spots for the kept woman and her lover. Knowing what sports, activities and places are fashionable is part of the superficial gentility of the kept relationship. What makes a particular commodity fashionable is difficult to say but it seems that some of the factors at work are qualities such as novelty, cost, exclusivity or rarity and its capacity to attract notice. Knowing where to eat, where to go on holiday, and where to gamble (and what to play), distinguish the man and reveal the circles in which he moves. The fashionable is esoteric; and knowing what is fashionable and being able to afford its pursuit allows the man to see himself as a man of the world. For the woman, pursuing fashionable activities in fashionable surroundings lends support to her idea of herself as someone who 'has arrived', to quote one of my respondents. The watering-holes of the wealthy are places where the members of the group can consolidate their corporate identity as a privileged elite.

The boundaries between the various groups are perhaps most clearly to be observed in their social activities and the 'closed courts' in which they take place. Even public places can be converted into the private haunts of a network group and, if in principle the setting is open to everyone, in practice the democratic policy is barely recognized. Preferential treatment by staff who tolerate the quirks of members in the in-group and the staff's identification with the in-group itself may form a metaphorical moat which others are discouraged from crossing. When the setting is the private house party, the group defines itself even more rigorously and deliberately seeks to protect its insularity. While at a social function the only criteria for inclusion may be the social climber's ability to pay the price of admission (for instance to a fund-raising ball), this will not necessarily qualify him to become the weekend guest of the people whose tables he shares. All men may have been created equal, but some are thought more obviously equal than others. So it is that a man may be the aristocrat of his particular network and a lowly serf in another. While large-scale social functions may bring together a variety of network groups they may not mingle to any great degree.

Social activities in themselves are interesting because they are thought to permit or promote vertical mobility – rising up the social ladder. They are not pursued for the sake of simple enjoyment. They also serve to integrate group members and provide for conspicuous consumption. If you cultivate interest in fox-hunting because you think that joining in the sport of kings marks you as a special sort of person, then the sport is unimportant and the main reason for following it is manifest self-aggrandizement. If it became terribly stylish to spear wild boars you might expect people who had previously shown little interest in the sport to go off boar-hunting. Whether any activity is done for pleasure or because fashion demands it is seldom readily apparent but the dictates of fashion do not apply only to dress.

Morton Hunt's *Affair: a Portrait of Extramarital Love in Contemporary America* suggests that having an affair can be a 'fashionable' activity:

> In certain wealthy and jet-set circles, an extramarital affair of some durability is a status activity, and virtually *de rigueur* for anyone of prestige and significance. In such circles, marriage is based on property and family... In the upper-class society of San Francisco, for instance, the status affair is quite openly accepted and the social newsnotes in San Francisco papers customarily list the names of extramarital couples who have been seen arriving together at some resort or major social event. Since everyone knows who is what to whom, the appearance of the linked names in the paper is a source not of embarrassment but of pride.

If having an affair is stylish, the etiquette of the gentleman should ensure that it is stylishly conducted with a veneer of gentility.

I would qualify Hunt's suggestion that the upper-class affair is flaunted rather than hidden, by saying that it is flaunted only within the confines of the participants' social sphere. My respondents certainly did not want to have their relationship highlighted in the gutter press. For men in the public eye, private sex has the potential of becoming public scandal. Lord Denning commented about the Profumo Affair that 'scandalous information about well-known people has become a marketable commodity – the greater the scandal, the higher the price'. If a man pursues a series of one-night stands he increases the number of women who could disclose information about his personal life. While a jilted mistress can often sell her story to a newspaper or a publisher, she may be discouraged from doing so by the treatment of the 'other woman' in the popular press. When the notorious American sex scandals in Washington became known the 'kept' lovers of men were strongly disparaged in the press as self-acknowledged whores. Women who parade the liaisons they have had in tell-tale autobiographies often become figures of fun. They may be thought liberated but hardly lady-like. When mud hits the fan it generally flies in all directions; if a woman does not want to be presented to the public as a woman of easy virtue she may conspire with the man to keep the relationship discreet rather than let it be known outside the in-group. One of the costs of keeping a woman is the price of privacy. Given that the average rent per month of the kept woman I interviewed was in excess of £500 it is unlikely that tender moments will be spied on by a flatmate arriving home unexpectedly.

At the turn of the century, London districts such as Maida Vale and St John's Wood were known for their proliferation of kept women, but in London to day there do not seem to be any such equivalents. Although there are pockets that have a higher than average number of kept women, at least in my experience, these are indistinguishable from the high-rent areas of

Belgravia, around St James's Palace, Chelsea, Knightsbridge and so on and they tend to be within central London rather than on the outskirts. One estate agent joked that if there were one single area for this purpose there would probably be a bus taking people round it on a sight-seeing tour. Given the popularity of the 'Tour of the Stars' or rather, their homes, in Beverly Hills, there may be good reason why the concentration of kept women has disappeared from St John's Wood. Although the selection of a flat does not seem deliberately influenced by the cachet of the area, there may be some awareness of it. One man noted:

> Of course the area is important – you'll invite your friends around so you look for a good area. I didn't want an area too close to my own because it could get awkward if people see you and if you're ridiculously indiscreet. [*Is there one area to your knowledge where there are lots of mistresses?*] No, if there was you'd never get in for the traffic. (*44-year-old man, London*)

Estate agents suggest additional reasons why there is no apparent concentration of mistresses in one area. London has become such a popular city that flat-seeking is relatively complicated. Should demand exceed supply in one district you must look for what you want in another. The avowed purpose of company flats is not, after all, to accommodate a man's mistress – even if that is often the use to which they are put. Finally, if the man does not wish to buy a flat on a long lease or freehold, his options steadily decrease. In such cases flats belonging to hotels or service flats are rented. These factors all influence the geographic distribution of kept women in London and contribute to the invisibility of the kept relationship in general.

However, while the behaviour of the kept woman and her lover may be unremarkable and indistinguishable from that of other couples, the disparity in their ages which is often present may itself result in the relationship being noticed. About 65 per cent of the relationships I investigated were characterized by an age difference of 20 years or more, the woman being the younger partner. The older the man, the more obvious this difference. An 80-year-old man with a 40-year-old woman may look like a cradle-snatcher although the woman is well above the age of consent, At times, also, the relationship almost brazenly announced itself by the wardrobe affected, the cars driven and so on. The gold Rolls Royce, the maroon limousine that arrives chauffeur-driven, the Lincoln Continental parked on a street cluttered with Mini-Metros and Volkswagens are as conspicuous as a yacht in a harbour of dinghies. Similarly, a contingent of Arabs in national dress, though common enough in London, still attracts notice.

The dangers of recognition by others include the possibilities that the man's wife will be informed or that there will be attempts at blackmail.

Either eventuality may cause the termination of the relationship. Blackmail may be directed either at the mistress or at her lover. If she 'cheats' on him and is seen with other men, she becomes vulnerable to financial or sexual blackmail. If money is at stake, this may mean that the affair becomes a source of embarrassment for the man and his family. A wife who has been aware of the affair but has been pretending not to know about it may be forced to insist that it is brought to an end, or to divorce him for adultery to save face. The man's indiscretion is a *faux pas*; contravening the etiquette of the affair in this way may invite censure. However, people may recognize that the relationship exists but not betray the confidence. It is speculative how far the adulterous kept relationship remains a secret. It often seems that friends wear blinkers to avoid recognizing the relationship for what it is and stop themselves from expressing negative comments:

> Her lover was both a lawyer and the head of a large and profitable corporation with offices in San Francisco, L.A., Reno and Las Vegas. They met almost every day and both were friends of mine. She was desolate when he died and asked me to visit him in hospital. She felt she couldn't because his wife might be present. She still speaks fondly of him and has a large portrait of him in her home, doing him a bit more justice than he deserved. They took trips together, to Tahoe, Canada, Mexico and the Bahamas. I've no idea how he justified all of this to his wife and never asked. (*56-year-old man, San Francisco*)

> We're all adults and if he wants to keep a mistress, that's none of my business is it? If he doesn't see it as a problem why should I? (*51-year-old man, London*)

> [*Did you tell your friends?*] Some of them, my close friend and my sister. [*How did they react?*] Tactfully noncommital!! They had more respect for his money than for him. (*32-year-old woman, London*)

One man summed up his Sugar Daddy friend's behaviour with the proverb 'A fool and his money are soon parted' and then told me to forget he had said it. Similarly, a woman's friends, whatever their private opinion, may adopt a 'nothing unusual about that' attitude; so it is that on learning of a certain relationship they will say 'But I thought he was married?'. 'He is'. 'Oh'.

The sociologists Richard Hawkins and Gary Tiedeman suggest several reasons why even when rule-breaking behaviour is observed, people turn a blind eye to it:

> Children in American society are taught not to reveal others' transgressions. 'Don't squeal' or 'Don't tattle' are admonitions

regularly encountered. Extollment of the virtues of noninvolvement
– e.g. 'mind your own business' – as well as pronouncements of
loyalty to one's group may also produce a non-sanctioning bias:
'One does not look for trouble and should not do anything if it is
encountered'.

These authors also put forward, for example, moral and religious attitudes
to repentance whereby culprits are given a second chance, and the
possibilities of embarrassment.

Several other reasons may be put forward, such as a friend fearing that his
attitude will be thought 'holier than thou' or prudish and that he in turn will
be labelled a sanctimonious prig. Similarly, the social status of the Sugar
Daddy may discourage others from voicing opinions which are not
supportive. The underling who is over-concerned with the welfare of the
man's wife may be summarily dismissed, the friend who asks too many
questions may be ostracized for being a nosy parker. Losing a job or a friend
may be too high a price to pay for speaking your mind. By saying instead
'It's not my problem' or 'It's not my business how he wants to run his life'
people disclaim responsibility for someone else's behaviour. If various
friends know and yet say nothing, the individual may feel less obligation to
do so; the effect is that responsibility is diffused. A friend may also feel that
he has become an 'accessory after the fact', especially if he has been
recruited into a role which directly or indirectly supports the behaviour.
Friends who supported the relationship to start with can be called to task
for contradicting themselves later. The girlfriend who has previously
supported the woman's definition of the relationship as a love affair by
sympathetically murmuring 'Of course he loves you', will be called to
account for any reversal of support. The man who originally found it
acceptable to socialize with the man and his lover may be asked why he now
finds objectionable what was previously agreeable.

A final reason suggested for non-intervention can be termed the bearer-
of-bad-news complex. There may be an uneasy awareness that in times past
messengers of bad news were put to death or received ignominious
chastisement. While it is unlikely that the wife would physically assault the
friend or friends who break the news of her husband's affair she might well
resent them and identify them as a source of embarrassment and anguish.
The friends' news places the woman in the role of someone in need of
compassion and although the wife may need tea and sympathy she may also
resent being an object of pity and believe her friends to be patronizing and
obsequious. If the wife has known of the affair all along she may be forced
into publicly acknowledging a secret which she would rather not tell. An
outsider's knowledge may force her to do something about a situation with
which she herself is comfortable.

In *The Theory of the Leisure Class*, Thorstein Veblen commented that 'if decency is observed, morals are taken for granted'. Being seen or seeing yourself as an adulterer, a philanderer or a man who keeps a mistress is nevertheless unlikely to dislodge you from the self-image of an honourable man. A woman kept by a gangster may be known as a gangster's moll but the man's status remains unchanged. He may be thought of as 'a bit of a lad' or as spending his money foolishly, but none of the men I interviewed felt that what they were doing inflicted any social stigma on them. Perceiving the need for secrecy or feeling guilty is not the same as labelling the affair as fundamentally wrong. 'How can anything that feels so right be wrong?' Secrecy is part of the protocol of the affair, indeed it consolidates it, but no firm line is taken over whether adultery is shameful or a by-product of a society which has unreal expectations of the monogamous marriage and its capacity to satisfy the needs of the couple. So long as the affair is conducted with a veneer of gentility it is not thought to be anti-social or abnormal.

If the concept of the gentleman was originally a Christian *par excellence*, the term now denotes an elegance of manner and conduct. Boswell's *The Life of Johnson* makes the distinction between a 'gentleman' and 'gentility' clear.

> Boswell: A man may debauch his friend's wife very genteelly; he
>   may cheat at cards very genteelly.
> Hickey: I do not think *that* is very genteel.
> Boswell: Sir, it may not be like a gentleman but it may be genteel.
> Johnson: You are meaning two different things. One means
>   exterior grace, the other honour.

The distinction between 'gentility' and a 'gentleman' is interesting because social morality, which can allow the person to perceive that what he is doing is socially acceptable, is not identical to personal morality, which may make him feel guilty about having an affair. One of the men I interviewed commented:

> Concomitant with keeping a woman is guilt in our Western Judaeo-Christian culture. This is present at some time or another, or always in my experience and as told me by friends, clients, et al. This condition may not exist in other societies, or to a much less extent, such as in the Moslem world, or among the French or Italians or Mexicans, but it's a significant factor in our society.

On the other hand, another man suggested that the commandment 'Thou shalt not commit adultery' had never been intended to apply to men but simply to monitor women's behaviour. If a man is allowed to have as many wives as he wants, he argued, there is never the expectation that he contents himself with but one wife. In the first of these two examples the man's behaviour seems to be at odds with his personal morality while in the second the man denies that there is any cause for self-doubt or guilt. In both cases, however, the men do not define their behaviour as socially unacceptable or 'deviant' in any way. It was Kierkegaard who said: 'Marriage? All women should be married but no men.'

The responses of Arab men illustrate how outsiders, not defined as part of the Chosen or the Elect, can be treated with less ceremony and less cause for self-recrimination. When an Arab man has a white and/or non-Muslim girlfriend he tends to be rather flippant and dismissive of her. Arab men are frequently described by kept women as being a law unto themselves and when the Arab man is of royal birth, the kept woman is like a pawn in an elaborate chess game played by others whose duty it is to protect and serve the royal personage. The woman is often summoned by others who act on the man's request to invite the lady for dinner, to accompany him on an evening out, to have sex with him, to give her a farewell gift or to dismiss her abruptly when he tires of her. This may be consistent with the treatment of women in the Arab cultural background in that women are second-class citizens, like children, to be seen and not heard, so they can be treated somewhat dismissively. It might well be reinforced, however, by the fact that the non-Muslim is considered to be of an inferior class, like a servant. For example, one Arab man spoke sombrely and seriously about polygamy and stressed that the man was required to behave honourably with his wives. If he gave a gift to one wife he was expected to give the same gift or a gift of identical value to his other wives as well. The economics of this practice, he said, discouraged men from having as many wives as they might have wished for.

This same man felt entitled to treat non-Muslim women with little regard, however. He told me that the previous night he and a friend had hired a call girl, dismissed his mistress and told her to retire for the night, and then proceeded to engage in a triangular act of sexual intercourse with the call girl. Afterwards, the other man and himself settled the question of who would pay the girl by masturbating; the man who ejaculated last was required to pay the woman the agreed price of £400. The man found this anecdote unroariously funny and did not think the whole incident might have been degrading to either his mistress or to the call girl. This type of ethnocentricism may create one standard of behaviour for your own kind, and another for behaviour with outsiders. Just as the Arab may feel less cause for self-recrimination in treating a non-Muslim girlfriend contemptuously, a Jewish man may feel that a Gentile woman is the sort you can have affairs with but not be obliged to marry. This creates a certain laxity of moral conduct, making excusable and permissible where a woman of the Elect is not involved what is otherwise frowned upon. If the woman is defined as an outsider, the standards of 'moral conduct' and honourable behaviour may be less stringent than what is normally observed.

When interviewing men it was not unusual to hear them elaborate painstakingly on the idea that no one was wronged by their relationship.

Several factors may support the man in his view that he is not doing anything harmful or wrong. First, by accepting him and his financial support the kept woman herself generates the feeling of acceptance for his behaviour. Since her actions are voluntary – she has not been seduced or coerced – the mistress is not seen as a 'victim' in the relationship. The man's attitude is that the woman's knowledge of his marital status clears him of accusations that she is being victimized: 'She knew I was married from the start' . . . 'I told her not to get too serious' . . . 'She knows . . . I'd never leave my kids' and so on. Her complicity creates a code of etiquette which develops in the relationship itself. Juxtaposed with their belief that their families are not wanting for anything, honourable behaviour is defined by maintaining both the women in their lives at a comfortable level of existence. The argument is, 'she doesn't suffer for it' and 'I treat her well.' Ostensibly, the argument is seen as applicable to both the wife and the kept woman. Moreover, maintaining a kept woman is seen broadly as a prestige-conferring activity. Rather than being viewed as immoral behaviour ('Thou shalt not commit adultery'), keeping a woman is positively assessed as indicative of wealth, sexual virility and masculinity. A man's ability to support a wife and a mistress is seen as something to be admired, given the costs involved. For men to be sexually active is not considered unseemly but appropriate to his gender. The double standard reduces his culpability of moral trespass.

I suggest that men are not conditioned into being husbands, fathers or lovers but rather, into assuming a dominant status based on a professional identity. An important effect of work may be to isolate the successful 'corporate man' from his family, making it increasingly less likely that he will base his image of himself on his role within the family, other than as their provider. From my male respondents, it appears that neither the wife nor the kept woman commands as much of a commitment in terms of time or attention, as the man's professional career. The importance of keeping a woman may be reduced to being incidental to the work-role and the man's definition of himself in that role. Businessmen predominate as Sugar Daddies and the ethos of the business world seems to affect their non-work-roles.

Although the stereotype of the businessman is an ulcer-ridden 'work-aholic', it may simply be that the great investment of time and the intensity of commitment demanded by a career make the work-role a master status which is not easily discarded. The isolation of the corporate man from his family can be termed the country house syndrome. A man who is successful in his profession wins much esteem by purchasing a grand home outside London to house his family. As a result, he becomes a long-distance commuter. He leaves home earlier and returns later, spending less time with his family and more time at work or in the process of getting to and returning from work. Buying a country house may originally have been motivated by the man's desire to give his family a superior lifestyle, but in effect, the country house must compensate for the man's absence in the domestic life of his family. The cost of buying a country house results in the man having to channel yet more of his energies into his work. To pay for the extra petrol costs involved and finance the white elephant that marks him as successful, he must devote his energies into making his work more profitable.

If symbols of success such as the country house are the objects of admiration, the emphasis on acquiring possessions is not simply for the purpose of conspicuous consumption. For men, to be a good provider is mandatory. The corporate man is not only separated from his family by the physical distance between his work and his family home, but also by the symbolic country house which signifies the dichotomization of family life and work. It may be that men become so immersed in their career that they forego outside intimacies and replace them with ones in the workplace. Robert Whitehurst's study: 'Extramarital sex: Alienation or Extension of Normal Behaviour' in G. Neubeck's *Extramarital Relations* suggests that exposure to the 'fringe ethics' of the business world, and the opportunities created therein for adultery, may themselves lead to extramarital involvements. Similarly, perks of the man's employment such as company flats and expense accounts are conducive to keeping a mistress. It may be that the kept relationship is logically consistent with the ethos of the business environment and is facilitated by it.

The reasons why men keep women are much more complex than the authors of pulp fiction suggest. The importance of the kept relationship as a sexual one has received an inordinate amount of notoriety and attention. The kept relationship can emerge and survive for much the same reasons as marriage: love, friendship, loneliness, infatuation and habit. Marriage symbolizes respectability, responsibility and stability; to the men in my research, keeping a woman is a positive symbol of wealth, sexual virility and personal desirability.

As for the incidence of love in this context, there is rarely any consensus on its nature. For example, in the eighteenth century Proudhon suggested that: 'true love ripens slowly out of friendship; it does not happen suddenly or drastically'. In contrast, the mystic Khalil Gibran maintained: 'It is wrong to think that love comes from long companionship. Love is the offspring of spiritual affinity, and unless that affinity is created in a moment, it will not be created in years or even in generations.' My contacts themselves were conscious of the many interpretations which can be placed on the term 'love'. I shall leave the last word to one of my respondents, a 56-year-old man from California:

> Whether we were 'in love' is a much more complex question, and it
> may be that I can try to answer it. Is it caring and closeness? Is it
> sexual attraction? Is it something else or a combination of things?

You have to give me the guidelines. You ask if I was 'in love' with any mistress. Probably not, but the sexual attraction was an ineluctable factor. My wife was a rather cool lady, to put it mildly – I'm not. Most men might say the same thing but the performance might be quite different. With me it was not . . . The 'in love' concept is difficult because it can embrace many different factors from one relationship and one couple to another. Frequent or infrequent or no sexual congress may be involved. In my relationships sexual attraction was high and sex was frequent. Without doubt 'love' connotes caring and concern for the wellbeing of another in all senses: physical, emotional, financial, etc. The dictionary definitions of love are inadequate and simplistic: 'an intense affectionate concern for another' followed by 'an intense sexual desire for another person'. See how inadequate these definitions are? The ancient Greeks probably defined 'love' best. There were words which defined many types, or faces, of love, ranging from the simple 'agape' (to like a person, regardless of gender), to 'philos' (a friend of one treated with the same regard as a brother, and for which the city of Philadelphia is named), 'eros' or erotic love, symbolized by a special god. There are at least half a dozen more words they used (and which are still in use) in defining love. Implicit in the man and 'kept woman' context is . . . a realization that it is possible to love more than one person of the opposite sex at the same time: i.e. your wife and your mistress. All this is addressed to heterosexual relationships . . .

SELECT BIBLIOGRAPHY

Acton, William *Prostitution, Considered in its Moral, Social and Sanitary Aspects in London and Other Large Cities and Garrison Towns* (London, 1857, 1972; New York, 1870; New Jersey, 1972)

Anderson, R. and Rosenblatt, P. 'Human Sexuality in a Cross-Cultural Perspective' in *The Bases of Human Sexual Attraction* (Ed.) *Mark Cook (London and New York, 1981)*

Beach, Frank A. and Ford, Clellan S. *Patterns of Sexual Behavior* (New York, 1951; Connecticut, 1980; London, 1952, new edn 1980)

Beauvoir, Simone de *Le Deuxième Sexe* (Paris, 1953)/*The Second Sex*, transl. H. M. Parshley (London, 1953, rev. edn 1968; New York, 1953, 1974)

Becker, Howard *Outsiders: Studies in the Sociology of Deviance* (New York and London, 1963)

Benjamin, H. and Masters, R. *The Prostitute in Society* (New York, 1964)

Boswell, James *The Life of Samuel Johnson* (1791; new edn London, 1976; New Jersey, 1976, 1978)

Capote, Truman *Breakfast at Tiffany's* (New York, 1958; London, 1958; Middlesex, 1969)

Chesser, Eustace *Live and Let Live* (London, 1958)

Choisy (Clouzet), Maryse *Psychoanalysis of the Prostitute* (New York, 1961; London, 1962)

Comfort, Alex (Ed.) *The Joy of Sex: a Gourmet Guide to Lovemaking* (New York, 1972, 1974; London, 1974, rev. edn 1978)

175

Cooper, Cary L. and Davidson, Marilyn J. *High Pressure: Working Lives of Women Managers* (London, 1982)

Cuber, John F. and Harroff, Peggy B. *Significant Americans: A Study of Sexual Behavior Among the Affluent* (Connecticut, 1965; New York, 1966)

Davidson, Marilyn J. *see* Cooper, Cary L.

Dostoevsky, Fyodor M. *Notes from Underground* (1913; Middlesex, 1972; New York, 1981)

Douglas, Jack (Ed.) *Deviance and Respectability: Social Construction of Moral Meanings* (New York, 1970)

Dowling, Colette *The Cinderella Complex: Women's Hidden Fear of Independence* (New York, 1981, 1982)

Farley, Lin *Sexual Shakedown: the Sexual Harassment of Women on the Job* (New York, 1978)/*Sexual Shakedown: Sexual Harassment of Women in the Working World* (Buckinghamshire, 1980)

Fidler, John *The British Business Elite: Its Attitudes to Class, Status and Power* (London and Boston, Mass., 1981)

Fitzgerald, F. Scott 'The Rich Boy' (1926) in *The Diamond as Big as the Ritz* (London, 1974)

Flexner, Abraham *Prostitution in Europe* (New York, 1914; New Jersey, 1969; London, 1919)

Ford, Clellan S. *see* Beach, Frank A.

Glover, Edward *The Psychopathology of Prostitution* (London, 1945, 1969)

Grazia, Sebastian de *Of Time, Work and Leisure* (New York, 1962, 1964)

Greenwald, Harold *The Elegant Prostitute* (New York, 1970)

Harroff, Peggy B. *see* Cuber, John F.

Hawkins, Richard and Tiedeman, Gary *The Creation of Deviance: Interpersonal & Organizational Determinants* (Ohio, 1975)

Henslin, James M. (Ed.) 'Towards a Sociology of Sex' in *The Sociology of Sex* (New York, 1971)

Hunt, Morton *Affair: a Portrait of Extramarital Love in Contemporary America* (California, 1969)

James, Wendy and Kedgley, Susan Jane *The Mistress* (London, 1973; New York, 1974)

Jedburgh, Arabella 'High-Class Hostesses' in *Prostitutes*, see Sandford, Jeremy

Kartovaara, Leena – dissertation summarized in E. Haavio-Mannila's

'Finland: Economic, Political and Cutural Leadership' in *Access to Power: Cross-National Studies of Women and Elites* (Eds) Cynthia Fuchs Epstein and Rose Laub Coser (London and Massachusetts, 1980)

Kedgley, Susan Jane *see* James, Wendy

Klapp, Orrin E. *Symbolic Leaders: Public Dramas and Public Man* (New York, 1964)

Lipman-Blumen, J. 'A Homosocial Theory of Sex-Roles: an Examination of the Sex Segregation of Social Institutions' in *Women and the Workplace: the Implication of Occupational Segregation* (Eds) Martha Blaxall and Barbara Regan (London and Chicago, 1976)

Loizos, P. 'Images of Man' in *Not Work Alone: a Cross-Cultural Survey (View) of Activities Apparently Superfluous to Survival* (Eds) Jeremy Cherfas and Roger Lewin (London and California, 1980)

Lucian (AD *c.115–c.200*) 'Dialogues Among the Courtesans' (transl. 1905) in Lucian's *Works* Vol. 7 (London, 1961)

'M' *The Sensuous Man*' (London, 1971, new edn 1972; New York, 1972, 1982)

Maine, Charles Eric *World Famous Mistresses* (Middlesex, 1970)

Marañón, Gregorio *The Climacteric: the Critical Age* (Missouri, 1929)

Masters, R. *see* Benjamin, H.

Mills, C. Wright *The Power Elite* (New York, 1956)

Partridge, Eric *A Dictionary of the Underworld* (London, 1949, 3rd rev. edn 1968; New York, 1949, rev. edn 1961)

Ploscowe, M. *Sex and the Law* (New York, 1962)

Rosenblatt, P. *see* Anderson R.

Sandford, Jeremy *Prostitutes: Portraits of People in the Sexploitation Business* (London, 1975)

Sands, Melissa *The Mistress' Survival Manual* (New York, 1980); *The Making of the American Mistress* (New York, 1981)

Scott, George Ryley *A History of Prostitution from Antiquity to the Present Day* (London, 1936, rev. edn 1954; New York, 1936, 1972)

Seymour-Smith, Martin *Fallen Women* (London, 1969)

Spooner, John D. *Smart People: a User's Guide to Experts* (Boston, 1979)

Strauss, Anselm *Mirrors and Masks: the Search for Identity* (California, 1970; Oxford, 1977)

Szasz, Thomas S. *Sex: Facts, Frauds and Follies* (Oxford, 1981)

Tanner, Tracy *How to Find a Man . . . And Make Him Keep You* (New York, 1979)

Thackeray, William Makepeace *The Four Georges* (London, 1861, 1968; Boston, 1875; New York, 1968)

Thompson, Hunter Stockton *Hell's Angels* (Middlesex, 1967, 1970; New York, 1967, 1975)

Thompson, Michael *Rubbish Theory: the Creation and Destruction of Value* (Oxford and New York, 1979)

Thompson, V. A. *Modern Organization* (New York, 1961, 2nd edn Alabama, 1977)

Tiedeman, Gary *see* Hawkins, Richard

Veblen, Thorstein *The Theory of the Leisure Class* (New York, 1899, new impression, 1970; new edn London, 1971)

'Walter' *My Secret Life* (c.1890–94, new edn London, 1972; new edn New York, 1979)

Warhol, Andy with Bob Colacello *Andy Warhol's Exposures* (New York, 1979; London, 1980)

Whitehurst, Robert 'Extramarital Sex: Alienation or Extension of Normal Behavior' in *Extramarital Relations* (Ed.) *Gerhard Neubeck* (New Jersey and London, 1970)

Yablonsky, Lewis *The Extra-Sex Factor: Why Over Half of America's Men Play Around* (New York, 1978)

Periodical Articles

Cosmopolitan (British edn) Letter in Irma Kurtz's agony column (August 1982)

Cosmopolitan (U.S.) 'Playing the Mistress Game' by Patricia Morrisroe (August 1982)

Ethnology (U.S.) 'Publicity, Privacy and the Mehinacu Marriage' by T. Gregor (13:1979)

Journal of Marriage and the Family (U.S.) 'The Secret Ranking' by Hans L. Zetterberg (28 Part 2:1966)

Journal of Personality and Social Psychology (U.S.) 'Perceptions of Similarly and Dissimilarly Attractive Couples and Individuals' by D. Bar-Tal and L. Saxe (33:1976)

Saturday Review (U.S.) 'The Double Standard of Aging' by Susan Sontag (55:23 September 1972)

Smart Set Magazine (U.S.) 'The Secret of Success' by Donald Ogden Stewart (March 1922)

Spare Rib 'Our Greatest Occupational Hazard' by Jane Root (114: January 1982)

Telegraph Sunday Magazine 'Next to the Room at the Top' by Jane Ellison (280:7 February 1982)

Woman's World 'The Woman's World Guide to Office Romance' (November 1982)

AUTHOR'S ACKNOWLEDGMENTS

For reasons of confidentiality I am unable to thank by name various individuals whose help was greatly appreciated. Nevertheless, I would like to thank my respondents, the management and staff of the agencies, clubs and hotels I visited, and the editors who published my request for respondents in their newspapers and magazines.

I owe a tremendous debt of gratitude to Paul Rock, my Ph.D supervisor at the London School of Economics, for his total kindness, patience and invaluable help. I would also like to thank David Downes who read numerous drafts of the thesis on which this book is based and gave advice and continual assistance. Ken Plummer was extremely helpful and suggested how the thesis could be adapted as a book and my editor at Orbis Publishing, Marie-Jaqueline ('M-J') Lancaster, accomplished this task with infinite charm, tact and encouragement, ably assisted by her copy editor Suzy Powling. Only the stupidities in this work are solely my own and I accept full responsibility for them. Several organizations were extremely helpful and provided me with useful information. Special thanks are given to the librarians at the British Library, the British Library of Economics and Political Science, the Kensington/Chelsea Public Library, and the University of Manitoba Library.

I would also like to thank Robert Prus, Jessie Bernard, Douglas Sutherland and Melissa Sands for taking time to enter into correspondence and the departmental secretaries of Sociology at the London School of Economics, Anne Trowles and Jenny Law, for relaying messages and letters to me.

On a personal level, several individuals have been extraordinarily kind: Anne de Courcy's interest in my work and marked professionalism as a journalist have been inspiring; Alex Richter, though sorely tried, has been a valued and loyal friend; Gail Guyton acted as my chaperone, 'bodyguard' and comrade-in-arms on many occasions which turned out far different than we had anticipated; Marmie Longair read 101 drafts of the same chapter and, unknowingly, was not only kind and sympathetic to me but to my tutor Dr Rock as well; Denis Jones is a photographer capable of making Quasimodo look like Rhett Butler and my agent Carole Blake is worth much more than her commission rate – but I'll keep that secret. My thanks as well to: Leena Kore, Jane Green, Jill Jordanov, Debbie Rice, Tom James, Tony Fuller, Ken McCluskey, Dan Albas, Maxine White, Annette and Dipo Adebo, Deborah and Dwayne Noyse and John Lowman.

Finally, I would like to thank my parents who funded this research in its entirety and, as always, gave more than they themselves could imagine, my sister Reena – and always dear Bruce . . .

EDNA SALAMON
London, 1983

The publishers would like to thank the following for permission to reproduce extracts: Jonathan Cape Ltd *The Second Sex* by Simone de Beauvoir, translated by H.M. Parshley (1953, rev. edn 1968); Gerald Duckworth & Co. Ltd *The Collected Dorothy Parker* for the poem 'Epitaph for a Darling Lady' (1944, 1973); Grosset & Dunlap Inc. *Andy Warhol's Exposures* by Andy Warhol with Bob Colacello (1979); Hamish Hamilton Ltd *Breakfast at Tiffany's* by Truman Capote (1958); William Morris Agency, Inc. on behalf of the author 'Playing the Mistress Game' © 1982 Patricia Morrisroe; Secker and Warburg Ltd *Prostitutes: Portraits of People in the Sexploitation Business* by Jeremy Sandford (1975). Extract from Proverbs, Authorized King James Version of the Bible (Crown Copyright in England) is reproduced by permission of Eyre & Spottiswoode, Her Majesty's Printers. Although every effort has been made to trace the present copyright holders, we apologise in advance for any unintentional omission or neglect and will be pleased to insert the appropriate acknowledgment to companies or individuals in any subsequent edition of this publication.